Vocabulary Skills for the
TOEFL 2
iBT [Step-up]

Vocabulary Skills for the
TOEFL iBT 2 [Step-up]

저 자 윤창만, 손성균
발행인 고본화
발 행 반석출판사
2023년 1월 10일 초판 3쇄 인쇄
2023년 1월 15일 초판 3쇄 발행
홈페이지 www.bansok.co.kr
이메일 bansok@bansok.co.kr
블로그 blog.naver.com/bansokbooks

07547 서울시 강서구 양천로 583. B동 1007호
(서울시 강서구 염창동 240-21번지 우림블루나인 비즈니스센터 B동 1007호)
대표전화 02) 2093-3399 **팩 스** 02) 2093-3393
출 판 부 02) 2093-3395 **영업부** 02) 2093-3396
등록번호 제315-2008-000033호

Copyright ⓒ 윤창만, 손성균

ISBN 978-89-7172-751-5 (13740)

- 교재 관련 문의: bansok@bansok.co.kr을 이용해 주시기 바랍니다.
- 이 책에 게재된 내용의 일부 또는 전체를 무단으로 복제 및 발췌하는 것을 금합니다.
- 파본 및 잘못된 제품은 구입처에서 교환해 드립니다.

Vocabulary Skills for the
TOEFL 2
iBT [Step-up]

Bansok

머리말

TOEFL을 단시간에 효율적으로 공략하기 위해 가장 우선시 되어야 할 것이 기출어휘 암기이다. 기출어휘를 많이 알면 알수록 Reading뿐 아니라 Listening이나 Writing, Speaking을 공부할 때도 학습 효과는 배가 된다. 어휘력이 늘어날수록 다른 섹션에 대한 이해도 빠르고 쉬워진다.

하지만 어휘를 공부할 때 단순히 영어 단어와 우리말 뜻을 대입하여 암기해서는 안 된다. 처음에는 효과가 있을 수 있겠지만, 시간이 지나갈수록 그 효과는 분명히 떨어진다. 이 책은 효과적인 TOEFL 어휘 학습방법을 제시하며, 과거 20여 년간의 TOEFL 기출어휘를 총정리했다.

분야별 전문용어는 지문을 이해하는 데 반드시 필요하지는 않지만 핵심적인 부분이다. 전문용어를 익히는 가장 좋은 방법은 배경지식을 제공하는 지문을 많이 읽어보며 어휘를 정리하는 것이다. 그렇지 못할 경우에는 TOEFL의 Listening과 Reading에 자주 나오는 내용을 중심으로 지문을 많이 읽어보는 것이다. 이러한 분야별 어휘 학습을 돕기 위해 이 책의 예문들은 다양한 주제로부터 선정하였으며, 문맥에서 어휘의 뜻을 이해할 수 있도록 하기 위해 연습문제를 제시하였다.

어휘 학습은 하루에 30~50개가 적당하다. 처음에는 영어 단어와 한글 뜻, 이렇게 단순하게 외울 수 있지만, 이보다는 [영어 단어 → 동의어 ▶ 영어 단어 → 동의어(Definition) → 예문 ▶ 영어 단어의 어원관련 학습 ▶ 한글 뜻 → 영어 단어] 순으로 점차 그 범위를 넓혀가면서 기억용량(Memory Span)을 늘리다보면 어휘량은 무한히 늘어날 것이다. 어휘는 문맥 속에서 적절하게 사용해야 하기 때문에 한 가지 방법보다는 여러 가지 방법으로 어휘의 본래 의미와 용례 등을 학습해야 한다. 효율적인 어휘 학습을 돕기 위한 방법의 한 예로 어휘의 뜻을 그림으로 그려가며 하는 것도 도움이 될 것이다.

TOEFL 어휘는 시험을 보는 마지막 순간까지도 지속적으로 공부해야 할 것이다. 꾸준한 학습을 통하여 TOEFL 어휘를 공부하면서 TOEFL에 대한 두려움이 사라질 수 있기를 바란다. 이 책이 부족하지만 체계적인 TOEFL 어휘 학습을 위한 길라잡이가 되어 어휘 학습량을 늘려줄 수 있다면 저자로서 더 바랄 게 없다. 모두가 큰 축복 속에 평안하기 바란다.

2014년 7월

저자 윤창만, 손성균

목차

Vocabulary Skills for the TOEFL iBT 2

머리말	4
Day 01	7
Day 02	13
Day 03	19
Day 04	25
Day 05	31
Day 01-05 EXERCISE	37
Day 06	45
Day 07	51
Day 08	57
Day 09	63
Day 10	69
Day 06-10 EXERCISE	75
Day 11	83
Day 12	89
Day 13	95
Day 14	101
Day 15	107
Day 11-15 EXERCISE	113
Day 16	121
Day 17	127
Day 18	133
Day 19	139
Day 20	145
Day 16-20 EXERCISE	151
정답 해설	159

이 책의 특징 및 공부 방법

이 책은 지난 20여 년 동안의 TOEFL 기출어휘를 분석하여 1권당 800개(20유닛, 1유닛당 40개)를 선정, 총 2400개(총 3권)의 필수어휘를 제시하고 있다.

01. Daily Checkup

필수어휘 40개를 공부하기 전에, 자신의 어휘 실력을 테스트해볼 수 있도록 하기 위해 20개의 동의어 문제를 제공한다.

02. Voca Bank

하루치 40개의 단어를 선정하여 [동의어 – 반의어 – 한글 뜻 – 구문 및 예문] 등을 실었다. 구문 및 예문은 실제 시험에 출제되었던 내용을 요약·정리했기 때문에 반드시 암기해야 한다. 자주 출제되는 단어는 별표를 이용해서 출제 빈도를 표시했다.

03. Practice Test

Voca Bank에서 공부한 어휘를 테스트해볼 수 있다. 틀린 문제는 반드시 다시 한번 체크하기 바란다. 여기에 실린 문제들은 지면 관계상 본문에서 미처 다루지 못했던 예문을 대신하는 역할을 겸하기 때문에 문제 자체를 외우는 것도 문맥 파악을 위해 도움이 될 것이다.

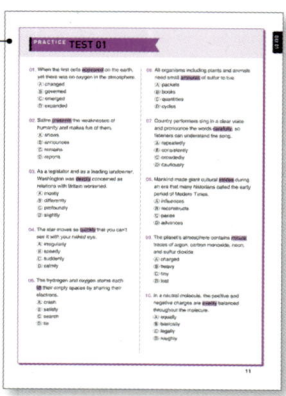

01

01. have a **lecture** from
    - Ⓐ degree
    - Ⓑ money
    - Ⓒ evidence
    - Ⓓ talk

02. the **spine** of a textbook
    - Ⓐ foot
    - Ⓑ backbone
    - Ⓒ hand
    - Ⓓ toe

03. decided to **extend** our trip
    - Ⓐ give up
    - Ⓑ achieve
    - Ⓒ change
    - Ⓓ lengthen

04. **plead** a person's case
    - Ⓐ regret
    - Ⓑ entreat
    - Ⓒ vary
    - Ⓓ reprove

05. a **lucid** explanation
    - Ⓐ unusual
    - Ⓑ ceaseless
    - Ⓒ plain
    - Ⓓ obscure

06. show signs of **decadence**
    - Ⓐ decline
    - Ⓑ corruption
    - Ⓒ improvement
    - Ⓓ recovery

07. **alter** a house into a store
    - Ⓐ stretch
    - Ⓑ diminish
    - Ⓒ add
    - Ⓓ transform

08. **tap** the ends of one's fingers together
    - Ⓐ fix
    - Ⓑ knock
    - Ⓒ augment
    - Ⓓ remove

09. a rare and **exotic** bird
    - Ⓐ common
    - Ⓑ well-known
    - Ⓒ foreign
    - Ⓓ prevalent

10. be getting better **gradually**
    - Ⓐ perpetually
    - Ⓑ permanently
    - Ⓒ slowly
    - Ⓓ commonly

11. a very **reliable** mechanic
    - Ⓐ dependable
    - Ⓑ fruitless
    - Ⓒ useless
    - Ⓓ barren

12. with a **dejected** air
    - Ⓐ serious
    - Ⓑ depressed
    - Ⓒ alien
    - Ⓓ joyful

13. an **impregnable** fortress
    - Ⓐ breakable
    - Ⓑ effective
    - Ⓒ remarkable
    - Ⓓ invincible

14. **application** for admission to a school
    - Ⓐ money
    - Ⓑ inquiry
    - Ⓒ changing
    - Ⓓ essence

15. **transfer** a boy to another school
    - Ⓐ scold
    - Ⓑ tap
    - Ⓒ move
    - Ⓓ mutate

16. a **massive** block of stone
    - Ⓐ transparent
    - Ⓑ flawless
    - Ⓒ infinite
    - Ⓓ immense

17. There is something **scrapping** against the wall.
    - Ⓐ grinding
    - Ⓑ immersing
    - Ⓒ corrupting
    - Ⓓ quivering

18. **pervade** the air of the room
    - Ⓐ penetrate
    - Ⓑ fill
    - Ⓒ cleanse
    - Ⓓ breathe

19. receive a **rebuke**
    - Ⓐ scolding
    - Ⓑ gist
    - Ⓒ uniform
    - Ⓓ bark

20. **invariable** custom
    - Ⓐ depressed
    - Ⓑ primary
    - Ⓒ bizarre
    - Ⓓ constant

01 Voca Bank

표제어	품사	동의어와 예문	한글 뜻
1 **alloy** [ǽlɔi]	v	mix, combine; debase, impair **alloy** the copper with zinc 구리와 아연을 합금하다	합금하다 / (품위를) 떨어뜨리다
2 **alter**** [ɔ́:ltər]	v	change, transform, modify, fix, mutate **alter** a store into a house 가게를 집으로 바꾸다	변경하다, 바꾸다
3 **application*** [æpləkéiʃən]	n	use, employment, exercise, inquiry practical **application** of the result 결과의 실용적인 응용 an **application** for a driver's license 운전면허를 위한 응시원서	응용, 신청, 응시원서
4 **attain***** [ətéin]	v	reach, acquire, achieve, procure, win **attain** to perfection 완벽의 경지에 이르다	달성하다, 획득하다
5 **burst*** [bə:rst]	v	explode, blow up **burst** the balloon aloft in the air 하늘 높이서 풍선이 터지다	폭발하다, 터지다
6 **capital*** [kǽpətl]	n a	money, funds, finances, investments, assets a **capital** fund 자본금 principal, chief, prime, primary, major, leading a **capital** idea for relocating of furniture 가구 재배치에 대한 좋은 생각	자본 주요한
7 **chamber** [tʃéimbər]	a	compartment, room stay in a particular **chamber** for debates 토론을 위해 특별한 방에서 머무르다	방, 실
8 **core*** [kɔ:r]	n	center, heart, essence, gist, substance the **core** of the apple 사과의 핵(중심)	핵, 중심
9 **decadence** [dékədəns]	n	deterioration, decline **decadence** of art 예술의 타락	타락, 쇠퇴
10 **dejected*** [didʒéktid]	a	depressed, discouraged with a **dejected** air 소침하여	낙담한, 우울증 있는
11 **delegate*** [déligət]	n	representative **delegate** from Korea to attend a conference 학회에 참석할 한국 대표	대표자
12 **deplore*** [diplɔ́:r]	v	grieve, regret, lament, mourn **deplore** the evils of the time 시대의 병폐를 개탄하다	한탄하다, 애도하다
13 **differentiate**** [difərénʃièit]	v	distinguish, make different, change **differentiate** man from brutes 인간을 짐승과 구별하다	구별 짓다
14 **eternal*** [itə́:rnəl]	a	perpetual, endless, everlasting, infinite, permanent **eternal** truth 영원한 진리	영원한, 지속적인

15	**everywhere*** [évrihwɛər]	ad	all around, all over, far and wide, the world over **Everywhere** we go, people are much the same. 어디를 가든지 인간은 별 차이가 없다.	도처에
16	**exotic*** [igzátik]	a	unusual, foreign, alien resemble **exotic** sea shells 이국적인 바다 조개와 유사하다	색다른
17	**extend*** [iksténd]	v	① stretch, expand, enlarge, range, augment ↔ contract, condense **extend** a road to the next city 다음 도시까지 도로를 확장하다 ② lengthen, prolong ↔ shorten **extend** a rehearsal 연습을 늘리다	① 확대하다 ② 연장하다
18	**famous*** [féiməs]	a	well-known, celebrated, acclaimed a **famous** writer 유명한 작가	유명한
19	**fiery** [fáiəri]	a	excitable, burning, ablaze a volcano's **fiery** discharge 한 화산의 분화(화염의 분출)	성미가 사나운, 불 같은, 화염의
20	**gradually*** [grǽdʒuəli]	ad	slowly, little by little, by degrees be getting better **gradually** 점차 나아지다	점차적으로
21	**grasp*** [græsp]	v	seize, hold, clasp, comprehend, grip, grab **grasp** the bike's handlebars 자전거의 핸들을 잡다	잡다, 이해하다
22	**impregnable*** [imprégnəbl]	a	invincible, unassailable an **impregnable** fortress 난공불락의 요새	난공불락의
23	**invariable** [invɛ́əriəbl]	a	unchangeable, constant, uniform **invariable** principle of education 교육의 철칙	지속적인, 변함없는
24	**lecture** [léktʃər]	n	give speech, talk, address, lesson, sermon get a **lecture** from ~에게서 훈계를 받다	강의, 설교, 훈계
25	**lucid** [lúːsid]	a	clear, transparent, intelligible, plain, obvious, distinct a **lucid** explanation 명쾌한 해설	맑은, 명료한
26	**magnitude*** [mǽgnətjùːd]	n	① degree, extent, measure, proportion of the first **magnitude** 일등성(星)의, 가장 중요한, 일류의 ② volume, size, mass, bulk, amplitude an earthquake of **magnitude** 7.0 규모 7.0 지진 ③ importance, consequence the **magnitude** of a problem in education 교육에 있어서 문제의 중대성	① 정도 ② 규모 ③ 중대함
27	**mask*** [mæsk]	v	veil, disguise assume a **mask** 가면을 쓰다, 정체를 감추다	가장하다, 가면을 씌우다
28	**massive*** [mǽsiv]	a	enormous, bulky, immense, huge, tremendous **massive** column 큰 기둥	크고 무거운, 육중한
29	**pervade*** [pərvéid]	v	permeate, penetrate, infiltrate Spring **pervaded** the air. 봄 기운이 대기에 충만하다.	널리 퍼지다
30	**plead** [pliːd]	v	entreat, beg, reason, defend, supplicate **plead** for help 도움을 간청하다	변론하다, 항변하다

31	**prophet** [práfit]	n	forecaster, oracle a **prophet** of doom 재앙을 예언하는 사람	예언자, 선지자
32	**purified*** [pjúərəfàid]	a	refined, clean sugar **purified** from the sugarcane 사탕수수로부터 정제한 설탕	깨끗이 하는, 정제한
33	**rebuke** [ribjúːk]	v	reprove, reprimand, censure, reproach, scold without **rebuke** 나무랄 데 없이	비난하다, 꾸짖다
34	**reliable*** [riláiəbl]	a	trustworthy, dependable, infallible a **reliable** source 유력한 소식통	믿을 수 있는
35	**scrape** [skreip]	v	graze, bark, rub, grind **scrape** away soil or sand to reveal relics 유물이 나타나도록 흙과 모래를 긁어내다	스치다, 문지르다
		n	predicament, awkward situation a **scrape** on one's knee 누구의 무릎에 찰과상	스치기, 곤경, 곤란, 궁지
36	**spine** [spain]	n	backbone, vertebrate I felt my **spine** go cold. 나는 등골이 오싹해졌다.	등뼈
37	**sterile*** [stéril]	a	barren, unproductive, fruitless a **sterile** year 흉년	불임의
38	**tap** [tæp]	v	draw upon; knock, beat, strike **tap** time 똑똑 치며 박자를 맞추다	떨어뜨리다 / 가볍게 두드리다
39	**transfer*** [trænsfə́ːr]	v	move, change, convey **transfer** a boy to another school 소년을 전학시키다	옮기다, 바꾸다
40	**unbecoming** [ʌnbikʌ́miŋ]	a	inappropriate, unsuitable **unbecoming** behavior 꼴사나운 짓	어울리지 않은

Practice Test 01

01. People can live almost everywhere on land.
    Ⓐ attempt
    Ⓑ lost
    Ⓒ all around
    Ⓓ reach

02. Too much salt masks the true flavor of the food.
    Ⓐ stimulates
    Ⓑ obscures
    Ⓒ preserves
    Ⓓ sauces

03. Copper and other minerals are purified by electrolysis.
    Ⓐ refined
    Ⓑ identified
    Ⓒ reproduced
    Ⓓ yielded

04. A volcano forms when magma, hot gases, and fragments of rock burst through the surface.
    Ⓐ emergence
    Ⓑ spurt
    Ⓒ show
    Ⓓ release

05. Cherokee women could attain a position of 'war woman' and participate in the war councils.
    Ⓐ contain
    Ⓑ maintain
    Ⓒ remain
    Ⓓ achieve

06. Most religions teach that salvation comes only once and is eternal.
    Ⓐ balanced
    Ⓑ traditional
    Ⓒ disciplined
    Ⓓ perpetual

07. Planetariums employ astronomers to lecture and conduct classes for the public.
    Ⓐ raise money
    Ⓑ arrange meetings
    Ⓒ write articles
    Ⓓ give speeches

08. Adams was determined to keep the United States neutral, and deplored the policy of Hamilton and his followers.
    Ⓐ emulated
    Ⓑ ridicule
    Ⓒ complimented
    Ⓓ nullified

09. A mule is a sterile offspring of a female horse and a male donkey.
    Ⓐ unfruitful
    Ⓑ aesthetic
    Ⓒ aseptic
    Ⓓ fertile

10. Sand particles driven by wind scrape and wear away rock surfaces.
    Ⓐ scratch
    Ⓑ pile
    Ⓒ collect
    Ⓓ pass

11. In Islam, people think that God selects prophets to urge people to worship only God, and to teach God's commandments, and not to foretell the future.
    Ⓐ forecasters
    Ⓑ masters
    Ⓒ noblemen
    Ⓓ beholders

12. By 1910, Hollywood had become the motion-picture capital of the world.
    Ⓐ knowledge
    Ⓑ manpower
    Ⓒ center
    Ⓓ technology

13. On the Richter scale, each increase in number in magnitude means that the energy release of the quake is about 32 times greater.
    Ⓐ degree
    Ⓑ volume
    Ⓒ value
    Ⓓ period

14. Although most of the information distributed over the Internet is reliable, some of it is biased or fictitious.
    Ⓐ convenient
    Ⓑ dependable
    Ⓒ accessible
    Ⓓ concise

15. Most airplane wings are made of metal, while the skeleton has a thin covering, usually made of aluminum alloy.
    Ⓐ mixture
    Ⓑ plate
    Ⓒ layer
    Ⓓ heat

16. Today, the Chinese government permits the practice of the religion so that followers are gradually increasing in number.
    Ⓐ slowly
    Ⓑ freely
    Ⓒ inevitably
    Ⓓ rapidly

17. Virgil tried to connect the origins of Rome to the events that followed the fiery destruction of Troy by the Greeks.
    Ⓐ inflamed
    Ⓑ ferment
    Ⓒ impetuous
    Ⓓ explosive

18. To understand the history of a country, it is not necessary to study the lives and work of its individual famous men.
    Ⓐ moving
    Ⓑ notorious
    Ⓒ religious
    Ⓓ well-known

19. Orangutans have long, curved fingers and toes that help them grasp branches, making them well-suited for life in trees.
    Ⓐ realize
    Ⓑ trickle
    Ⓒ grip
    Ⓓ perceive

20. Within the interior of the Earth, the temperature rises rapidly, reaching perhaps 2300°C inside the ocean and 7000°C in the rocky core.
    Ⓐ crust
    Ⓑ mantle
    Ⓒ ore
    Ⓓ center

DAY 02 Daily Checkup

01. a mild winter
    - Ⓐ severe
    - Ⓑ clear
    - Ⓒ gentle
    - Ⓓ draughty

02. give support to
    - Ⓐ birth
    - Ⓑ aid
    - Ⓒ benefit
    - Ⓓ advice

03. leap out
    - Ⓐ jump
    - Ⓑ provoke
    - Ⓒ limit
    - Ⓓ ripe

04. conform to the custom
    - Ⓐ opposite
    - Ⓑ agree
    - Ⓒ direct
    - Ⓓ confront

05. an imaginary enemy
    - Ⓐ humiliating
    - Ⓑ robust
    - Ⓒ amiable
    - Ⓓ visionary

06. a local autonomous entity
    - Ⓐ unit
    - Ⓑ extent
    - Ⓒ myth
    - Ⓓ hindrance

07. a terrific party
    - Ⓐ superb
    - Ⓑ kindly
    - Ⓒ coarse
    - Ⓓ stylish

08. provoke a riot
    - Ⓐ constrain
    - Ⓑ exasperate
    - Ⓒ astonish
    - Ⓓ hinder

09. too frail to travel
    - Ⓐ hot
    - Ⓑ energetic
    - Ⓒ selfish
    - Ⓓ meek

10. condense milk
    - Ⓐ boil
    - Ⓑ warn
    - Ⓒ dissolve
    - Ⓓ concentrate

11. a stern voice
    - Ⓐ unfit
    - Ⓑ strict
    - Ⓒ tender
    - Ⓓ harsh

12. linger over one's work
    - Ⓐ teach
    - Ⓑ join
    - Ⓒ remain
    - Ⓓ wander

13. a genial household
    - Ⓐ cordial
    - Ⓑ diligent
    - Ⓒ sluggish
    - Ⓓ animate

14. be blinded by greed
    - Ⓐ corruption
    - Ⓑ avarice
    - Ⓒ failure
    - Ⓓ murder

15. stunned by the bad news
    - Ⓐ compressed
    - Ⓑ separated
    - Ⓒ bewildered
    - Ⓓ acceded

16. stint oneself in sleep
    - Ⓐ patronize
    - Ⓑ limit
    - Ⓒ astound
    - Ⓓ awaken

17. the predominant figure in the business
    - Ⓐ tiny
    - Ⓑ sympathetic
    - Ⓒ intimidating
    - Ⓓ principal

18. the inevitable result
    - Ⓐ positive
    - Ⓑ firm
    - Ⓒ unavoidable
    - Ⓓ unreal

19. stale beer
    - Ⓐ friendly
    - Ⓑ old
    - Ⓒ visionary
    - Ⓓ rotten

20. aid to destitute families
    - Ⓐ affluent
    - Ⓑ wealthy
    - Ⓒ depressed
    - Ⓓ poor

DAY 02 Voca Bank

표제어	품사	동의어와 예문	한글 뜻
1 **abject** [ǽbdʒekt]	a	humiliating, contemptible, base, mean **abject** poverty 극빈	비천한, 비열한, 모욕적인
2 **administer** [ədmínistər]	v	manage, govern, conduct, execute, direct, monitor, supervise **administer** justice to him 그를 재판하다	관리하다, 운영하다
3 **arid** [ǽrid]	a	dry, draughty, thirsty, dusty an **arid** plot of land 불모지	메마른, 불모의
4 **assent** [əsént]	v	accede, consent force to **assent** to their demands 그들의 요구를 들어주기를 강요하다	동의하다, 찬성하다
5 **attach** [ətǽtʃ]	v	fasten, adhere, affix, join, secure ↔ separate, detach **attach** a price tag on each article 각 상품에 가격표를 달다	첨부하다, 붙이다
6 **certificate** [sərtífikeit]	n	document, authorization, credentials, diploma a **certificate** of birth 출생증명서	증명서
7 **condense** [kəndéns]	v	compress, concentrate **condense** milk 우유를 농축하다	응축하다
8 **conform** [kənfɔ́:rm]	v	comply, yield, agree, assent; meet **conform** to the custom 관례를 지키다	동의하다 / 순응하다
9 **destitute** [déstətjù:t]	a	impoverished, poor, devoid be left **destitute** 곤궁에 빠져 있다	빈곤한, 결핍한
10 **distinctly** [distíŋktli]	ad	clearly, definitely, markedly, noticeably **distinctly** heard 분명히 들은	분명히, 명백하게
11 **enrich** [inrítʃ]	v	enhance, make, wealthy, augment **enrich** soil (with phosphate) (인산 비료로) 토지를 비옥하게 하다	부유하게 하다
12 **entity** [éntəti]	n	unit, puzzle, object a local autonomous **entity** 지방 자치단체	존재, 실체
13 **failing** [féiliŋ]	n	shortcoming, defect, flaw His health was **failing** rapidly. 그의 건강이 급격히 나빠지고 있다.	단점, 결점
14 **frail** [freil]	a	weak, feeble, fragile a **frail** girl 연약한 소녀	약한, 노쇠한
15 **genial** [dʒí:njəl]	a	sympathetic, cordial, friendly, kindly a **genial** disposition 싹싹한 성질	친근한, 상냥한
16 **greed** [gri:d]	n	avidity, avarice, covetousness the intoxication of **greed** and success 탐욕과 성공의 중독	욕심, 탐욕

17	**imaginary** [imǽdʒənèri]	a	fanciful, visionary, unreal an **imaginary** enemy 가상의 적	상상의
18	**improper** [imprápər]	a	unfit, inappropriate **improper** conduct 버릇없는 행동	적절치 않은
19	**inevitably** [inévitəbli]	ad	unavoidably, as a result, certainly **inevitably** end up competing other stores 어쩔 수 없이 다른 가게와 경쟁을 끝내다 an **inevitable** conclusion 당연한 결론	필연적으로, 확실히
20	**leap** [liːp]	v	jump, bound, spring, vault, hop **leap** to one's feet 후다닥 일어서다	껑충 뛰다, 뛰어넘다
21	**legend** [lédʒənd]	n	fable, myth according to **legend** 전설에 따르면	전설
22	**linger** [líŋgər]	v	remain, wait, stay, delay ↔ vacate, depart **linger** to say goodbye 작별을 망설이고 있다	남아있다, 꾸물거리다
23	**mild** [maild]	a	amiable, gentle, temperate, clement, tender ↔ stormy, violent, spicy a **mild** voice 부드러운 목소리	온화한
24	**murky** [məːrki]	a	dark, cloudy, dim, dull **murky** smoke 검은 연기	어두운
25	**output** [áutput]	n	production, yield, outcome, product, result the total **output** 총생산고	산출량, 결과
26	**predominant** [pridámənənt]	a	principal, major, essential, prevailing, prevalent a **predominant** trait 눈에 띄는 특징	널리 퍼진, 두드러진, 지배적인
27	**provoke** [prəvóuk]	v	arouse, cause, elicit, enrage, exasperate, vex, irritate **provoke** a riot 폭동을 선동하다	화나게 하다, 자극하여 ~시키다
28	**range** [reindʒ]	n	extent, scope, compass within the **range** of 사정거리 안에, 손에 닿는	범위, 정렬, 줄
29	**shame** [ʃeim]	n	embarrassment, discredit, humiliation suffer the **shame** of humble job 미천한 직업을 수치스러워하다 **shameful** behavior 부끄러워 해야 할 행동	수치심
30	**short-lived** [ʃɔ́ːrtláivd]	a	does not last long about her **short-lived** marriage 길지 않은 그녀의 결혼생활에 대해서	단명한, 일시적인
31	**stale** [steil]	a	old, dry, decayed, musty, moldy, uninteresting, trite ↔ fresh **stale** bread 신선하지 않은 빵	상한, 진부한
32	**stern** [stəːrn]	a	strict, firm, adamant, unrelenting, harsh mother's **stern** instructions not to boast 과장하지 않는 어머니의 단호한 가르침	단호한, 강경한
33	**stint** [stint]	v	limit, restrict, be frugal **stint** oneself in sleep 수면을 줄이다	제한하다, 절약하다

34	**stray** [strei]	v	wander, rove, roam, ramble, straggle, meander **stray** far from the truth 진실에서 겉리 멀어지다	다른 길로 들어서다
		a	lost, wandering, homeless, unwanted a **stray** sheep 길 잃은 양	헤매는
35	**stun** [stʌn]	v	amaze, astound, astonish, bewilder, stupefy be **stunned** into silence 놀라서 할 말을 잃다	어리벙벙하게 하다
36	**support** [səpɔ́:rt]	n	aid, help, assistance ↔ hindrance count on the **support** of his party 그의 모임의 지원에 의존하다	보조, 도움, 지원
		v	① help, maintain, assist, back, patronize, abet ↔ oppose **support** the family 가족을 부양하다	① 도와주다
			② confirm, reinforce, substantiate, corroborate **supported** the decision 그 결정을 지지하다	② 지지하다
			③ bear, uphold, carry, brace, buttress, prop, stay **support** the weight 무게를 유지하다	③ 받치다, 유지하다
37	**tame** [teim]	a	domesticated, mild, docile ↔ wild **tame** a wild animal 야생동물을 길들이다	길들인, 온순한
38	**terrific** [tərífik]	a	splendid, glorious, superb, marvelous, sensational; huge He is a **terrific** athlete and a brilliant jumper. 그는 놀라운 선수이며 훌륭한 도약 경기 선수이다.	훌륭한, 아주 멋진 / 엄청난
39	**vigorous** [vígərəs]	a	strong, robust, sturdy, energetic, powerful **vigorous** young man 건장한 젊은이	건장한, 힘찬
40	**whole** [houl]	a	entire, complete, intact, unbroken, sound ↔ partial, incomplete a **whole** year 꼬박 1년	전체의

Practice Test 02

01. Horses had been tamed for riding by about 3000 B.C.
    A hunted
    B acclimatized
    C domesticated
    D threatened

02. The more vigorous the activity, the more calories it burns.
    A strong
    B justifiable
    C initial
    D delicate

03. About 1900's, Latin American artists began to develop painting styles that were distinctly that of Latin American.
    A definitely
    B surprisingly
    C separately
    D logically

04. Most bacteria are surrounded by a cell wall, which is attached to the eukaryotic cell membrane.
    A augmented
    B fastened
    C removed
    D included

05. State governments support public schools through taxes and administer them through local school districts.
    A manage
    B recognize
    C oppose
    D justify

06. Although the world as a whole has plenty of fresh water, some regions still have a water shortage.
    A harmonious
    B altogether
    C partly
    D greatly

07. Adams supported Jackson's foreign policy and also his stern resistance to nullification.
    A excessive
    B consistent
    C strict
    D malicious

08. To begin the long jump, the competitor sprints down a long runway and leaps from a take-off board.
    A jump
    B see
    C hear
    D call

09. The minister resigned last night after a stunning defeat in Monday's vote.
    A amusing
    B amazing
    C frightening
    D offending

10. An improper or inadequate diet increases the risk of various diseases.
    A appropriate
    B immoral
    C scant
    D unsuitable

11. Indian children were praised when they behaved well and shamed when they misbehaved.
    A scolded
    B restricted
    C embarrassed
    D reckless

12. The airplane is an engine-driven machine that can fly through the air supported by air flow around its wings.
    A protected
    B consistent
    C burdened
    D sustained

13. When warm, moist air moves up a windward slope of a mountain, it cools down while the water vapor it holds condenses into water droplets.
    A penetrates
    B filtrates
    C compresses
    D spreads

14. Many works of poor quality have strayed far from the truth, presenting only the most sensational parts of frontier life.
    A cleared
    B maligned
    C impeded
    D deviated

15. Watergate differed from most previous political scandals because personal greed apparently did not play an important role.
    A superiority
    B profit
    C covetousness
    D salute

16. In arid areas, the sandy soil quickly erodes after the protective covering of vegetation is removed.
    A dirty
    B dry
    C harsh
    D soggy

17. The geological records of ancient times remain somewhat murky, yet many geologists still believe that the sea level stood about five meters higher than it does now.
    A coaxed
    B dusty
    C hazy
    D mingled

18. The governments of most nations require international travelers to show certificates of vaccination and inoculation before allowing them to enter their country.
    A authorizations
    B guarantee
    C assurances
    D specifications

19. Young people seldom feel compelled to take certain action, adopt certain values, or otherwise conform to be accepted by the group.
    A allow to
    B feel to
    C agree to
    D surpass to

20. As Venus travels around the sun, it rotates very slowly on its axis, an imaginary line drawn through its center.
    A unexpected
    B uncommon
    C unusual
    D unreal

DAY 03 Daily Checkup

01. be convenient for work
    - Ⓐ calm
    - Ⓑ handy
    - Ⓒ quiet
    - Ⓓ reasonable

02. experiments in chemistry
    - Ⓐ molecules
    - Ⓑ errors
    - Ⓒ addition
    - Ⓓ tests

03. elude the law
    - Ⓐ inspect
    - Ⓑ obey
    - Ⓒ evade
    - Ⓓ betray

04. a spacious house
    - Ⓐ roomy
    - Ⓑ impractical
    - Ⓒ spiritual
    - Ⓓ magnificent

05. splendid talents
    - Ⓐ impractical
    - Ⓑ artistic
    - Ⓒ spiritual
    - Ⓓ magnificent

06. part time and adjunct teaching position at college
    - Ⓐ clever
    - Ⓑ useful
    - Ⓒ additional
    - Ⓓ careless

07. ban smoking in all offices
    - Ⓐ prohibit
    - Ⓑ determine
    - Ⓒ choose
    - Ⓓ reflect

08. incompatible colors
    - Ⓐ simple
    - Ⓑ blurred
    - Ⓒ inconsistent
    - Ⓓ bright

09. implore God for mercy
    - Ⓐ imagine
    - Ⓑ entreat
    - Ⓒ deem
    - Ⓓ enact

10. The seasons rotate.
    - Ⓐ resemble
    - Ⓑ change
    - Ⓒ test
    - Ⓓ turn

11. slaughter the newborn animals
    - Ⓐ care
    - Ⓑ massacre
    - Ⓒ raise
    - Ⓓ protest

12. the sum of our knowledge
    - Ⓐ evolution
    - Ⓑ amount
    - Ⓒ accumulation
    - Ⓓ creation

13. ruin one's career
    - Ⓐ heighten
    - Ⓑ ignore
    - Ⓒ murder
    - Ⓓ spoil

14. adopt a method
    - Ⓐ take on
    - Ⓑ classify
    - Ⓒ alter
    - Ⓓ study

15. the segments of an orange
    - Ⓐ tastes
    - Ⓑ portions
    - Ⓒ scents
    - Ⓓ colors

16. in extreme danger
    - Ⓐ fable
    - Ⓑ gained
    - Ⓒ reaped
    - Ⓓ ultimate

17. by the medium of
    - Ⓐ sector
    - Ⓑ sum
    - Ⓒ means
    - Ⓓ mistaking

18. tears of indignation
    - Ⓐ happiness
    - Ⓑ wrath
    - Ⓒ sorrow
    - Ⓓ joy

19. a negligible loss that we need not worry about
    - Ⓐ extreme
    - Ⓑ fatal
    - Ⓒ suitable
    - Ⓓ careless

20. study wholeheartedly
    - Ⓐ carelessly
    - Ⓑ enthusiastically
    - Ⓒ inconsistently
    - Ⓓ excessively

03 Voca Bank

	표제어	품사	동의어와 예문	한글 뜻
1	**adjunct (to)*** [ǽdʒʌŋkt]	n	addition (to) an **adjunct** to the main computer 메인 컴퓨터의 부속물	부가물, 부속물
2	**adopt*** [ədápt]	v	enact, take on, choose **adopt** laws requiring democracy 민주주의가 요구하는 법을 채택하다	채용하다, 제정하다
3	**attitude*** [ǽtitjùːd]	n	① position, bearing, pose, posture with an **attitude** toward critics 비평가들에 대한 입장으로 ② air, demeanor, disposition, presence She has a calm **attitude**. 그녀는 냉담한 태도를 하고 있다.	① 입장 ② 태도, 자세
4	**backbone** [bǽkbòun]	n	spine, back, column, vertebrate from **backbone** of our company 우리 회사의 중견이 되다	등뼈, 중견
5	**ban**** [bæn]	v	forbid, prohibit, inhibit, bar, exclude, banish ↔ allow, permit **ban** smoking in all offices 모든 사무실에서 금연하다	금지하다, 억제하다
6	**bar*** [bɑːr]	v	stem, hinder, obstruct, deter, stop, impede be **barred** from ~을 금지 당하다	방해하다, 저지하다
7	**blunder**** [blʌ́ndər]	v	make a mistake, err, slip up **blunder** away one's chance 좋은 기회를 놓치다	실수를 하다
		n	mistake, slip, error, gaffe a fatal **blunder** 치명적인 과실	실수, 과실
8	**confuse** [kənfjúːz]	v	disturb, perplex, bewilder, baffle, confound, mislead ↔ clarify **confuse** Charlie with another 찰리와 다른 사람을 혼동하다	혼동하다, 당황하다
9	**convenient**** [kənvíːnjənt]	a	handy, opportune, appropriate, suitable, useful ↔ bothersome a simple and **convenient** article 간편한 물건	편리한, 적당한
10	**diagnose** [dáiəgnòus]	v	analyze, identify, determine **diagnose** a person's illness as cancer 암이라고 진단하다	분석하다, 진단하다
11	**diffract** [difrǽkt]	v	break into parts, break up, divide **diffract** X rays by the flat surface of the crystal 수정의 편평한 표면에 의해 X 선을 분산시키다	분산시키다, 나누다
12	**elevate***** [éləvèit]	v	① exalt, raise, heighten, lift, increase, enhance ↔ lower, depress **elevate** our spirits 우리의 정신을 고양시키다 ② promote, upgrade, advance, boost ↔ demote, downgrade **elevate** to a higher-paying job 고임금 일로 승진시키다	① 높이다, 고양하다 ② 향상시키다

13	**elude** [ilúːd]	v	avoid, escape, evade, shun, dodge **elude** the law 법망을 뚫다	피하다
14	**erroneous**** [iróuniəs]	a	incorrect, mistaken, false prove his statement to be **erroneous** 그의 진술이 잘못된 것을 증명하다	실수의, 거짓의
15	**experiment*** [ikspérəmənt]	n	investigation, test, trial, research, study **experiments** in chemistry 화학실험	실험
16	**extreme**** [ikstríːm]	a	ultimate, excessive, unreasonable **extreme** penalty 극형	극도의, 과도한
17	**fable** [féibl]	n	legend, parable Aesop's **Fables** 이솝우화	전설, 우화
18	**implore** [implɔ́ːr]	v	supplicate, beseech, entreat, crave, beg, solicit **implore** a judge for mercy 판사의 자비를 탄원하다	탄원하다
19	**incompatible***** [ìnkəmpǽtəbl]	a	inconsistent, contradictory, inharmonious, unable, incapable **incompatible** with its mainframe 컴퓨터 본체와 맞지 않는	조화되지 않은
20	**incorporate*** [inkɔ́ːrpərèit]	v	combine, integrate, include, contain **incorporated** with another company 다른 회사와 합병하다	포함시키다
21	**indignation** [ìndignéiʃən]	n	wrath, anger, resentment tears of **indignation** 비분의 눈물	분노
22	**medium*** [míːdiəm]	a	stone or wood, water, means the **medium** of circulation 통화의 수단 * stone or wood, water가 문맥상에서 정답으로 쓰이는 경우가 있음	수단, 매개물
23	**mirror** [mírə(r)]	v	resemble, reflect hold the **mirror** up to nature 자연 그대로 비추다	비추다, 반영하다
24	**mistake**** [mistéik]	n	blunder, error, slip, oversight, offense, fault by **mistake** 잘못하여, 실수로	잘못, 틀림
25	**negligence*** [néglidʒəns]	n	carelessness owing to one's **negligence** 불찰로	부주의
26	**reaped** [riːpid]	a	gained, harvested **reaped** the fruits of one's action 자업자득한	거두어 들이는
27	**reckon**** [rékən]	v	① count, compute, calculate, enumerate be **reckoned** at about 5 times 5배 정도라고 계산되었다 ② consider, regard, deem He **reckoned** he was still fond of her. 그는 아직도 그녀를 좋아한다고 생각했다.	① 세다, 계산하다 ② 간주하다
28	**resist**** [rizíst]	v	① fight, oppose, confront, counteract ↔ yield, surrender **resist** the enemy 적을 격퇴하다 ② withstand, ignore, stand, thwart ↔ submit **resist** the temptation 유혹을 물리치다 **resist** law 법을 거스르다	① 반항하다 ② 저항하다

29	**rotate*** [róuteit]	v	turn, spin, revolve, wheel, roll The seasons **rotate**. 사계절은 돌고 돈다.		회전하다
30	**ruin** [rú:in]	v	downfall, spoil, demolish, destroy, decay, damage **ruin** every relationship 모든 관계를 망치다 rapine and red **ruin** 약탈과 화재		파멸하다
31	**scorch** [skɔ:rtʃ]	v	burn, parch, roast, sear **scorch** rice 밥을 태우다		태우다
32	**segment** [ségmənt]	n	portion, sector the **segment** of an orange 오렌지 조각		구획, 단편
33	**slaughter** [slɔ́:tər]	v	massacre, murder, slay, butcher, kill **slaughtered** for commercial gain 상업적 이득을 위해 도살하다		도살하다
		n	massacre, carnage, bloodbath the **slaughter** of war 전쟁에 의한 대량 살인		대학살
34	**slay** [slei]	v	kill, slaughter, massacre, murder, butcher, assassinate **slay** a man 사람을 죽이다		살해하다
35	**spacious*** [spéiʃəs]	a	ample, capacious, extensive, roomy, vast a **spacious** house 넓은 집		넓은, 풍부한
36	**specimen** [spésəmən]	n	sample, model, pattern a fine **specimen** 훌륭한 표본		견본, 표본
37	**splendid*** [spléndid]	a	magnificent, gorgeous, sumptuous, dazzling ↔ dreadful **splendid** talents 뛰어난 재능		찬란한, 훌륭한
38	**sum** [sʌm]	n	total, amount a **sum** of money 돈의 총액		총액, 합계
39	**via** [váiə]	prep	by way of **via** Canada 캐나다를 경유하여		경유하여
40	**wholeheartedly*** [hóulhá:rtidli]	ad	enthusiastically study **wholeheartedly** 전심전력으로 공부하다		전심전력의

Practice

01. Specific tariffs are levied on certain imported products as a sum of money.
    Ⓐ amount
    Ⓑ service
    Ⓒ debt
    Ⓓ list

02. The majority of Roman roads fell into ruin during the following centuries.
    Ⓐ delay
    Ⓑ tax
    Ⓒ destroy
    Ⓓ reroute

03. Someone who was trying to discover a comet could easily mistake a nebula for a comet.
    Ⓐ observe
    Ⓑ think
    Ⓒ nominate
    Ⓓ confuse with

04. Many news services deliver reports to news organizations via communication satellites.
    Ⓐ off
    Ⓑ by way of
    Ⓒ near
    Ⓓ in line with

05. A good driver is someone with a proper attitude, which means a willingness to share the road with others.
    Ⓐ bearing
    Ⓑ affection
    Ⓒ disposition
    Ⓓ intention

06. The earth takes a day to rotate on its axis, an imaginary line that goes through the North and South poles.
    Ⓐ shift
    Ⓑ distort
    Ⓒ move
    Ⓓ spin

07. Hardness is the trait of a material to scratch another substance or to resist being scratched by them.
    Ⓐ isolate
    Ⓑ damage
    Ⓒ withstand
    Ⓓ strengthen

08. The beam was diffracted by the flat surfaces of the crystal.
    Ⓐ shared
    Ⓑ deflected
    Ⓒ reflected
    Ⓓ divided

09. In microscope, the mirror reflects light through an opening in the stage to illuminate the specimen.
    Ⓐ example
    Ⓑ surface
    Ⓒ simple
    Ⓓ production

10. Global warming, which has so far played a negligible role in West Antarctica's fate, is bound to wield greater influence in the future.
    Ⓐ undetermined
    Ⓑ insignificant
    Ⓒ unusual
    Ⓓ indisputable

11. In 1906, movement along another faulty segment resulted in a major earthquake in San Francisco.
    Ⓐ core
    Ⓑ layer
    Ⓒ section
    Ⓓ problem

12. Classical composers have incorporated folk melodies into their work.
    Ⓐ assigned
    Ⓑ combined
    Ⓒ indicated
    Ⓓ evidenced

13. In many fables, the moral is told in the form of a proverb at the end of story.
    Ⓐ dramas
    Ⓑ plays
    Ⓒ poetry
    Ⓓ parables

14. Physicians use a variety of electronic instruments and machines to diagnose and treat disorders.
    Ⓐ heal
    Ⓑ relieve
    Ⓒ analyze
    Ⓓ control

15. In our own economic system, money gives a universal measure of values, a convenient medium of exchange through which we can buy and sell almost anything.
    Ⓐ means
    Ⓑ milieu
    Ⓒ center
    Ⓓ funds

16. People with dyslexia often confuse letters or words and may read or write words and sentences in the wrong order.
    Ⓐ ruin
    Ⓑ astonish
    Ⓒ perplex
    Ⓓ falter

17. People throughout the world were made aware to the fact that thousands of elephants were being slaughtered each year to provide ivory jewelry and carvings.
    Ⓐ isolated
    Ⓑ tested
    Ⓒ vaccinated
    Ⓓ killed

18. A monosaccharide such as glucose has a backbone of six carbon atoms, with hydrogen and oxygen atoms attached, giving it the chemical symbol C6H12O6.
    Ⓐ chain
    Ⓑ frame
    Ⓒ spinal cord
    Ⓓ particle

19. Soft drinks have been made available in more convenient packages, such as metal cans and many types of glass and plastic containers.
    Ⓐ neat
    Ⓑ various
    Ⓒ handy
    Ⓓ small

20. The plays vividly mirror the Wars of the Roses - the series of bloody conflicts between the houses of York and Lancaster for control of the English throne.
    Ⓐ reflect
    Ⓑ distort
    Ⓒ restrict
    Ⓓ deny

DAY 04 Daily Checkup

01. the primary stage of civilization
    - Ⓐ intermediate
    - Ⓑ introductory
    - Ⓒ inert
    - Ⓓ lowered

02. bore a hole in the board
    - Ⓐ confess
    - Ⓑ captivated
    - Ⓒ drill
    - Ⓓ prohibit

03. forge a sword
    - Ⓐ cover
    - Ⓑ prohibit
    - Ⓒ polish
    - Ⓓ make

04. muse on the meaning of life
    - Ⓐ ponder
    - Ⓑ forge
    - Ⓒ enjoy
    - Ⓓ bleach

05. compete with others for a prize
    - Ⓐ captivate
    - Ⓑ contest
    - Ⓒ hamper
    - Ⓓ shake

06. have a tacit understanding
    - Ⓐ explicit
    - Ⓑ tangled
    - Ⓒ powerful
    - Ⓓ implicit

07. anti-imperialist sentiment
    - Ⓐ government
    - Ⓑ emotion
    - Ⓒ nation
    - Ⓓ uproar

08. The log was rotted away.
    - Ⓐ weared
    - Ⓑ gnarled
    - Ⓒ decayed
    - Ⓓ composed

09. a rude reply
    - Ⓐ impolite
    - Ⓑ pointless
    - Ⓒ crude
    - Ⓓ modest

10. a feeble mind
    - Ⓐ romantic
    - Ⓑ timorous
    - Ⓒ hot tempered
    - Ⓓ delicate

11. a deluge of congratulations
    - Ⓐ flood
    - Ⓑ kinship
    - Ⓒ rotation
    - Ⓓ eruption

12. transcend human power
    - Ⓐ copy
    - Ⓑ elevate
    - Ⓒ go beyond
    - Ⓓ restrict

13. be fascinated by the scenic beauty of
    - Ⓐ scared
    - Ⓑ charmed
    - Ⓒ comforted
    - Ⓓ pleased

14. lead a gay life
    - Ⓐ nomadic
    - Ⓑ carefree
    - Ⓒ pleasant
    - Ⓓ anxious

15. honor one's ancestors
    - Ⓐ successor
    - Ⓑ citizens
    - Ⓒ human being
    - Ⓓ forefather

16. acknowledge one's mistake
    - Ⓐ reject
    - Ⓑ exclude
    - Ⓒ admit
    - Ⓓ ignore

17. lost an appreciable amount of blood
    - Ⓐ significant
    - Ⓑ allowed
    - Ⓒ contemplated
    - Ⓓ diverse

18. awakening the dormant buds
    - Ⓐ inactive
    - Ⓑ mythical
    - Ⓒ elaborate
    - Ⓓ flying

19. The market is extremely stagnant.
    - Ⓐ arousing
    - Ⓑ corrupt
    - Ⓒ wild
    - Ⓓ inactive

20. tangle oneself in one's own share
    - Ⓐ deliberate
    - Ⓑ twist together
    - Ⓒ revolt
    - Ⓓ decay

DAY 04 Voca Bank

표제어	품사	동의어와 예문	한글 뜻
1 **acknowledge***** [æknálidʒ]	v	admit, confess, own **acknowledge** a favor 호의에 감사하다	인정하다
2 **ancestor*** [ǽnsestər]	n	forefather, forebear a philosophical **ancestor** 철학의 사표	선조
3 **appreciable*** [əprí:ʃiəbl]	a	significant, considerable, appropriate, pertinent an **appreciable** change 뚜렷한 변화	중요한, 적절한
4 **balmy*** [bá:mi]	a	mild, warm, calm, moderate **balmy** weather 온화한 날씨	온화한
5 **bore** [bɔ:r]	v	drill; weary, tire He **bores** me to death. 저 남자에게는 진절머리가 난다.	구멍을 뚫다 / 지루하게 하다, 피곤하게 만들다
6 **compete** [kəmpí:t]	v	contest, contend, rival, vie **compete** with others for a prize 상을 타려고 남과 겨루다	경쟁하다
7 **complex**** [kəmpléks]	a	complicated, elaborate, involve, tangled, intricate ↔ clear, plain a **complex** system 복합 시스템	복잡한
	n	a group of buildings department store **complex** 백화점 건물 집합체	건물 집합체
8 **cover** [kʌvər]	v	envelop, overlay, disguise, clothe **cover** the wound 상처를 감추다	덮어주다
9 **deluge**** [délju:dʒ]	n	flood, inundation, overflowng a **deluge** of fire 불바다	대홍수
10 **depressed*** [diprést]	a	lowered, melancholy, gloomy, disheartened, blue ↔ happy Business is **depressed**. 경기가 나쁘다.	우울한, 기가 죽은
11 **dip*** [dip]	v	plunge, immerse, sink, submerge; decline, fall **dip** a dress 옷을 담가서 물들이다	담그다 / 기울다
12 **disturbance** [distə́:rbəns]	n	agitation, disorder, confusion, uproar a **disturbance** of the public peace 치안 방해	방해, 혼란
13 **dormant**** [dɔ́:rmənt]	a	inactive, inert, latent, asleep, suspended, hibernating a **dormant** volcano 휴화산	활동하지 않는
14 **dramatically**** [drəmǽtikəli]	ad	radically, impressively, climactically **dramatically** increased 급격히 상승된	극적으로
15 **enable*** [inéibl]	v	help, allow, permit, authorize, empower, qualify Money **enables** one to do a lot of things. 돈이 있으면 많은 일을 할 수 있다.	할 수 있게 하다, 가능하게 하다

#	Word		Synonyms / Example	Meaning (Korean)
16	**fade*** [feid]	v	① **lose color, pale, bleach** The book's paper **faded** over time. 책 종이가 시간이 지남에 따라 바랬다. ② **weaken, wither, decline, decay** **fade** away 사라져 버리다	① 창백해지다 ② 시들다, 쇠퇴하다
17	**fanciful** [fǽnsifəl]	a	**unreal, imaginary, mythical,** romantic a **fanciful** scheme 공상적인 계획	공상의, 기발한
18	**fascinate**** [fǽsənèit]	v	**charm, enchant, captivate, allure,** delight, intrigue Ancient Egypt has always **fascinated** me. 고대 이집트는 언제나 나를 매혹시켰다.	매료시키다, 사로잡다
19	**feeble*** [fíːbl]	a	① **weak, delicate, fragile, frail,** unsubstantial He was **feeble** after his illness. 그는 병을 앓은 후에 약해졌다. ② **unconvincing, flimsy, inadequate,** insufficient, lame **feeble** light 희미한 빛	① 허약한 ② (소리, 빛 등이) 약한
20	**forge** [fɔːrdʒ]	v	**create, falsify, copy** **forge** a sword 검을 벼리다	꾸며내다, 단조하다
21	**gay** [gei]	a	**homosexual, carefree, colorful** **gay** liberation 동성 연애자의 해방	동성애의, 명랑한
22	**grandeur** [grǽndʒər]	n	**magnificence, splendor,** dignity, majesty insanity of **grandeur** 과대 망상증	웅장
23	**habitual*** [həbítʃuəl]	a	**usual, regular, customary, accustomed** her **habitual** tardiness 그녀의 습관적인 지각	습관적인, 규칙적인
24	**kinship** [kínʃip]	n	**relationship, affinity** trace the degree of **kinship** 촌수를 캐다	친족, 연대감
25	**leave behind*** [liːv biháind]	a	**leave, leave alone** rinse out the poison **left behind** by noxious herb 독초가 남겼던 독을 씻어내다	두고 가다, 남기고 가다, 통과하다
26	**muse*** [mjuːz]	v	**meditate, ponder, contemplate, deliberate, brood** time to **muse** 심사숙고할 시간	생각하다, 숙고하다
27	**numerous*** [njúːmərəs]	a	**many, countless;** various, diverse **numerous** students 많은 학생들	셀 수 없는 / 다양한
28	**prevent** [privént]	v	① **avoid, hinder, hamper, impede,** thwart, interrupt ↔ **encourage** **prevent** an accident 사고를 방지하다 ② **prohibit, forbid,** block ↔ **permit** **prevent** deer hunting 사슴 사냥을 금지하다	① 막다, 방해하다 ② 금지하다
29	**primary*** [práiməri]	a	**fundamental, elementary, principal, basic** the **primary** stage of civilization 문명의 초기 단계	근본적인, 기초의

DAY 04

30	**revolution** [rèvəlúːʃən]	n	① revolt, rebellion, mutiny, uprising on the eve of a **revolution** 혁명 전야에 ② rotation, movement, circuit, cycle one **revolution** around the sun 태양 주위를 한 번 순환	① 혁명, 대변혁 ② 순환
31	**rot*** [rat]	v	decay, corrupt, degenerate, spoil, decompose, putrefy The log was **rotting** away. 재목은 썩어가고 있었다.	썩다, 부패하다
32	**rude** [ruːd]	n	impolite, coarse, ill-mannered, uncivil ↔ polite, courteous a **rude** customer 무례한 소비자	버릇없는
33	**sentiment** [séntəmənt]	n	emotion, sentimentality, sensibility anti-imperialist **sentiment** 반제국주의 감정	감정, 심정
34	**shelter*** [ʃéltər]	n	safety, retreat, roof, asylum, refuge, sanctuary a nuclear bomb **shelter** 핵 대피호	피난 장소, 대피소
		v	protect, guard, cover, safeguard, shield, harbor ↔ expose, reveal **shelter** the wild animals in the deep forest 깊은 산속에서 야생동물을 보호하다	보호하다
35	**sometimes**** [sʌmtàimz]	ad	occasionally, now and then, at time Drop me a line **sometimes**. 가끔 편지라도 한 통 보내주세요.	때때로
36	**stagnant** [stǽgnənt]	a	inert, inactive, dull The market is extremely **stagnant**. 시장 거래가 심하게 정체되어 있다.	정체된, 침체한
37	**tacit** [tǽsit]	a	implicit, implied, inferred **tacit** law 관습법	암묵의
38	**tangle** [tǽŋgl]	v	twist together, interweave, mesh, snarl **tangle** the knit wool by a baby 아기에 의해 털실이 엉켜지다	얽히게 하다
39	**transcend*** [trænsénd]	v	go beyond, surpass, eclipse, exceed, outdo **transcend** human power 인력을 초월하다	능가하다, 초월하다
40	**tremble** [trémbl]	v	shake, shudder, shiver, quiver, quaver, quake Her voice **trembled** over the phone. 전화기 너머로 그녀의 목소리가 떨렸다.	전율하다, 떨다

Practice Test 04

01. Alcohol is a powerful drug, and habitual drinking can lead to many health problems.
    - (A) rhythmical
    - (B) intermittent
    - (C) customary
    - (D) casual

02. Today, angiosperms (flowering plants) are one of the most numerous plants on earth.
    - (A) international
    - (B) familiar
    - (C) difficult
    - (D) many

03. Like the mitochondria, these organelles are complex in structure.
    - (A) crucial
    - (B) compress
    - (C) fascinate
    - (D) complicate

04. A moving airplane creates disturbances in pressure while in the air.
    - (A) impact
    - (B) infringements
    - (C) turbulences
    - (D) depressions

05. Ozone absorbs most of the ultraviolet rays from the sun, preventing them from reaching the earth.
    - (A) averting
    - (B) holding
    - (C) spreading
    - (D) projecting

06. Some Indian artists acknowledge that their world has changed, and they reflect that development in their work.
    - (A) find
    - (B) conceal
    - (C) inform
    - (D) admit

07. Latin America's economy grew rapidly during the 1960's and 1970's but slowed dramatically in the 1980's.
    - (A) comparatively
    - (B) occasionally
    - (C) radically
    - (D) continuously

08. The ancient warming may have brought forth conditions that were a bit more balmy than at present.
    - (A) mild
    - (B) changeable
    - (C) humid
    - (D) dry

09. Water covers about 70 per cent of the earth's surface and land covers about 30 per cent.
    - (A) uses
    - (B) wraps
    - (C) circulates
    - (D) remains

10. The house is a building that provides shelter, comfort, and protection for its inhabitants.
    - (A) residue
    - (B) calm place
    - (C) security
    - (D) camouflage

11. The plot becomes increasingly tangled until Sebastian, Viola's twin brother, appears.
    Ⓐ twisted
    Ⓑ well-balanced
    Ⓒ formed
    Ⓓ lowered

12. NASA sent the Extreme Ultraviolet Explorer aloft in 1992 to study wavelengths of 7 to 76 nanometers.
    Ⓐ intact
    Ⓑ on high
    Ⓒ out of danger
    Ⓓ maneuverable

13. Many imaginative writers proposed fanciful techniques to travel through space.
    Ⓐ familiar
    Ⓑ imaginative
    Ⓒ apparent
    Ⓓ logical

14. A jackknife wagon can be of any size, and it is sometimes as wide as the proscenium opening itself.
    Ⓐ totally
    Ⓑ usually
    Ⓒ secretly
    Ⓓ occasionally

15. In contemporary society, people often apply the word family to any group that feels a sense of kinship.
    Ⓐ family history
    Ⓑ friends
    Ⓒ affinity
    Ⓓ apathy

16. Memory B lymphocytes enable the immune system to respond more rapidly to infection if the same type of antigen is encountered at a later time.
    Ⓐ remind
    Ⓑ force
    Ⓒ provoke
    Ⓓ allow

17. The icecap's thickest parts are located over deep basins that dip far below sea level.
    Ⓐ immersed momentarily
    Ⓑ dry thoroughly
    Ⓒ plunge
    Ⓓ float

18. Since the 1960's, many families have moved from economically depressed rural areas to new settlements.
    Ⓐ cheered
    Ⓒ downhearted
    Ⓒ narrowed
    Ⓓ diminished

19. The air gets thinner as it gets farther away from the earth and fades into space about 1,000 kilometers above the earth.
    Ⓐ penetrates
    Ⓑ dwindles
    Ⓒ darkens
    Ⓓ evaporates

20. Oxygen first entered the atmosphere in appreciable quantities some two billion years ago, progressively rising to each a stable level at around 1.5 billion years ago.
    Ⓐ miniscule
    Ⓑ considerable
    Ⓒ unbelievable
    Ⓓ recognizable

DAY 05 Daily Checkup

01. **marvelous** sight of nature
    - Ⓐ rounded
    - Ⓑ wonderful
    - Ⓒ offensive
    - Ⓓ generous

02. **savage** customs
    - Ⓐ familiar
    - Ⓑ ferocious
    - Ⓒ old-fashioned
    - Ⓓ modern

03. **intimate** friends
    - Ⓐ adverse
    - Ⓑ elaborate
    - Ⓒ extraordinary
    - Ⓓ close

04. suffer from a **disaster**
    - Ⓐ border
    - Ⓑ job
    - Ⓒ violation
    - Ⓓ calamity

05. by a narrow **margin**
    - Ⓐ space
    - Ⓑ thought
    - Ⓒ fashion
    - Ⓓ demeanor

06. **grossly** underused
    - Ⓐ entirely
    - Ⓑ somewhat
    - Ⓒ concisely
    - Ⓓ wonderfully

07. a **sightless** person
    - Ⓐ dumb
    - Ⓑ talkative
    - Ⓒ witty
    - Ⓓ blind

08. get a **grueling**
    - Ⓐ intimating
    - Ⓑ tormenting
    - Ⓒ bondage
    - Ⓓ diagnosing

09. It's **somewhat** different.
    - Ⓐ wonderful
    - Ⓑ rather
    - Ⓒ mammoth
    - Ⓓ almost

10. **complicate** the assignment
    - Ⓐ distribute
    - Ⓑ check
    - Ⓒ reward
    - Ⓓ intricate

11. **avert** his eyes
    - Ⓐ prevent
    - Ⓑ supply
    - Ⓒ torment
    - Ⓓ hurt

12. **trigger** the chemical reaction
    - Ⓐ watch
    - Ⓑ intricate
    - Ⓒ provide
    - Ⓓ activate

13. **escalate** into a major conflict
    - Ⓐ fall
    - Ⓑ pledge
    - Ⓒ rise
    - Ⓓ examine

14. a **liberal** view
    - Ⓐ narrow-minded
    - Ⓑ surprising
    - Ⓒ blunt
    - Ⓓ generous

15. **appease** a person by kindness
    - Ⓐ deter
    - Ⓑ soothe
    - Ⓒ confine
    - Ⓓ enrage

16. be **sure** of a person's honesty
    - Ⓐ ambiguous
    - Ⓑ brutal
    - Ⓒ certain
    - Ⓓ ferocious

17. maintain a correct **posture**
    - Ⓐ dimension
    - Ⓑ attitude
    - Ⓒ calamity
    - Ⓓ thought

18. **spawning** time of salmon
    - Ⓐ spending
    - Ⓑ unrelenting
    - Ⓒ wasting
    - Ⓓ laying egg

19. **recompense** her for her time and effort
    - Ⓐ furnish
    - Ⓑ reward
    - Ⓒ entangle
    - Ⓓ intricate

20. feelings **indigenous** to human beings
    - Ⓐ native
    - Ⓑ foreign
    - Ⓒ cold-blooded
    - Ⓓ barbarous

DAY 05 Voca Bank

표제어	품사	동의어와 예문	한글 뜻
1 **abreast** [əbrést]	a	alongside stand **abreast** 옆으로 나란히 서다	나란히
2 **absent-minded*** [æbsəntmáindid]	a	**uninterested, oblivious,** inattentive even more **absent-minded** 게다가 정신이 없는	정신이 나간
3 **adolescent*** [ædəlésnt]	a	**juvenile, immature, young, junior,** childish be aimed primarily at **adolescent** readers 젊은 독자들을 우선적으로 목표로 하다	청춘의, 한참 젊은
4 **analyze*** [ǽnəlàiz]	v	**diagnose, examine,** study, break down, dissect **analyze** water quality 수질을 조사하다	분석하다
5 **appease** [əpíːz]	v	**pacify, quiet, soothe,** calm, tranquilize **appease** a person with a present 선물로 누구를 달래다	완화시키다, 진정시키다
6 **avert** [əvə́ːrt]	v	**prevent, deter,** avoid **avert** people's eye 세상의 이목을 꺼리다	돌리다, 피하다
7 **beneath*** [biníːθ]	prep	**below, under, underneath,** inferior to **beneath** notice 주목할 가치도 없는	아래의
8 **blunt*** [blʌnt]	a	**dull, rounded,** unsharpened be **blunt** of speech 말버릇이 불퉁스럽다(퉁명스럽다)	무딘
9 **captivity** [kæptívəti]	n	**bondage, confinement** adapt well to life in **captivity** 포로 생활에 잘 적응하다	포획, 감금
10 **complicate***** [kámpləkèit]	v	**intricate, make difficult, confuse, entangle,** perplex ↔ simple, easy **complicate** matters 사태를 복잡하게 만들다	복잡하게 되다
11 **dehydrate** [diːháidreit]	v	**dry, desiccate** **dehydrated** vegetables 건조 야채	건조시키다
12 **disaster**** [dizǽstər]	n	**catastrophe, calamity, adversity,** mishap carry out the relief of victims of a **disaster** 이재민을 구호하다	재난, 불운
13 **engaged*** [ingéidʒd]	a	**betrothed,** pledged; busy an **engaged** couple 약혼한 남녀	약혼한 / 바쁜
14 **escalate** [éskəlèit]	v	**rise, increase,** heighten Cost can **escalate** terrifyingly. 가격이 끔찍하게 오를 수 있다.	오르다
15 **furnish** [fə́ːrniʃ]	v	**provide, supply** **furnish** out (충분히) 준비를 갖추다, (필요품을) 공급하다	공급하다
16 **gigantic*** [dʒaigǽntik]	a	**enormous, colossal, mammoth, vast,** prodigious, titanic ↔ small, tiny **gigantic** statue 거대한 조상(彫像)	거대한

17	**grossly** [gróusli]	ad	entirely, totally, greatly, wholly **grossly** underused 거의 사용하지 못한	크게, 심하게
18	**grueling** [grúːəliŋ]	a	exhausting, tormenting This fighting is more **grueling**. 이번 시합은 더욱 녹초로 만들었다.	녹초로 만드는, 엄한
19	**inadequate**** [inǽdikwət]	a	deficient, insufficient, unsatisfactory, lacking ↔ enough an **inadequate** excuse 부적당한 변명	부적당한
20	**indigenous***** [indídʒənəs]	a	native, aboriginal, original feelings **indigenous** to human beings 인간 고유의 감정	고유한, 원산인, 타고난
21	**intimate**** [íntəmət]	a	close, familiar **intimate** secrets 개인적인 비밀	가까운, 친밀한
22	**liberal** [líbərəl]	a	tolerant, broad-minded, magnanimous, generous in **liberal** quantities 충분히	관대한, 너그러운, 풍부한
23	**manner**** [mǽnər]	n	① method, mode, fashion, way, demeanor, air a **manner** of speaking 말하는 방법 in a **manner** 어떤 의미로는, 어느 정도는 ② behavior, aspect, appearance a polite **manner** 예의 바른 태도	① 방식, 방법 ② 행동, 태도
24	**margin*** [máːrdʒin]	n	edge, border, rim by a narrow **margin** 아슬아슬하게, 간신히	가장자리, 물가
25	**marvelous**** [máːrvələs]	a	wonderful, extraordinary, amazing, astonishing, surprising a **marvelous** show 멋진 쇼	놀라운, 신기한
26	**posture** [pástʃər]	n	pose, attitude, upright, stance straight **posture** 꼿꼿한 자세	자세, 포즈
27	**preeminence** [priémənəns]	n	superiority, prominence, supremacy, prestige, dominance procure a steady stride toward **preeminence** in space 우주에서 우위 유지를 위한 꾸준한 전진을 확보하다	탁월, 현저, 우위
28	**proportion** [prəpɔ́ːrʃən]	n	size, extent, dimensions, amount **proportion** of three to one 3대 1의 비율	크기, 면적
29	**recompense**** [rékəmpèns]	v	compensate, reward **recompense** a person for his losses 남의 손실을 보상하다	보답하다, 갚다
30	**savage** [sǽvidʒ]	a	① brutal, violent, ferocious, fierce, cold-blooded a **savage** attack 야만적인 공격 ② wild, uncultivated, barbarous a **savage** person 무례한 사람	① 야만적인, 야만인의 ② 무례한
31	**sightless** [sáitlis]	a	blind, invisible a **sightless** person 눈먼 사람	시력이 없는, 보이지 않는
32	**somewhat***** [sʌ́mhwʌt]	ad	rather, to some degree It's **somewhat** different. 그건 다소 다르다.	어느 정도, 다소

DAY 05

33	**spawn*** [spɔːn]	v	produce, lay eggs, hatch, generate Her novels **spawned** both movies and the play. 그녀의 소설은 영화와 연극으로 만들어졌다. a good environment to **spawn** new business 새로운 사업이 생겨날 좋은 환경	(알을) 낳다, 야기하다
34	**straightforward** [streitfɔ́ːrwərd]	a	honest, candid, direct, open a **straightforward** man 대쪽같이 결이 바른 사람	정직한
35	**succinct*** [səksíŋkt]	a	concise, brief, compact a **succinct** outline of artificial intelligence AI(인공지능)의 간결한 요약	간결한
36	**sure*** [ʃuər]	a	① certain, definite, positive, proven, unfailing ↔ doubtful, uncertain a **sure** success 확실한 성공 ② safe, secure ↔ unprotected, dangerous a **sure** place to hide 감추기에 안전한 장소 ③ dependable, reliable, faithful, tested, trustworthy ↔ untrustworthy a **sure** friend 믿을 수 있는 친구	① 확신하는 ② 안전한 ③ 믿을 수 있는
37	**survey** [sərvéi]	v	watch, inspect, examine, scrutinize **survey** a situation 상황을 살펴보다	조사하다
38	**trigger*** [trígər]	v	set off, activate **trigger** an immune response 면역 반응을 유발하다/촉발하다	유발하다
39	**unpleasant*** [ʌnplézənt]	a	disagreeable, offensive, repulsive an **unpleasant** smell 불쾌한 냄새	불쾌한
40	**unrelenting** [ʌnriléntiŋ]	a	relentless, implacable, inexorable, merciless, ruthless an **relenting** downpour of rain 무자비하게 내리는 비	무자비한, 가차없는

Practice Test 05

01. Everyone was quite sure she would become very beautiful.
    Ⓐ curt
    Ⓑ compulsory
    Ⓒ confident
    Ⓓ adulterate

02. Many mythologies predict the end of the world by some great disaster, such as a fire or flood.
    Ⓐ catastrophe
    Ⓑ tsunami
    Ⓒ holocaust
    Ⓓ portent

03. Videotapes of live sports events allow sportscasters to rerun and analyze key plays immediately after they happen.
    Ⓐ estimate
    Ⓑ speculate
    Ⓒ investigate
    Ⓓ conjecture

04. Television news services furnish visual of world events for televised news.
    Ⓐ replace
    Ⓑ provide
    Ⓒ consume
    Ⓓ supplement

05. Unlike many earlier operas, La Traviata has realistic characters who have complicated emotions.
    Ⓐ crucial
    Ⓑ involved
    Ⓒ fascinated
    Ⓓ complex

06. Scientists pointed out that large animals, particularly gigantic dinosaurs, lost their body heat slowly.
    Ⓐ remarkable
    Ⓑ colossal
    Ⓒ infinitesimal
    Ⓓ unexceptional

07. Although many ghosts are evil and unpleasant, some may be helpful.
    Ⓐ nasty
    Ⓑ heedless
    Ⓒ uncanny
    Ⓓ occult

08. Many publishers conduct surveys to find out what groups of people read their magazines.
    Ⓐ inquiries
    Ⓑ details
    Ⓒ purveys
    Ⓓ presses

09. The sun has a magnetic field that somewhat resembles the pattern of a bar magnet, especially near the sun's poles.
    Ⓐ rather
    Ⓑ still
    Ⓒ partly
    Ⓓ exactly

10. To save time and space, food for combat troops is dehydrated and prepackaged in airtight containers.
    Ⓐ furnished
    Ⓑ dried
    Ⓒ fumigated
    Ⓓ over burned

11. Inadequate brain development or vision or hearing defects can cause reading difficulties.
    Ⓐ abundant
    Ⓑ nonexistent
    Ⓒ substantial
    Ⓓ insufficient

12. Most fats from animal sources contain a large proportion that is said to be highly saturated.
    Ⓐ length
    Ⓑ sequence
    Ⓒ number
    Ⓓ amount

13. The allergist injects small doses of common allergens in separate areas just beneath the skin.
    Ⓐ below
    Ⓑ through
    Ⓒ out of
    Ⓓ near

14. That perspective now offers some fascinating new insights into the marvelously complex evolution of the earth.
    Ⓐ wonderfully
    Ⓑ terribly
    Ⓒ disappointedly
    Ⓓ wholeheartedly

15. To keep an encyclopedia abreast of events in all fields of knowledge, the publisher must revise it on a regular basis.
    Ⓐ irrelevant of
    Ⓑ informed about
    Ⓒ well-known
    Ⓓ important

16. This upright posture enabled dinosaurs to walk on all four legs without dragging their bellies on the ground.
    Ⓐ niche
    Ⓑ standing
    Ⓒ postulate
    Ⓓ pattern

17. When affected by the Hungtington's Disease, people become more and more absent-minded and begin to display involuntary gestures, especially when under psychological or physical stress.
    Ⓐ forgetful
    Ⓑ eccentric
    Ⓒ oblivious
    Ⓓ disinterest

18. Predicting the response of Antarctic ice sheets to the changing climate and the impact on sea level is not always straightforward.
    Ⓐ predictable
    Ⓑ candid
    Ⓒ curved
    Ⓓ simple

19. During the early to mid-1900's, Latin American Indians engaged in protests and armed uprisings to demand social, political, economic, and land reform.
    Ⓐ trained
    Ⓑ involved in
    Ⓒ described as
    Ⓓ evaluated

20. The teeth of meat-eaters have sharp edges for cutting and slicing through meat, while plant-eaters often have broad, blunt teeth for grinding plant material, which may include tough fibers
    Ⓐ weak   Ⓑ broken
    Ⓒ dull   Ⓓ rough

DAY 01-05 Exercise

01. **improper** way of doing
    - Ⓐ apt
    - Ⓑ illeal
    - Ⓒ moral
    - Ⓓ inappropriate

02. **attain** to perfection
    - Ⓐ hush
    - Ⓑ explode
    - Ⓒ reach
    - Ⓓ grasp

03. **inadequate** equipment
    - Ⓐ appropriate
    - Ⓑ perplexing
    - Ⓒ deficient
    - Ⓓ wonderful

04. Business is **depressed**.
    - Ⓐ expanding
    - Ⓑ gloomy
    - Ⓒ insufficient
    - Ⓓ magnificent

05. a region too **arid** for farming
    - Ⓐ dry
    - Ⓑ cloudy
    - Ⓒ damp
    - Ⓓ rainy

06. the **numerous** voice of the people
    - Ⓐ monotonous
    - Ⓑ dramatically
    - Ⓒ weary
    - Ⓓ various

07. the **magnitude** of the task
    - Ⓐ essence
    - Ⓑ extent
    - Ⓒ content
    - Ⓓ difficulty

08. **reckon** up the names
    - Ⓐ create
    - Ⓑ erase
    - Ⓒ enumerate
    - Ⓓ eliminate

09. an unnecessary **disturbance**
    - Ⓐ tools
    - Ⓑ agitation
    - Ⓒ jobs
    - Ⓓ uprising

10. an apple rotten at the **core**
    - Ⓐ center
    - Ⓑ peel
    - Ⓒ surface
    - Ⓓ seed

11. **habitual** courtesy
    - Ⓐ ill-mannered
    - Ⓑ convenient
    - Ⓒ customary
    - Ⓓ regular

12. to **purify** the mixture
    - Ⓐ alter
    - Ⓑ modify
    - Ⓒ refine
    - Ⓓ form

13. one's **attitude** of mind
    - Ⓐ pose
    - Ⓑ worry
    - Ⓒ resentment
    - Ⓓ development

14. **incorporated** with another company
    - Ⓐ resembled
    - Ⓑ integrated
    - Ⓒ examined
    - Ⓓ spoiled

15. a **blunt** answer to your question
    - Ⓐ liberal
    - Ⓑ dull
    - Ⓒ wonderful
    - Ⓓ clear

16. a very **tame** party
    - Ⓐ splendid
    - Ⓑ sturdy
    - Ⓒ strong
    - Ⓓ boring

17. an **appreciable** change
    - Ⓐ dominative
    - Ⓑ harmonious
    - Ⓒ colorful
    - Ⓓ significant

18. have **backbone**
    - Ⓐ spine
    - Ⓑ stomach
    - Ⓒ muscle
    - Ⓓ brain

19. a **gigantic** hole in the ground
    - Ⓐ amazing
    - Ⓑ intricate
    - Ⓒ huge
    - Ⓓ invisible

20. put on a **mask**
    - Ⓐ veil
    - Ⓑ soothsayer
    - Ⓒ clearness
    - Ⓓ awkward

Practice Test 01-05

01. By the late 1600's, England produced about 80 percent of the world's total coal output.
    Ⓐ conservation
    Ⓑ profit
    Ⓒ export
    Ⓓ production

02. Today, sulfur is used in a wide variety of products and industrial processes.
    Ⓐ recycle
    Ⓑ wrapped in
    Ⓒ various
    Ⓓ as substitutes for

03. In the early 1860's, the United States government decided to extend rail lines across the country.
    Ⓐ range
    Ⓑ expand
    Ⓒ expend
    Ⓓ offer

04. Babies differ in the rate and manner of growth and development.
    Ⓐ way
    Ⓑ behavior
    Ⓒ stage
    Ⓓ range

05. Diamonds can cut, grind, and bore very hard metal quickly and accurately.
    Ⓐ trim
    Ⓑ drill
    Ⓒ melt
    Ⓓ slice

06. In wet tropical areas, moisture causes wood shelters to rot within a few years.
    Ⓐ collect
    Ⓑ decay
    Ⓒ expand
    Ⓓ cultivated

07. Many private companies have begun to develop launch services to compete with the national and international organizations.
    Ⓐ contest
    Ⓑ work
    Ⓒ effect
    Ⓓ complicate

08. In 1977, the FDA (Food and Drug Administrations) took steps to ban saccharin use in the United States.
    Ⓐ study
    Ⓑ feedback
    Ⓒ sponsor
    Ⓓ prohibit

09. Hydrogen can be stored in liquid form, but a substantial amount of energy is needed to chill it to the extremely low temperatures required (- 253 °C or - 423 °F).
    Ⓐ extraordinarily
    Ⓑ energetically
    Ⓒ Celsius degree
    Ⓓ gracefully

10. In the twentieth century, the scientific revolution extended to many other areas of science.
    Ⓐ prospect   Ⓑ change
    Ⓒ innovation   Ⓓ consideration

11. The United Kingdom has a mild climate, even though it lies as far north as the bitterly cold Labrador.
    Ⓐ bizarre
    Ⓑ frigid
    Ⓒ moderate
    Ⓓ rainy

12. In the Institutes gave lectures on mathematics and its applications.
    Ⓐ instruments
    Ⓑ habits
    Ⓒ usages
    Ⓓ duties

13. The fossil record shows a gradual increase in the complexity of animals and plants.
    Ⓐ sporadic
    Ⓑ momentary
    Ⓒ steady
    Ⓓ quick

14. The Orient Express, one of the most famous European passenger trains, began operation between Paris, France, and Istanbul, Turkey, in 1883.
    Ⓐ moving
    Ⓑ remarkable
    Ⓒ religious
    Ⓓ well-known

15. Mammals are important not only to people but also to the whole system of life on the earth.
    Ⓐ entire
    Ⓑ organized
    Ⓒ incomplete
    Ⓓ individual

16. Although most light looks white to the eye, it is actually a mixture of three primary colors: blue, green, and red.
    Ⓐ principal
    Ⓑ original
    Ⓒ prior
    Ⓓ sole

17. The simplest organisms consists of only one cell, but such complex living things as dogs and human possess billions of cells.
    Ⓐ variable
    Ⓑ large
    Ⓒ complicated
    Ⓓ functioning

18. Although the management of most news organizations are politically conservative, many journalists tend to be liberal.
    Ⓐ lavish
    Ⓑ expensive
    Ⓒ deceptive
    Ⓓ progressive

19. The study of the spectrum enables chemists to analyze materials and determine what elements they contain.
    Ⓐ examine
    Ⓑ skim
    Ⓒ dissect
    Ⓓ spread

20. Scientists measure the relative tilt of a planet at the right angle of the orbital plane, an imaginary surface that touches all points of the orbit.
    Ⓐ unexpected
    Ⓑ unreal
    Ⓒ unusual
    Ⓓ uncommon

Intensive Practice

01. Wealthy Egyptians built beautiful, spacious homes of brick and wood.
    Ⓐ open
    Ⓑ capacious
    Ⓒ specious
    Ⓓ inclusive

02. Despite recent successes, stem cell therapy is still highly experimental.
    Ⓐ precious
    Ⓑ practical
    Ⓒ speculative
    Ⓓ competitive

03. The substances that trigger an immune response are called antigens.
    Ⓐ alleviate
    Ⓑ endure
    Ⓒ activate
    Ⓓ cover up

04. Confessional poets wrote about intimate personal experiences, such as sexual relationships and mental illness.
    Ⓐ private
    Ⓑ wealthy
    Ⓒ influential
    Ⓓ charismatic

05. John Adams (1735-1826) played a leading role in the adoption of the Declaration of Independence, and also signed the historic document.
    Ⓐ regulation
    Ⓑ announce
    Ⓒ initiation
    Ⓓ approbation

06. Efforts by government to raise taxes provoked heated protest from the people.
    Ⓐ demanded
    Ⓑ appreciated
    Ⓒ defied
    Ⓓ caused

07. The smell of dead bodies lingered in the air, and rats become a constant problem.
    Ⓐ stayed
    Ⓑ wandered
    Ⓒ discontinued
    Ⓓ linked

08. Farmers had difficulty finding wood for shelter, fuel, and building fences.
    Ⓐ fortification
    Ⓑ cover
    Ⓒ hide
    Ⓓ shade

09. The inevitable result of pumping the sky full of greenhouse gases is global warming.
    Ⓐ unavoidable
    Ⓑ distinct
    Ⓒ regular
    Ⓓ actual

10. Most neutron stars are thought to originate as a massive but otherwise ordinary star, being between eight to 20 times heavier than the sun.
    Ⓐ abrupt
    Ⓑ enormous
    Ⓒ long term
    Ⓓ overdue

11. Christian moral views have had a predominant influence on U.S. laws because most of the nation's people are Christians.
    A) principal
    B) predictable
    C) necessary
    D) routine

12. A writer should always use reliable sources so that the article presents accurate information.
    A) convenient
    B) dependable
    C) accessible
    D) concise

13. All Muslims acknowledge such heroes as Muhammad and Ali as saints.
    A) yield
    B) accept
    C) respect
    D) praise

14. In the tragic opera in The Bohemian by Giacomo Puccini, four poor but carefree young men live a bohemian life together in Paris 1830, and Mimi, a frail young girl in poor health, is their neighbor.
    A) small
    B) tall
    C) weak
    D) dead

15. One of the most savage racial persecutions in history occurred in the 1930's and 1940's, when Nazi Germany killed about 6 million Jews.
    A) primitive
    B) undomesticated
    C) uncivilized
    D) cruel

16. Today's light rail vehicles can run underground, on elevated tracks, or on tracks built alongside city streets.
    A) revised
    B) researched
    C) enlivened
    D) raised

17. Historians further mention the blunderings of politicians and the d sorder in the American political party system during the 1850's.
    A) mistakes
    B) attempts
    C) insults
    D) arguments

18. When the typist preparing a manuscript, he or she should doub e space and leave margins on the top, bottom, and sides of every page.
    A) centers
    B) peripheries
    C) covers
    D) contents

19. Sometimes the symptoms and knowledge of the weather allow us to readily diagnose the disorder.
    A) denounce
    B) relieve
    C) analyze
    D) control

20. The formation of NASA helped forge an agreement between competing interests, including military branches, universities, the aerospace industry, and politicians.
    A) study
    B) form
    C) search
    D) use

Related Words 01-05

핵, 중심	- core, center, heart, gist, hub
뼈대	- backbone, spine, spinal, skeleton, column, vertebrate
큰 실수	- blunder, mistake, fault, error, fiasco, slipup
증명서	- certificate, document, authorization, credentials, diploma
피난처	- shelter, safety, retreat, roof, asylum, refuge, sanctuary
온화한	- balmy, mild, warm, calm, moderate
편리한	- convenient, handy, opportune, appropriate, suitable, useful
널찍한	- spacious, ample, capacious, extensive, roomy, vast
성숙한	- adult, mature, fully grown, completely ripened
청춘의	- adolescent, juvenile, immature, young, junior, childish, pubescence
필연적인	- inevitable, unavoidable, as a result, certainly
훌륭한	- splendid, magnificent, gorgeous, sumptuous, dazzling
조화되지 않는	- incompatible, inconsistent, contradictory, inharmonious, unable, incapable
매료시키다	- fascinate, charm, enchant, captivate, allure, delight, intrigue
복잡하게 되다	- complicate, intricate, difficult, confuse, entangle, perplex
한탄하다	- deplore, grieve, regret, lament, mourn
혼동하다	- confuse, disturb, perplex, bewilder, baffle, confound, mislead
탄원하다	- implore, supplicate, beseech, entreat, crave, beg, solicit
도살하다	- slaughter, massacre, murder, slay, butcher, kill
관리하다	- administer, manage, govern, conduct, execute, direct, monitor, supervise

Knowledge based Vocabulary 01-05

INSECTS

Humans regard certain insects as ❶ pests, and attempt to ❷ control them using insecticides and a host of other techniques. Some insects do damages on numerous crops by feeding on ❸ sap, leaves or fruits. A few parasitic species are ❹ pathogenic. Some insects perform ❺ complex ecological roles; blow-flies, for example, help consume carrion but also spread diseases. Insect pollinators are essential to the life-cycle of many flowering plant species on which most organisms, including humans, are at least partly dependent; without them, the ❻ terrestrial portion of the biosphere (including humans) would be ❼ devastated. Many other insects such lady beetle, lacewing and mantis as natural enemies are considered ecologically beneficial as predators and a few provide direct ❽ economic benefit. Silkworms and honey bees have been used ❾ extensively by humans for the production of silk and honey, respectively. In some cultures, the larvae or adults of certain insects are a food-source for humans. We called these as ❿ edible insects.

What is closest meaning to left word?

1. pests   Ⓐ vermins   Ⓑ curse   Ⓒ immorality   Ⓓ wickedness
2. control   Ⓐ supremacy   Ⓑ regulation   Ⓒ instrument   Ⓓ design
3. sap   Ⓐ pouch   Ⓑ beverage   Ⓒ ooze   Ⓓ plant fluid
4. pathogenic   Ⓐ good conditions Ⓑ omnivorous   Ⓒ infective   Ⓓ delicate
5. complex   Ⓐ elementary   Ⓑ complicated   Ⓒ a group of building Ⓓ synthesis

6. terrestrial Ⓐ aquatic   Ⓑ amphibious   Ⓒ earthly   Ⓓ celestial
7. devastated   Ⓐ destroyed   Ⓑ overcome   Ⓒ capsized   Ⓓ disappeared
8. economic   Ⓐ current   Ⓑ monetary   Ⓒ productive   Ⓓ expensive
9. extensively Ⓐ intensively   Ⓑ deeply   Ⓒ unnoticeably   Ⓓ extendedly
10. edible   Ⓐ visible   Ⓑ eatable   Ⓒ profitable   Ⓓ lovely

곤충

인간은 어떤 곤충들을 해충으로 간주하며regard as pests 살충제insecticides와 다수의 다른 기술들a host of other techniques을 사용하여 방제하려고 시도한다attempt to control. 일부 곤충은 즙액이나 잎과 과실을 섭식하여by feeding on sap, leaves or fruits 무수히 많은 작물에 피해를 준다do damages on numerous crops. 소수의 기생성parasitic 종은 병원성이 있다pathogenic. 어떤 곤충들은 복잡한 생태적 역할을 수행하는데perform complex ecological roles 예를 들면 검정파리는 썩은 고기를 먹으면서consume carrion 질병을 퍼뜨린다spread disease. 화분매개곤충insect pollinators은 인간을 포함하여 대부분의 유기체organisms가 적어도 부분적으로 의존적인at least partly dependent 많은 현화식물many flowering plant 종들의 생활사에 있어서 필수적이다. 그들이 없다면 (인간을 포함한) 생물권의 육지부분the terrestrial portion of the biosphere은 황폐화될 것이다would be devastated. 천적으로서as natural enemies 무당벌레lady beetle, 풀잠자리와 사마귀와 같은 많은 다른 곤충들은 포식자predators로서 생태적으로 유익한 것으로 여겨지고are considered ecologically beneficial 소수는 직접적으로 경제적 이득을 제공한다provide direct economic benefit. 누에와 꿀벌silkworms and honey bees은 각각 실크와 꿀의 생산을 위해 인간에 의해 널리 사용되어 왔다have been used extensively by humans. 어떤 문화에서는 특정 종의 유충과 성충the larvae and adults of certain insects은 인간에게 음식원food-source이 된다. 우리는 이런 곤충을 먹을 수 있는(식용) 곤충edible insects이라고 부른다.

1. Ⓐ 2. Ⓑ 3. Ⓓ 4. Ⓒ 5. Ⓑ
6. Ⓒ 7. Ⓐ 8. Ⓑ 9. Ⓓ 10. Ⓑ

DAY 06 Daily Checkup

01. possess a vote
    - Ⓐ help
    - Ⓑ assault
    - Ⓒ own
    - Ⓓ evaluate

02. blaze a trail to pioneer
    - Ⓐ endower
    - Ⓑ originator
    - Ⓒ president
    - Ⓓ governor

03. an extensive order
    - Ⓐ broad
    - Ⓑ forcing
    - Ⓒ bestowing
    - Ⓓ reconciling

04. stringent laws
    - Ⓐ useless
    - Ⓑ voluptuous
    - Ⓒ constricted
    - Ⓓ general

05. the trail of a slug
    - Ⓐ demonstration
    - Ⓑ nudeness
    - Ⓒ load
    - Ⓓ drag

06. persuade oneself
    - Ⓐ convince
    - Ⓑ endure
    - Ⓒ breed
    - Ⓓ blend

07. assist a person with parcels
    - Ⓐ draw
    - Ⓑ help
    - Ⓒ force
    - Ⓓ give

08. a frugal but nourishing meal
    - Ⓐ rich
    - Ⓑ poor
    - Ⓒ artistic
    - Ⓓ thrifty

09. You are endowed with wealth.
    - Ⓐ desperate
    - Ⓑ suffered
    - Ⓒ bestowed
    - Ⓓ splendid

10. grow to university status
    - Ⓐ major
    - Ⓑ club
    - Ⓒ position
    - Ⓓ professor

11. at one's own charge
    - Ⓐ cost
    - Ⓑ prestige
    - Ⓒ reputation
    - Ⓓ ability

12. if a plant or animal flourishes
    - Ⓐ conveys
    - Ⓑ thrives
    - Ⓒ destroys
    - Ⓓ waves

13. a slim meal
    - Ⓐ economical
    - Ⓑ fertile
    - Ⓒ light
    - Ⓓ ample

14. judged the distance to be thirty feet
    - Ⓐ expended
    - Ⓑ evaluated
    - Ⓒ combined
    - Ⓓ demonstrated

15. noxious fumes of carbon monoxide
    - Ⓐ toxin
    - Ⓑ materials
    - Ⓒ smokes
    - Ⓓ property

16. convenient garment
    - Ⓐ chair
    - Ⓑ clothes
    - Ⓒ pants
    - Ⓓ desk

17. carried a great burden
    - Ⓐ passenger
    - Ⓑ explanation
    - Ⓒ assault
    - Ⓓ load

18. deliberate on a problem
    - Ⓐ consider
    - Ⓑ blame
    - Ⓒ carry
    - Ⓓ force

19. reconcile two enemies
    - Ⓐ regard
    - Ⓑ conciliate
    - Ⓒ influence
    - Ⓓ stimulate

20. barely audible
    - Ⓐ intentionally
    - Ⓑ extensively
    - Ⓒ generally
    - Ⓓ hardly

DAY 06 Voca Bank

	표제어	품사	동의어와 예문	한글 뜻
1	**anomaly** [ənáməli]	n	**irregularity**, abnormality, eccentricity This kind of opera is an **anomaly** in Europe. 이런 종류의 오페라는 유럽에서는 이상한 것이다.	변칙, 예외적인 것
2	**assist**** [əsíst]	v	**help, aid, support, cooperate with** **assist** a person financially 누구를 재정적으로 돕다	돕다
3	**bare*** [bɛər]	a	① **naked, nude,** unclothed ↔ clothed a **bare** body 벗은 몸 ② **empty, plain, barren** ↔ lush a **bare** landscape 휑한 풍경	① 발가벗은 ② 비어 있는
	barely [bɛ́əli]	ad	**hardly, scarcely** **barely** audible 간신히 들을 수 있는	간신히
4	**bear**** [bɛər]	v	① **overcome, endure, last,** stand, suffer, tolerate try to **bear** the pain 고통을 참도록 노력하다 ② **yield, produce,** render, propagate **bear** testimony 증언하다, 증거를 내세우다 ③ **carry, transport, convey,** support **bear** the flag 깃발을 옮기다	① 참다 ② 생산하다 ③ 옮기다
5	**blend*** [blend]	v	**mingle, mix, combine** **blend** red with some white 빨강에다 흰색을 섞다	섞다, 혼합하다
6	**breakthrough***** [bréikθru:]	n	**advance, development, discovery** a significant **breakthrough** in China 중국의 상당한 발전	발전
7	**burden*** [bə́:rdn]	n	**load** ship of **burden** 화물선	부담, 짐
8	**charge**** [tʃa:rdʒ]	n	① **price, cost** ② **attack, assault** The team captain led the **charge**. 팀장은 공격을 이끌었다. ③ **accusation** He was jailed on a **charge** of robbery. 그는 도둑죄로 감옥에 갔다.	① 비용 ② 공격 ③ 변명
		v	① **attack, assault** **charge** the fort 요새를 공격하다 ② **accuse, blame** **charge** with the crime 범죄로 기소하다	① 습격하다 ② 비난하다
9	**collaborate*** [kəlǽbərèit]	v	**work jointly, work together (on)** **collaborate** on a project 과제물을 협동하다	협동하다
10	**culture** [kʌ́ltʃər]	n	**civilization, society, lifestyle; cultivation, farming** a man of **culture** 교양 있는 사람 **culture** the peppers, soybeans and corns in the backyard 뒷마당에 고추, 콩과 옥수수를 재배하다	문화, 교양 / 재배, 경작

11	**deliberate**** [dilíbərət]	a	**careful, thoughtful, cautious, intentional** a **deliberate** policy to introduce 도입하기에 신중한 정책	신중한, 고의적인
		v	**consider, cogitate** **deliberate** how to do it 그것을 하는 방법을 숙고하다	숙고하다
	deliberately [dilíbərətli]	ad	**intentionally, consciously, on purpose** **deliberately** frustrated his effort 그의 노력을 고의로 좌절시킨	계획적으로
12	**endow** [indáu]	v	**confer, bestow**, give be **endowed** with ~을 타고나다, ~이 부여되다	수여하다, 주다
13	**estate** [istéit]	v	**property, land, area** real **estate** 부동산	자산
14	**extensive** [iksténsiv]	a	**wide, broad, spacious**, vast an **extensive** order 대량주문	광범위한, 넓은
15	**flourish*** [flə́:riʃ]	v	**thrive, prosper, succeed** in full **flourish** 한창인, 원기 왕성하여, 융성하여 Business **flourished** within six months. 사업이 6개월 내에 번창했다.	번창하다
16	**foster*** [fɔ́:stər]	v	**rear, breed, nourish**, raise, promote **foster** global economic growth 세계 경제 성장을 조장하다	키우다, 자양분을 주다
17	**frugal*** [frú:gəl]	a	**economical, thrifty** a **frugal** student 근검한 학생	절약하는
18	**fumes** [fju:mz]	n	**gas, smoke, exhaust, pollution** poisonous **fumes** of carbon monoxide (CO) 일산화탄소의 유독 연기	연기, 증기, 연무
19	**garment** [gá:rmənt]	n	**clothes, apparel, gear**, uniform, costume, dress a handy **garment** 단출한 옷	의복
20	**grateful** [gréitfəl]	a	**appreciative, thankful**, obliged a **grateful** letter 감사의 편지	감사하는
21	**infringement*** [infríndʒmənt]	n	**violation, contravention**, breach an **infringement** of copyright 출판권의 침해	위반
22	**jam** [dʒæm]	v	**pack, force**, squeeze A rope **jammed** the boat's propeller. 밧줄이 배의 프로펠러를 움직이지 않게 하다.	막히다, 강제하다
23	**judge*** [dʒʌdʒ]	n	**referee, umpire**, arbitrator the **judge** of the elections 선거의 심사원	심판
		v	**evaluate, consider, regard**, scrutinize, sentence, condemn **judge** a reputation for honesty 정직에 대한 평판을 평가하다	평가하다
24	**mammoth** [mǽməθ]	a	**huge, gigantic, immense, colossal** **mammoth** debt 막대한 빚	거대한
25	**monetary***** [mánətèri]	a	**pecuniary, financial, capital** tighten **monetary** policy 재정 정책을 조이다	금전상의, 화폐의
26	**nibble*** [níbl]	v	**gnaw, bite, eat** **nibble** at one's nails 손톱을 물어뜯다	갉아먹다
27	**persuade*** [pərswéid]	v	**induce, entice, convince**, influence, coax, urge ↔ **dissuade** **persuade** oneself 확신하다	설득하다

DAY 06

28	**pioneer*** [pàiəníər]	n	originator, founder, settler, explorer, innovator a **pioneer** in science 과학의 선구자	개척자, 창시자
29	**possess*** [pəzés]	v	① own, have **possess** three cats 고양이 3마리를 소유하다 ② demonstrate, evidence, manifest **possess** great musical talent 대단한 음악적 재능을 증명하다	① 소유하다 ② 증명하다
30	**productive**** [prədʌ́ktiv]	a	fertile, fruitful **productive** land 비옥한 땅	생산적인, 비옥한
31	**reconcile*** [rékənsàil]	v	conciliate, appease **reconcile** a dispute 논쟁을 조정하다	화해하다
32	**sensual** [sénʃuəl]	a	sensuous, voluptuous **sensual** delight 관능적 즐거움	관능적인, 세속적인
33	**set**** [set]	n	① setting, scene, backdrop the **set** for a play 연극을 위한 무대 ② collection, group, bunch a **set** of dishes 접시 한 세트	① 무대, 장면 ② 수집, 세트
		v	① situate, prescribe put, place, locate, lay **Set** it down on the table. 테이블 위에 올려놓다(배치하다) ② fix, establish, settle, determine, regulate, adjust **set** the price 가격을 조정하다	① 배치하다 ② 조정하다, 고정된,
		a	firm, unchanging, unyielding, adamant	대담한
34	**slim** [slim]	a	① thin, slender ↔ fat, corpulent, plump, chubby a **slim** man 호리호리한 사람 ② small, trifling, insignificant a **slim** chance for survival 생존할 수 있는 적은 기회 a **slim** income 빈약한 수입	① 가냘픈, 가는 ② 적은
35	**sly** [slai]	a	cunning, artful **sly** humor 익살맞은 유머	교활한, 간교한, 익살맞은
36	**status** [stéitəs]	n	prestige, position, standing, rank social **status** of women 여성의 사회적 지위	지위, 신분
37	**stretch**** [stretʃ]	v	① tighten, pull, strain ↔ contract **stretch** a rope 로프를 잡아당기다 ② extend, lengthen, increase, elongate at a **stretch** 단숨에 ③ exaggerate **stretch** the truth 진실을 과장하다	① 늘이다 ② 뻗치다 ③ 과장하다
38	**stringent*** [stríndʒənt]	a	strict, severe constricted, tight, strict **stringent** laws 엄한 법률	엄중한, 절박한
39	**trail** [treil]	n	drag, draw hit the **trail** (속어) 여행 떠나다, 가버리다, 떠나다	끌고 간 자국
40	**widely** [wáidli]	ad	generally, extensively **widely** believed 광범하게 믿어지고 있는	넓게, 크게

Practice

01. Scientific advances since the 1800's have made farming increasingly productive.
    A develop
    B infertile
    C fruitful
    D progressive

02. During the football season, thousands of fans jam packs the stadiums every Saturday.
    A settle
    B crowd
    C vote
    D disperse

03. The fox was often pictured as sly, and the owl as wise.
    A cunning
    B energetic
    C swift
    D vicious

04. American Indians judge folk songs by their power, not by their beauty.
    A impress
    B encourage
    C record
    D consider

05. The National Advertising Review Board fosters self-regulation among the advertising industry.
    A endangers
    B monitors
    C discovers
    D promotes

06. Some department stores and furniture outlets hire interior designers to assist customers and to help sell merchandise.
    A help
    B house
    C employ
    D encourage

07. Ancient Roman society flourished around 2,000 years ago.
    A discovered
    B gained
    C benefited
    D prospered

08. A central bank, known as the European Central Bank, conducts all monetary policies for all Economic and Monetary Union members.
    A contemporary
    B political
    C pecuniary
    D economical

09. New York's coastline stretches 204 kilometers along the Atlantic Ocean.
    A units
    B joins
    C extends
    D develops

10. The Allies nibbled away at its empire until Japan agreed to surrender in August 1945.
    A ruined
    B reached
    C climbed
    D gnawed

11. Laura Ingalls Wilder wrote a series of nine novels about pioneer life during the late 1800's.
    - Ⓐ artist
    - Ⓑ champion
    - Ⓒ explorer
    - Ⓓ publisher

12. Clothing had to be practical, so most people wore the same plain garments day after day.
    - Ⓐ apparatus
    - Ⓑ apparel
    - Ⓒ means
    - Ⓓ organs

13. Most masks represent standard characters from myth or folklore and are widely recognized by the audience.
    - Ⓐ impressively
    - Ⓑ extensively
    - Ⓒ conveniently
    - Ⓓ specifically

14. During the 1840's, the great landlords began the process of breaking up their estates into small independent farms.
    - Ⓐ foundations
    - Ⓑ hunting ground
    - Ⓒ forests
    - Ⓓ properties

15. The widespread popularity of the Townsend Plan helped persuade the U. S. Congress to pass the Social Security Act of 1935.
    - Ⓐ convince
    - Ⓑ assert
    - Ⓒ insist
    - Ⓓ desire

16. The Inca built an extensive system of roads through the Andes Mountains to connect the distant cities of their empire.
    - Ⓐ spacious
    - Ⓑ plentiful
    - Ⓒ widespread
    - Ⓓ progressive

17. Gabon is an African anomaly, as a relatively prosperous, politically stable nation and the least densely populated country in central Africa.
    - Ⓐ existence
    - Ⓑ standard
    - Ⓒ abnormal country
    - Ⓓ regularity

18. Advances in DNA sequencing and data processing have driven some of the most significant breakthroughs in recent biomedical science.
    - Ⓐ drops
    - Ⓑ developments
    - Ⓒ guarantees
    - Ⓓ decreases

19. Bernini combined emotional and sensual freedom with theatrical presentation and photographic naturalism.
    - Ⓐ susceptible
    - Ⓑ dramatic
    - Ⓒ physical
    - Ⓓ perceptible

20. A copyright owner whose copyright is violated may file a lawsuit to stop further infringements.
    - Ⓐ meeting
    - Ⓑ violations
    - Ⓒ happiness
    - Ⓓ publication

DAY 07 Daily Checkup

01. a radical difference
    - Ⓐ lucid
    - Ⓑ empty
    - Ⓒ basic
    - Ⓓ incompetent

02. a concise statement
    - Ⓐ excellent
    - Ⓑ forceful
    - Ⓒ brief
    - Ⓓ oral

03. an abundant crop
    - Ⓐ water
    - Ⓑ harvest
    - Ⓒ game
    - Ⓓ vegetable

04. a vacant position
    - Ⓐ important
    - Ⓑ void
    - Ⓒ central
    - Ⓓ unstable

05. a radiant smile
    - Ⓐ cunning
    - Ⓑ limpid
    - Ⓒ bright
    - Ⓓ fearful

06. come to a conclusion
    - Ⓐ result
    - Ⓑ feature
    - Ⓒ period
    - Ⓓ trend

07. a transparent glass door
    - Ⓐ shining
    - Ⓑ complicated
    - Ⓒ clear
    - Ⓓ fragile

08. in the realm of science
    - Ⓐ intersection
    - Ⓑ field
    - Ⓒ sphere
    - Ⓓ mistake

09. a sacred concert
    - Ⓐ immodest
    - Ⓑ bright
    - Ⓒ immoral
    - Ⓓ divine

10. Lead can accumulate in the body.
    - Ⓐ pile up
    - Ⓑ protect
    - Ⓒ change
    - Ⓓ contribute

11. partition the country
    - Ⓐ decrease
    - Ⓑ divide
    - Ⓒ endow
    - Ⓓ increase

12. modify a contract
    - Ⓐ deny
    - Ⓑ alter
    - Ⓒ follow
    - Ⓓ accede

13. the volume of air
    - Ⓐ purity
    - Ⓑ quality
    - Ⓒ amount
    - Ⓓ density

14. a problem with many phases
    - Ⓐ business
    - Ⓑ worker
    - Ⓒ aspects
    - Ⓓ company

15. quite a considerable additional income
    - Ⓐ substantial
    - Ⓑ fundamental
    - Ⓒ clear
    - Ⓓ unstable

16. a haughty sneer
    - Ⓐ arrogant
    - Ⓑ polite
    - Ⓒ friendly
    - Ⓓ nervous

17. an abundance of the heart
    - Ⓐ lack
    - Ⓑ lost
    - Ⓒ plenty
    - Ⓓ deficiency

18. an opportune remark
    - Ⓐ visible
    - Ⓑ glittering
    - Ⓒ vacant
    - Ⓓ timely

19. summon parliament
    - Ⓐ change
    - Ⓑ call
    - Ⓒ impaired
    - Ⓓ separate

20. inept at dealing with people
    - Ⓐ incompetent
    - Ⓑ extensive
    - Ⓒ defective
    - Ⓓ reasonable

07 Voca Bank

#	표제어	품사	동의어와 예문	한글 뜻
1	**abundant**** [əbʌ́ndənt]	a	plentiful, ample, bountiful, copious an **abundant** supply of cheap labor 값싼 노동력의 풍부한 공급	풍부한
		ad	in great numbers, generously a plant that grow **abundantly** in Jeju 제주에서 아주 많이 자라는 식물	풍부하게
2	**accumulate*** [əkjúːmjulèit]	v	collect, gather, pile up, heap up, amass, assemble, aggregate **accumulate** virtuous deeds 공덕을 쌓다	모으다, 쌓다
3	**character*** [kǽriktər]	n	element, distinct, feature a man of **character** 인격자	성격, 특징
4	**conclusion**** [kənklúːʒən]	n	end, result, outcome, consequence draw **conclusions** 단안을 내리다, 추단하다	결론
	conclusive* [kənklúːsiv]	a	decisive, convincing, definite, final There is no **conclusive** evidence. 확실한 증거가 없다.	결정적인
5	**code** [koud]	n	cipher, cryptograph; rules, system understanding the genetic **code** 유전적 암호를 이해하는	암호 / 규율
		v	encode ↔ decode, interpret, make out **code** information to determine hereditary characters 유전 특성을 결정하기 위해 정보를 암호화하다	암호로 하다
6	**concisely*** [kənsáisli]	ad	succinctly, briefly, in short, in brief a **concisely** statement 간명한 진술	간결하게
7	**considerable***** [kənsídərəbl]	a	sensitive, substantial, important, much a fairly **considerable** portion of my life 내 인생에 있어서 꽤 중요한 부분	중요한, 상당한
8	**crop** [krap]	n	harvest, product, yield an abundant **crop** 풍작	수확물, 농산물, 작물
9	**crossroads** [krɔ́ːsroudz]	n	central meeting place stand at the **crossroads** 기로 [갈림길]에 서다	교차로
10	**dense*** [dens]	a	thick, compact, crowded, lush, impenetrable ↔ sparse a **dense** forest 빽빽한 산림 a **dense** population 조밀한 인구	밀집한
11	**dim*** [dim]	a	weak, obscure, faint, dark, dull, faded ↔ bright a **dim** sound 희미한 소리	희미한, 애매모호한
12	**donate** [dóuneit]	v	contribute, give, present, endow, grant **donate** blood 헌혈하다	기부하다

#	Word	PoS	Synonyms / Example	Korean
13	**elaborate*** [ilǽbərət]	a	① **decorated, ornate, detailed,** intricate ↔ plain an **elaborate** design 공들인 디자인 ② **effective; complicated, intricate,** involved, difficult, detailed ↔ simple **elaborate** arrangement of 효율적으로 정리한 He tackled the **elaborate** problem. 그가 복잡한 문제를 다루었다.	① 공들인, 정교한 ② 자세한 / 복잡한
14	**emphatic** [imfǽtik]	a	**forcible, strong** an **emphatic** tone 강한 어조	강조의, 강한
15	**fatal*** [féitl]	a	**deadly, mortal, lethal,** disastrous ↔ life-giving, beneficial a **fatal** disease 불치의 병, 죽을 병	치명적인
16	**guard** [ga:rd]	v	**protect, shield,** defend, shelter **guard** the herds of sheep against mountain lions and bands of rustlers 퓨마와 가축도둑에 대항하여 양의 무리를 보호하다	보호하다, 막다
17	**haughty** [hɔ́:ti]	a	**proud, arrogant** a **haughty** air 거만한 태도	거만한
18	**hence** [hens]	a	**as a result** five years **hence** 이제부터 5년 후에	결과적으로
19	**imperfect*** [impə́:rfikt]	a	**flawed, damaged, defective,** impaired **imperfect** vision 불완전한 시력	불완전한
20	**inclination*** [ìnklənéiʃən]	n	**tendency, trend,** preference have an **inclination** toward conservatism 보수적 경향이 있다	경향
21	**increase**** [inkrí:s]	v	**enlarge, amplify, grow, augment** ↔ lessen, reduce **increase** one's efforts 노력을 더하다	증가시키다, 증대하다, 확대하다
22	**indecent** [indí:snt]	a	**vulgar, coarse, rude,** immodest **indecent** language 추잡한 말씨	무례한, 저속한
23	**inept** [inépt]	a	**inapt, unsuitable, inappropriate,** incompetent **inept** at dealing with people 사람들을 다루는 데 능숙하지 못한	부적당한, 서투른
24	**modify**** [mádəfài]	v	**alter, vary, change** **modify** a contract 계약을 일부 변경하다	변경하다, 수정하다
25	**note**** [nout]	n	① **eminence, distinction, repute, celebrity, reputation,** know be an biologist of great **note** 유명한 생물학자가 되다 ② **record, memo, message, letter** make a **note** of her e-mail address 그녀의 이메일 주소를 메모하다 ③ **musical tone,** touch, sound detect a **note** of delight in his voice 그의 목소리에서 즐거움의 어조를 감지하다	① 명성, 평판 ② 기록, 메모, 편지 ③ 음정, 어조, 악보

DAY 07

53

26	**opportune** [àpərtjúːn]	a	timely, seasonable an **opportune** remark 때에 맞은 말		시기가 좋은, 알맞은
27	**partition** [paːrtíʃən]	n	division, separation, segregation the **partition** of profits 이익 분배		분배, 분할
		v	divide, separate		분배하다, 분할하다
28	**patch** [pætʃ]	v	mend, repair, fix **patch** a bedclothes 이불을 수선하다		수선하다, 고치다
29	**phase*** [feiz]	n	period, stage; aspect the first **phase** of trials of the vaccine 백신 실험의 첫 번째 단계		기간, 단계 / 국면, 양상
30	**radiant*** [réidiənt]	a	shining, bright, brilliant, beaming **radiant** heat 복사열		빛나는, 찬란한
31	**radical*** [rædikəl]	a	① fundamental, basic a **radical** difference 근본적인 차이 ② extreme, revolutionary period of **radical** change 급진적인 변화의 시기		① 근본적인 ② 급진적인
32	**realm*** [relm]	n	domain; sphere, province, field the **realm** of England 잉글랜드 왕국		왕국 / 범위, 영역
33	**sacred** [séikrid]	a	frightened, fearful, panicky, divine a **sacred** concert 종교 음악회		두려움을 느끼는, 신성한, 종교적인, 겁 먹은
34	**sparkle** [spáːrkl]	n	spark, glitter, twinkle **sparkling** gems 반짝이는 보석		섬광, 불꽃
35	**summon** [sʌmən]	v	call, bid, convene, convoke **summon** parliament 의회를 소집하다		호출하다, 소환하다
36	**transparent*** [trænspɛ́ərənt]	a	clear, pellucid, lucid, limpid, crystalline **transparent** colors 투명 그림물감		투명한
37	**unsettled*** [ʌnsétld]	a	unstable, unsteady, shaky, changeable, unfixed, infirm The trouble has been **unsettled**. 쟁의는 미해결인 채로 있다.		변하기 쉬운, 불안정한
38	**vacant** [véikənt]	a	empty, void, unoccupied that **vacant** house 빈 집		빈, 공허한
39	**volume*** [váljuːm]	n	size, measure, magnitude, mass a **volume** of mail 다량의 우편물		용적, 용량
40	**wedge*** [wedʒ]	n	chock a **wedge** of pie 쐐기 모양으로 자른 파이		쐐기
		v	cram, squeeze, force, lodge, crowd **wedge** a door open 문을 열어 쐐기로 고정하다		쐐기로 고정하다

Practice

01. The dim sunlight of the outer planets requires a lengthy camera exposure.
    Ⓐ blurred
    Ⓑ static
    Ⓒ harsh
    Ⓓ deep

02. Bacterial endocarditis is fatal unless it is treated with antibiotics.
    Ⓐ immortal
    Ⓑ lethal
    Ⓒ natural
    Ⓓ active

03. The sodium atom donates the electron which chlorine is able to accept.
    Ⓐ contributes
    Ⓑ takes
    Ⓒ recipients
    Ⓓ approved

04. Cowboys constantly guarded their herds against mountain lions and bands of rustlers.
    Ⓐ traveled
    Ⓑ observed
    Ⓒ protected
    Ⓓ hurled

05. In any object, the moving atoms or molecules create waves of radiant energy.
    Ⓐ fascinating
    Ⓑ luminous
    Ⓒ visible
    Ⓓ well-known

06. Some minerals have classlike surfaces that sparkle with color.
    Ⓐ shine
    Ⓑ mirror
    Ⓒ refract
    Ⓓ shock

07. Composers often use a short series of notes, called a motive as the base for developing their musical ideas.
    Ⓐ manuscripts
    Ⓑ scores
    Ⓒ poets
    Ⓓ memos

08. The wedge is placed in the hole with the pointed end upward.
    Ⓐ weed
    Ⓑ knife
    Ⓒ chock
    Ⓓ coin

09. Korea was partitioned into two different countries in 1945.
    Ⓐ independent
    Ⓑ united
    Ⓒ jointed
    Ⓓ segregated

10. In early 1616, Galileo was summoned to Rome for a hearing on the orthodoxy of his views.
    Ⓐ exiled
    Ⓑ called
    Ⓒ flown
    Ⓓ expelled

11. The office becomes vacant if the vice president dies, resigns, or is unable to carry out the duties of office.
    - Ⓐ costly
    - Ⓑ shady
    - Ⓒ small
    - Ⓓ empty

12. On Earth, the most familiar observation made is that of the moon's phases, including the full moon, half moon, and crescent.
    - Ⓐ stages
    - Ⓑ notion
    - Ⓒ pattern
    - Ⓓ alternative

13. Industrial-grade diamonds include stones that are imperfectly formed, contain many inclusions or other flaws, or have poor color.
    - Ⓐ flawless
    - Ⓑ charmingly
    - Ⓒ incompletely
    - Ⓓ exceedingly

14. When light passes through air to a denser substance, like a transparent gem, it slows down.
    - Ⓐ thicker
    - Ⓑ more foamy
    - Ⓒ more transparent
    - Ⓓ smaller

15. The vast Great Plains between the Missouri River and the Rockies remained unsettled until the 1860's.
    - Ⓐ thrilled
    - Ⓑ unoccupied
    - Ⓒ refreshed
    - Ⓓ frightened

16. In certain primitive societies, when an animal is killed during a hunt, the relatives of the hunter have a right to a share of the carcass.
    - Ⓐ horn
    - Ⓑ prey
    - Ⓒ hind leg
    - Ⓓ dead body

17. There is no question about the fact that much of the genetic information is actually a code for the many enzymes and structural proteins of the cell.
    - Ⓐ word
    - Ⓑ memory
    - Ⓒ cipher
    - Ⓓ letter

18. The accuracy of the scientist's conclusion depends on the accuracy and completeness of the principles or rules he uses.
    - Ⓐ result
    - Ⓑ repetition
    - Ⓒ act
    - Ⓓ intermission

19. Ancient scholars produced elaborate schemes to account for the observed movements of the stars, sun, moon, and planets.
    - Ⓐ extravagant
    - Ⓑ frightful
    - Ⓒ intricate
    - Ⓓ simple

20. Although rock 'n' roll was extremely popular, its lyrics and performance style that went with it were still considered indecent by many adults.
    - Ⓐ pure
    - Ⓑ acceptable
    - Ⓒ splendid
    - Ⓓ coarse

DAY 08 Daily Checkup

01. cruising **velocity**
    - A scene
    - B shape
    - C speed
    - D boat

02. in **elegant** velvet robes
    - A suffocated
    - B graceful
    - C choked
    - D contaminated

03. a married **couple**
    - A woman
    - B relatives
    - C fellow
    - D pair

04. a **spectacular** scene
    - A sensational
    - B dangerous
    - C infectious
    - D inventive

05. be in **raptures**
    - A profit
    - B anxiety
    - C rapidity
    - D delight

06. Language is **peculiar** to mankind.
    - A helpful
    - B particular
    - C reactive
    - D sensational

07. **dismiss** a boy from school
    - A rescue
    - B linger
    - C surmise
    - D discharge

08. **unpredictable** weather
    - A spoken
    - B eccentric
    - C uncertain
    - D matchless

09. **repent** of one's rashness
    - A enhance
    - B anguish
    - C assurance
    - D atone

10. a **handsome** school boy
    - A good-looking
    - B blue
    - C tasteful
    - D primary

11. **contaminate** the public moral
    - A conserve
    - B enact
    - C stain
    - D amend

12. an **expert** surgeon
    - A novice
    - B drunken
    - C amateurish
    - D veteran

13. **detach** a locomotive from a train
    - A augment
    - B separate
    - C whirl
    - D affix

14. **stifle** a yawn
    - A notice
    - B smother
    - C cause
    - D produce

15. an **oversight** on our part
    - A perfection
    - B plan
    - C component
    - D blunder

16. feel **constrain** to follow orders
    - A free
    - B compel
    - C vitalize
    - D release

17. **spin** on its own axis
    - A speak
    - B rotate
    - C certify
    - D coerce

18. **undergo** medical treatment
    - A demand
    - B invent
    - C experience
    - D provide

19. an **original** thinker
    - A conventional
    - B novel
    - C functional
    - D bootless

20. The flag **undulates** in the breeze.
    - A wave
    - B strangle
    - C constrain
    - D roll

DAY 08 Voca Bank

표제어	품사	동의어와 예문	한글 뜻
1 **assure*** [əʃúər]	v	① **convince**, **promise**, **pledge**, **affirm**, **guarantee**, **certify** **assure** the safety of the crew 선원들의 안전을 확신하다 ② **encourage**, **enthuse**, **hearten** **assure** the worried children 걱정하는 아이들을 안심시키다	① 보장하다, 확신시키다 ② 격려하다, 안심시키다
2 **attribute*** [ətríbju:t]	n	**trait**, **quality**, **characteristics**, **feature**, **property** **attributes** of special significance to a society 사회에 대한 특별한 의미의 성질	성질
3 **burrow** [bə́:rou]	v	**dig**, **hole**, **den**, **excavate** **burrow** underground 땅 밑으로 굴을 파다	굴을 파다
4 **characteristics*** [kæriktərístiks]	n	**elements**, **distinction**, **features** an innate **characteristics** 타고난 특성	특성, 특질, 특징
5 **constrain** [kənstréin]	v	**compel**, **coerce**, inhibit **constrain** obedience 복종을 강요하다	구속하다, 강제하다
6 **contaminate*** [kəntǽmənèit]	v	**pollute**, **stain**, **corrupt**, infect **contaminate** the water 수질을 오염시키다	오염시키다, 부패시키다
7 **couple** [kʌpl]	n	**pair**, two, duo, twin a married **couple** 결혼한 두 사람, 부부	한 쌍
8 **detach*** [ditǽtʃ]	v	**separate**, **split**, **disjoin**, **disconnect**, sever, divide ↔ attach **detach** oneself from the main body 본대에서 분리되다	분리하다, 떨어뜨리다
9 **dismiss*** [dismís]	v	① **fire**, **discharge**, **unseat**, release ↔ hire, employ **dismiss** an employee 고용인을 해고하다 ② **discard**, **reject**, **expel**, decline ↔ accept, retain, embrace **dismiss** an idea 아이디어를 거절하다	① 방출하다 ② 거절하다
10 **distress*** [distrés]	n	① **pain**, **anxiety**, **agony**, **anguish** He felt **distress** over the loss of his job. 그는 직업을 잃는 고통을 느꼈다. ② **trouble**, **worry**, **adversity** signal of **distress** 조난 신호	① 고통 ② 어려움, 곤경
11 **elegant*** [éligənt]	a	**tasteful**, **refined**, **polished**, graceful life of **elegant** ease 단아하고 안락한 생활	우아한

12	**expert*** [ékspəːrt]	n	specialist, authority, master, veteran ↔ beginner, novice an **expert** on flesh plant culture 다육식물 재배 전문가	전문가
		a	experienced, skillful, competent, deft, proficient ↔ inept be **expert** to make the slide for the presentation 발표용 슬라이드를 만드는 데 능력이 있다	능력 있는
13	**genius** [dʒíːnjəs]	n	brilliance, ability, gift, talent a man of **genius** 천재	천재, 비범한 재능
14	**handsome** [hǽnsəm]	a	good-looking a **handsome** boy 잘생긴 소년	멋있는, 잘생긴
15	**lag (behind)*** [læg]	v	linger, delay, decrease, trail, diminish **lag** behind in an embarrassment 당혹하여 꾸물거리다 **lag** behind in time 시대에 뒤쳐진	꾸물거리다, 뒤쳐지다
16	**masterpiece** [mǽstərpiːs]	n	great work the greatest **masterpiece** in recent years 근래의 명작	명작
17	**oral** [ɔ́ːrəl]	a	verbal, spoken, vocal an **oral** examination 구술 시험	구두의, 구술의
18	**original*** [ərídʒənl]	a	① inventive, creative, novel, fresh an **original** design 독창적인 디자인	① 독창적인, 참신한
			② first, primary, initial the **original** cast of the play 연극의 초기 배역	② 초기의
19	**oversight** [óuvərsait]	n	mistake, blunder, slip, error, inattention an **oversight** on our part 우리 편의 실수	간과, 실수
20	**peculiar*** [pikjúːljər]	a	distinctive, strange, odd, queer, eccentric, bizarre a substance of **peculiar** smell 특이한 냄새가 나는 물질	독특한, 특별한
21	**physician** [fizíʃən]	n	doctor, specialist, general practitioner a practicing **physician** 개업(내과)의	의사
22	**prior to*** [práiər tu]	a	preceding, before damp clothes **prior to** ironing 다림질하기 위해 옷을 축축하게 하다	앞선, 이전의
23	**propose** [prəpóuz]	v	suggest, advise, offer, project **propose** a new method 새로운 방법을 제안하다	제안하다, 제시하다
24	**rapture** [rǽptʃər]	n	ecstasy, joy, delight, bliss, exultation with **rapture** 황홀하여	황홀, 환희
25	**repent** [ripént]	v	regret, atone **repent** of one's rashness 경솔을 뉘우치다	후회하다, 뉘우치다
26	**silhouette*** [sìluét]	n	outline, form, profile, shape line a **silhouette** 실루엣을 그리다	외곽선, 윤곽, 개요
27	**spectacular*** [spektǽkjulər]	a	dramatic, sensational, impressive a **spectacular** scene 장관	장관인, 시선을 집중시키는

28	**speculation*** [spèkjuléiʃən]	n	guess, supposition, conjecture, surmise a report based on **speculation** rather than facts 사실보다는 추측에 근거한 보고	심사숙고, 추측
29	**spin*** [spin]	v	whirl, turn, rotate The Earth **spins** on its own axis. 지구는 지구의 축으로 돈다. **spin** a coin (내기 등으로) 동전을 던져 돌리다	회전시키다
30	**splotch*** [splatʃ]	n	spot, blotch, blot, smudge, smear smudge a large **splotches** with blue color 파란색으로 커다란 얼룩이 지다	얼룩, 오점
31	**stifle** [stáifl]	v	smother, suffocate, strangle, choke **stifle** free expression 표현의 자유를 억압하다	숨막히게 하다, 억누르다
32	**termite*** [tə́:rmait]	n	white ant, insect catch **termites** by inserting a twig into a termite mound 흰개미 언덕에 나뭇가지를 삽입하여 흰개미를 잡다	흰개미
33	**threshold** [θréʃhould]	n	entrance, start, minimum at the **threshold** of ~의 시초에	발단, 입구, 기준점
34	**undergoing*** [ʌndərgouiŋ]	a	experiencing, suffering, bearing, enduring **undergoing** radical change in the church 교회에서 급진적인 변화를 겪고 있는	경험을 한, 겪고 있는
35	**undulating** [ʌndʒuléitiŋ]	a	fluctuate, wavelike an **undulating** plain 기복이 있는 평야	물결 같은
36	**unequaled*** [ʌní:kwəld]	a	matchless, unparalleled, peerless **unequal** to the task 그 일에 경쟁자가 없는	경쟁자가 없는 (그 정도로 잘하는)
37	**unpredictable*** [ʌnpridíktəbl]	a	inconstant, chance, changeable Britain's **unpredictable** weather 영국의 예측하기 힘든 날씨	변덕스러운, 예측할 수 없는
38	**upheaval*** [ʌphi:vl]	n	breakthrough, violent disturbance an **upheaval** of society 사회의 격변	대변동, 동요
39	**velocity*** [vəlásəti]	n	speed, pace, rapidity, celerity cruising **velocity** 경제속도	속도, 빠르기
40	**wallow** [wálou]	v	roll, flounder **wallow** in luxury 사치에 빠지다	허우적거리다, 바둥거리다

Practice Test 08

01. The discovery of analytical geometry is usually attributed to Descartes and Fermat.
    Ⓐ related
    Ⓑ revealed
    Ⓒ stated
    Ⓓ ascribed

02. Prior to 1900, carmakers used skilled workers to assemble each automobile.
    Ⓐ In spite of
    Ⓑ During
    Ⓒ Earlier than
    Ⓓ Nevertheless

03. The president proposes legislations dealing with foreign aid and other international activities.
    Ⓐ demands
    Ⓑ suggests
    Ⓒ addresses
    Ⓓ guides

04. Spain's agriculture remains the weakest part of its economy, and it's farming lags behind most other European countries.
    Ⓐ fall behind
    Ⓑ leaving back
    Ⓒ obsolete
    Ⓓ date back

05. A growing number of museums employ people who are experts in the history of photography.
    Ⓐ amateurs
    Ⓑ novices
    Ⓒ professionals
    Ⓓ narrators

06. Growth is the orderly increase in size that organisms undergo as they mature.
    Ⓐ request
    Ⓑ experience
    Ⓒ repeat
    Ⓓ include

07. Political and social upheavals overturned many long established governments.
    Ⓐ bump
    Ⓑ vendor
    Ⓒ violent disturbance
    Ⓓ boulder

08. Comets typically pass the earth with a relatively high velocity.
    Ⓐ speed
    Ⓑ orbit
    Ⓒ weight
    Ⓓ diameter

09. Most scholars agree that the New Deal relieved much of the economic distress and brought about a large measure of recovery.
    Ⓐ difficulties
    Ⓑ inconvenience
    Ⓒ agony
    Ⓓ digression

10. Ground squirrels, prairie dogs, and many other small mammals rush into a burrows or other hiding place.
    Ⓐ squares
    Ⓑ shifts
    Ⓒ rivers
    Ⓓ dens

11. Medical photographers provide information that the physicians use to diagnose and treat illnesses.
    - Ⓐ doctors
    - Ⓑ physicists
    - Ⓒ athletes
    - Ⓓ prayers

12. Religious ideas generated some of the earliest philosophic speculations about the nature of life and the universe.
    - Ⓐ practices
    - Ⓑ certainties
    - Ⓒ tales
    - Ⓓ conjectures

13. Desert termites which are subterranean occasionally damage the wood of buildings, poles, and fence posts.
    - Ⓐ scorpions
    - Ⓑ moths
    - Ⓒ white ants
    - Ⓓ bugs

14. Back lighting can be used deliberately to create silhouettes.
    - Ⓐ darkness
    - Ⓑ lights
    - Ⓒ outlines
    - Ⓓ pictures

15. Great works of art produced today cannot take the place of the masterpieces of the past.
    - Ⓐ great works
    - Ⓑ favorite models
    - Ⓒ headquarters
    - Ⓓ memorials

16. Shakespeare's genius as a poet enabled him to express ideas both concisely and colorfully.
    - Ⓐ effort
    - Ⓑ success
    - Ⓒ talent
    - Ⓓ fiasco

17. No one knows exactly why we laugh or why anything that is funny should cause us to make such a peculiar noise.
    - Ⓐ original
    - Ⓑ unusual
    - Ⓒ unnatural
    - Ⓓ strange

18. The Milky Way is a splotchy band of bright and dark areas that stretch across the sky.
    - Ⓐ sign
    - Ⓑ blot
    - Ⓒ splendid
    - Ⓓ splash

19. Secular music which flourished in the colonies was passed down orally from person to person, without being published.
    - Ⓐ secretly
    - Ⓑ complicatedly
    - Ⓒ vocally
    - Ⓓ anciently

20. Integrated Pest Management is a concept of employing the optimum combination of control methods to reduce a pest population to below an economic threshold.
    - Ⓐ entrance
    - Ⓑ verge
    - Ⓒ upper limit
    - Ⓓ lower limit

DAY 09 Daily Checkup

01. **improve** one's health
    - Ⓐ deteriorate
    - Ⓑ measure
    - Ⓒ subordinate
    - Ⓓ ameliorate

02. false **scent**
    - Ⓐ odor
    - Ⓑ conjecture
    - Ⓒ price
    - Ⓓ taste

03. a **useful** member of the firm
    - Ⓐ obedient
    - Ⓑ homely
    - Ⓒ unimpaired
    - Ⓓ serviceable

04. The plan is **subject** to your approval.
    - Ⓐ horrible
    - Ⓑ submissive
    - Ⓒ theoretival
    - Ⓓ profitable

05. **curse** and swear
    - Ⓐ biting
    - Ⓑ calamity
    - Ⓒ damn
    - Ⓓ debating

06. **insult** a person's behavior
    - Ⓐ dispute
    - Ⓑ coerce
    - Ⓒ scorn
    - Ⓓ evacuate

07. on the **rims**
    - Ⓐ reliance
    - Ⓑ horror
    - Ⓒ edges
    - Ⓓ sound

08. **heighten** a description
    - Ⓐ make
    - Ⓑ advance
    - Ⓒ detail
    - Ⓓ furnish

09. a **valuable** friend
    - Ⓐ subordinate
    - Ⓑ important
    - Ⓒ careless
    - Ⓓ harsh

10. **argue** along lines
    - Ⓐ fight
    - Ⓑ talk
    - Ⓒ struggle
    - Ⓓ discuss

11. the **acrid** stench of burning rubber
    - Ⓐ tender
    - Ⓑ potent
    - Ⓒ apparent
    - Ⓓ bitter

12. The evidence **manifests** the guilt.
    - Ⓐ displays
    - Ⓑ banishs
    - Ⓒ shock
    - Ⓓ agree

13. a **detriment** to health
    - Ⓐ bitter
    - Ⓑ ominous
    - Ⓒ insufficient
    - Ⓓ beginning

14. a feeling of **dread**
    - Ⓐ happiness
    - Ⓑ delight
    - Ⓒ awe
    - Ⓓ pleasure

15. voice **trivial** objections to the plan
    - Ⓐ unimportant
    - Ⓑ colossal
    - Ⓒ positive
    - Ⓓ critical

16. keep **intact**
    - Ⓐ complete
    - Ⓑ alive
    - Ⓒ unchanged
    - Ⓓ changeable

17. be **ominous** of failure
    - Ⓐ worried
    - Ⓑ foreboding
    - Ⓒ vigorous
    - Ⓓ frightened

18. a vote of **confidence**
    - Ⓐ belief
    - Ⓑ honor
    - Ⓒ reason
    - Ⓓ dishonest

19. piano sonata, **opus** 1, No. 2
    - Ⓐ masterpiece
    - Ⓑ virtuoso
    - Ⓒ work
    - Ⓓ compostion

20. **dilapidated** furniture
    - Ⓐ brand new
    - Ⓑ antique
    - Ⓒ modern
    - Ⓓ run-down

DAY 09 Voca Bank

	표제어	품사	동의어와 예문	한글 뜻
1	**abstract***** [ǽbstrækt]	a	**theoretical, unpracticed, hypothetical,** speculative some **abstract** concept of justice 정의의 일부 요약적인 개념	추상적인
2	**acrid*** [ǽkrid]	a	**bitter** in **acrid** tones 신랄한 어조로	고통스러운, 쓴, 신랄한
3	**ally** [əlái]	v	**align, confederate, join,** combine, affiliate, conjoin **ally** with 동맹을 맺다	동맹을 맺다, 연합하다, 제휴하다
4	**argue**** [á:rgju:]	v	**debate, discuss, dispute,** disagree ↔ agree **argue** along lines 일정한 줄거리를 따라 논하다	논쟁하다, 논의하다
5	**bite** [bait]	v	**gnaw, chew,** nip **bite** one's lips 입술을 깨물다	깨물다
6	**blow*** [blou]	n v	**shock, calamity, disaster,** bash ① **fan,** ruffle **blow** your hair dry 바람 불어서 머리카락을 말리다 ② **goof, bungle, flub,** fumble **blow** the exam 시험을 망치다	타격, 재난 ① 바람 불다 ② 망치다
7	**coerce**** [kouá:rs]	v	**pressurize, compel, constrain,** force, squeeze **coerce** obedience 복종을 강요하다	강요하다
8	**common** [kámən]	a	① **average, ordinary, commonplace,** regular, customary ↔ rare Jogging is a **common** activity. 조깅은 일상적인 활동이다. a **common** complaint 평범한 불평 ② **popular, public, prevailing** the most **common** beverage 가장 대중적인 음료	① 공동의, 평범한 ② 대중적인
9	**confidence** [kánfədəns]	n	**trust, belief,** faith, reliance a vote of **confidence** 신임투표	자신감, 믿음
10	**curse** [kə:rs]	v	**damn, imprecate, anathematize,** scourge **curse** and swear 악담을 퍼붓다	저주하다
11	**desert** [dézərt]	v	**abandon, forsake, quit, defect,** evacuate **desert** one's job 직장을 포기하다	버리다, 포기하다
12	**detrimental**** [dètrəméntl]	a	**damaging, destructive, harmful,** averse, pernicious, prejudicial be **detrimental** to society 사회에 유해하다	해로운, 불리한
13	**dilapidated**** [dilǽpədèitid]	a	**run-down, ruined,** derelict **dilapidated** building 황폐한 건물	황폐한, 파손된

14	**discrete*** [diskrí:t]	a	distinct, separate **discrete** quantity 분리량	별개의, 분리된
15	**dread*** [dred]	a	fear, awe, horror have a **dread** of ~을 두려워하다	무서운, 경외의
16	**expel** [ikspél]	v	oust, banish, exile **expel** a student from a college 학생을 대학에서 퇴학시키다	추방하다
17	**full-blown**** [fulbloun]	a	completely ripened, mature, fully grown a **full blown** rose 만발한 장미	만발한, 완전히 성숙한
18	**heighten** [háitn]	v	increase, advance, amplify, augment **heighten** a color 색을 밝게 하다(강화하다)	증대하다
19	**improve**** [imprú:v]	v	ameliorate, better **improve** one's health 건강을 증진시키다	향상시키다, 개선시키다
20	**in the midst of** [in ðə midst əv]	a	during, undergoing **in the midst of** her busy schedule 그녀의 바쁜 스케줄 중에도	~의 가운데
21	**insult** [insʌlt]	v	scorn, slander, abuse **insult** one's behavior 누구의 행동을 모욕하다	모욕을 주다
22	**intact**** [intǽkt]	a	unchanged, uninjured, unimpaired, sound keep **intact** 손을 대지 않고 그대로 두다	손상되지 않는, 온전한 건드리지 않은
23	**loose*** [lu:s]	a	untied, slack **loose** bond with other male 다른 수컷들과 느슨한 결합	헐거운, 풀린
24	**manifest**** [mǽnəfèst]	a	evident, obvious, apparent, plain, clear, distinct the **manifest** failure of the policies 정책상의 명백한 실패	명백한, 분명한
		v	display, reveal ↔ conceal **manifest** one's sincerity 누구의 성실함을 보이다	표명하다
25	**mighty** [máiti]	a	powerful, potent a **mighty** wind 강풍	강력한, 힘센
26	**ominous*** [ámənəs]	a	foreboding an **ominous** report from the doctor 의사로부터의 불길한 소식	불길한, 전조의
27	**opus** [óupəs]	n	work, composition, creation one's magnum **opus** 필생의 역작	음악 작품, 작품 번호
28	**orator** [ɔ́:rətər]	n	speaker, lecturer the great **orator** of Russian Revolution 러시아 혁명의 위대한 연설자	연설자
29	**rare**** [rɛər]	a	scarce, infrequent, exceptional, extraordinary, uncommon a **rare** disease 희귀 병	드문, 진기한
30	**rim** [rim]	n	edge, border, brim, brink the **rim** of crater 분화구의 가장자리	가장자리
31	**scanty**** [skǽnti]	a	meager, insufficient, inadequate, deficient ↔ adequate a **scanty** amount of food 부족한 양의 음식	부족한, 불충분한

DAY 09

32	**scent** [sent]	n	odor, perfume cold **scent** 희미한 냄새(자취)	냄새, 향기, 기미, 낌새
33	**silent** [sáilənt]	a	noiseless, quiet, tranquil, calm ↔ boisterous **silent** during the visit 방문하는 동안에 조용한	고요한, 말을 안하는
34	**stout** [staut]	a	stalwart, sturdy, athletic, vigorous **stout** resistance 완강한 저항	튼튼한, 용감한
35	**strive*** [straiv]	v	endeavor, try, struggle, toil **strive** for the best 최고를 위해 노력하다	노력하다, 얻으려 애쓰다
36	**subject*** [sʌ́bdʒikt]	a	subordinate, subjected, submissive, obedient Prices may be **subject** to alteration. 가격은 변동에 영향을 받는다.	지배를 받는, 복종하는
37	**trivial** [tríviəl]	a	unimportant, little, small, minor, slight a **trivial** matter 사소한 일	하찮은
38	**ugly** [ʌ́gli]	a	unsightly, homely, unlovely an **ugly** face 못생긴 얼굴	추한, 못생긴
39	**useful** [júːsfəl]	a	advantageous, profitable, beneficial a **useful** member of the firm 회사의 유능한 사원	쓸모 있는, 유익한
40	**valuable*** [vǽljuəbl]	a	very useful, very thoughtful, useful a **valuable** gift 소중한 선물	귀중한

Practice Test 09

01. A solitary predator can hunt its prey more silently than can a group.
    - Ⓐ friendly
    - Ⓑ easily
    - Ⓒ loudly
    - Ⓓ inaudibly

02. Most people want to work hard and improve the lives of their families.
    - Ⓐ enjoy
    - Ⓑ possess
    - Ⓒ decline
    - Ⓓ ameliorate

03. A diamond can be broken cleanly with a sharp, accurate blow due to its cleavage.
    - Ⓐ break
    - Ⓑ bash
    - Ⓒ separation
    - Ⓓ engraving

04. Large craters are rimmed by mountains and have steep, terraced walls.
    - Ⓐ surrounded
    - Ⓑ ruined
    - Ⓒ bordered
    - Ⓓ formed

05. A diode can be built into an integrated circuit, or can form a discrete component of a conventional circuit.
    - Ⓐ separate
    - Ⓑ new
    - Ⓒ fused
    - Ⓓ numerous

06. Raspberries cultivated in greenhouses have a less acrid taste than wild raspberries.
    - Ⓐ bitter
    - Ⓑ gratifying
    - Ⓒ defined
    - Ⓓ recognizable

07. As the Nile flows northward through Egypt, it creates a narrow ribbon of fertile land in the midst of a great desert.
    - Ⓐ in vicinity of
    - Ⓑ in the middle of
    - Ⓒ on the verge of
    - Ⓓ at a distance of

08. Coffee and tea were too expensive for most frontier families to drink except on rare occasions.
    - Ⓐ explosive
    - Ⓑ physical
    - Ⓒ uncommon
    - Ⓓ affordable

09. Hyenas leave solid body wastes and scents produced by special glands to mark their boundaries.
    - Ⓐ tastes
    - Ⓑ touch
    - Ⓒ order
    - Ⓓ fragrance

10. The official name of a composition may identify the form of the work and often includes an opus number.
    - Ⓐ tour de force
    - Ⓑ job
    - Ⓒ writing
    - Ⓓ piece

11. The principal speaker was Edward Everett, one of the greatest orators of his time.
    A artists
    B public speakers
    C musicians
    D dancers

12. Lincoln came to acquire a quiet confidence in his own judgment as he met the trials of war.
    A assurance
    B doubt
    C timidity
    D misgiving

13. Some scientists argue that the buildup of atmospheric CO_2 due to human activities has caused the warming trend.
    A object
    B demonstrate
    C dispute
    D contradict

14. A United Nations military force would be useful even though it could not be strong enough to coerce the Great Powers.
    A attack
    B fight
    C combine
    D compel

15. Even a person who claims that the consideration of philosophic questions is a waste of time is in itself expressing what is important, worthwhile, or valuable.
    A various
    B delicious
    C organic
    D useful

16. The candidates and their followers strive to develop voter support through publicity, advertising, and personal appearances.
    A attest
    B endeavor
    C respire
    D admonish

17. When late summer rains were scanty, farmers had difficulty finding wood for shelter, fuel, and building fences.
    A meager
    B indeterminate
    C implicit
    D theoretical

18. Many ghost stories play on the reader's fear of death and their dread of uncomfortable, strange places, such as deserted mansions or medieval castles.
    A fortune
    B fright
    C notice
    D prediction

19. Conservation include the ways a performers conserve his power and heightens the role to a climax.
    A carries
    B diminishes
    C increases
    D considers

20. Mountains are the most visible manifestation of the powerful tectonic forces at work and the vast time spans over which those forces have operated.
    A work
    B result
    C hint
    D display

DAY 10 Daily Checkup

01. She is apt to learn.
    - Ⓐ is approach to
    - Ⓑ get into
    - Ⓒ is easily finish to
    - Ⓓ s liable to

02. I cannot account for facts.
    - Ⓐ approve by
    - Ⓑ understand by
    - Ⓒ explain
    - Ⓓ rely on

03. He was back and forth, lost in thoughts.
    - Ⓐ to and fro
    - Ⓑ hurried away
    - Ⓒ confused
    - Ⓓ now and then

04. You can count on Tom.
    - Ⓐ meet
    - Ⓑ recant
    - Ⓒ vilify
    - Ⓓ trust

05. coral reefs teem with fish
    - Ⓐ swarm with
    - Ⓑ are slimy with
    - Ⓒ are poisonous to
    - Ⓓ are uninhabited by

06. photograph that were worn out
    - Ⓐ old-fashioned
    - Ⓑ no longer usable
    - Ⓒ for display only
    - Ⓓ well known

07. do away with my book
    - Ⓐ do without
    - Ⓑ dispense
    - Ⓒ get rid of
    - Ⓓ recycle

08. a wide range of books
    - Ⓐ allows
    - Ⓑ a variety of
    - Ⓒ associated with
    - Ⓓ do away with

09. coincide with the start of the dry season
    - Ⓐ collide with
    - Ⓑ be similar to
    - Ⓒ occurred at the same time as
    - Ⓓ taken from

10. hard to deal with
    - Ⓐ succumb to
    - Ⓑ stick to
    - Ⓒ concern
    - Ⓓ respond to

11. very susceptible to injury
    - Ⓐ count on
    - Ⓑ subject to
    - Ⓒ worry about
    - Ⓓ concern over

12. He piled up huge debt.
    - Ⓐ to and fro
    - Ⓑ is full of
    - Ⓒ is free of
    - Ⓓ heap up

13. in the midst of her busy schedule
    - Ⓐ understand
    - Ⓑ in the middle of
    - Ⓒ besides
    - Ⓓ surpass

14. master up to 50 pages a day
    - Ⓐ arrange for
    - Ⓑ devoid of
    - Ⓒ a maximum of
    - Ⓓ make up for

15. carry out the procedure correctly
    - Ⓐ perform
    - Ⓑ call for
    - Ⓒ break apart
    - Ⓓ bring about

16. The Galaxy consists of 100 billion stars.
    - Ⓐ substituted for
    - Ⓑ purpose
    - Ⓒ composes
    - Ⓓ regards as

17. derived from Greek word
    - Ⓐ recovered from
    - Ⓑ benefited from
    - Ⓒ separated from
    - Ⓓ stemmed from

18. licenses as well as ordering the equipment
    - Ⓐ in addition to
    - Ⓑ as good as
    - Ⓒ instead of
    - Ⓓ as substitute for

19. Chocolate comes from cacao tree.
    - Ⓐ crucial for
    - Ⓑ contrary to
    - Ⓒ originates from
    - Ⓓ keeps from

20. costs may be trimmed at the expense of patent
    - Ⓐ criticize
    - Ⓑ disadvantage
    - Ⓒ agree with
    - Ⓓ elevate

DAY 10 Voca Bank

표제어	동의어와 예문	한글 뜻
1 **be apt to** [bi æpt tu]	be prone to He **was apt to** boast of his job. 그는 자기 직업을 과장하는 경향이 있다.	~하기 쉽다
2 **a wide range of**** [əwáid reindʒ əv]	a variety of, a myriad of, an army of **a wide range of** chemicals 다양한 화학약품	다양한, 많은
3 **account for**** [əkaunt fər]	explain, consider as, deem, reckon, regard There s no **account for** them. 그것을 설명할 사람이 아무도 없다.	~을 설명하다
4 **adjust to** [ədʒʌst tu]	fit, adapt, suit, accommodate **adjust** expenses **to** income 수입구 지출을 맞추다	~에 적응하다, ~에 조절하다
5 **as well as***** [æz wel æz]	in addition to, moreover He gave us clothes **as well as** focd. 그는 우리에게 음식뿐만 아니라 옷도 주었다.	게다가, ~뿐 아니라
6 **at the expense of** [æt ði: ikspéns əv]	disadvantage, cost, charge, price, expenditure He did it **at the expense of** his health. 그는 건강을 희생시켜 그것을 했다. **at the expense of** ~을 희생하여	~의 비용으로, ~의 희생으로
7 **back and forth** [bǽkənfɔ́:rθ]	crisscross, to and fro, side by side The teacher is walking **back and forth** on the platform. 선생님이 교단 위를 왔다갔다 걷고 계신다.	왔다갔다, 좌우로
8 **carry out** [kǽri aut]	perform, fulfill, attain, perform, achieve, serve **carry out** the procedure correctly 절차를 바르게 실행하다	~을 실행하다, ~을 이행하다
9 **coincide with*** [kòuinsáid wíð]	happened (occurred) at the same time as, correspond Your view exactly **coincides with** mine. 너의 견해가 나의 견해와 부합된다.	~와 동시에 발생하다
10 **come up with** [kʌm ʌp wíð]	① reach, overtake, approach **come up with** a something to drive the industry forward 산업을 발전시킬 새로운 것에 접근하다 ② supply, produce; present, propose **come up with** new antibiotics to replace old one 기존 것을 대체하기 위해 새로운 항생제로 브슝하다	① ~에 접근하다 ② ~을 보충 [제안]하다
11 **comes from*** [kʌmz frəm]	originate from The word paper **comes from** papyrus. 종이란 단어는 파피루스에서 생겨났다.	(결과로서) 생기다, 원인이 있다
12 **compared to** [kəmpɛ́ərd tu]	liken to, correlate to, equal to, identify with Shakespeare **compared** the world **to** a stage. 셰익스피어는 세상을 무대에 비유하였다.	~와 비교하다, ~와 대조하다

#	Term	Definitions / Examples	Meaning
13	**confronted with**** [kənfrʌ́ntid wíð]	① **adhere to, encounter, confront, face** **confront with** the witness against him 그에게 증인으로서 대면하다 ② **withstand, oppose, counteract, rebuff** **confront with** a difficulty 난관에 대항하다	① ~에 대면하다 ② ~에 대항하다
14	**consist of**** [kənsíst əv]	**be made up of, make up, constitute, compose, form, comprise** Water **consists of** hydrogen and oxygen. 물은 수소와 산소로 되어 있다.	~로 구성하다
15	**count on** [kaunt ən]	**trust, rely on, accredit** Don't **count on** me for any help. 나에게 어떤 도움도 기대하지 마라.	~을 의존하다
16	**deals with*** [di:ls wíð]	**concern, involve, relate to** hard to **deal with** 다루기 어려운	~을 다루다
17	**derived from** [diráivd frəm]	**stem from** The word 'pan' is **derived from** Portuguess. 빵이란 말은 포르투갈어에서 유래했다.	~에서 유래되다
18	**be filled with** [bi fíld wíð]	**pack with** **be filled with** exciting episodes, suspense and powerful verse 흥미로운 에피소드, 서스펜스와 힘찬 운문으로 채우다	~로 채우다, ~로 가득하다
19	**in addition to** [in ədíʃən tu]	**as well as, besides, moreover, coupled with, further, furthermore** eat meat **in addition to** fruits, insects, and plants 고기뿐만 아니라 과일, 곤충, 식물도 먹다	더욱이, 더불어
20	**in spite of*** [in spait əv]	**despite, (even) though, notwithstanding, regardless of** **in spite of** oneself 저도 모르게, 무심코	~에도 불구하고
21	**join together** [dʒɔin təgéðər]	**combine** **join together** in the process of fermentation 발효과정에서 함께하다	함께하다
22	**keep pace with** [ki:p peis wíð]	**hold pace with, at the same speed as** We can **keep pace with** scientific development. 우리는 과학의 발전에 보조를 맞출 수 있다.	~와 보조를 맞추다
23	**knack for** [næk fər]	**aptitude, trick, tact** Cheolsu has the **knack for** gardening. 철수는 정원을 가꾸는 데 재주가 있다.	~에 대한 소질 [재주]
24	**of our own time** [əv auər oun taim]	**Independently; contemporary** deny all inequalities **of their own time** 자기재량으로 모든 불평등을 거부하다 gain a better understanding **of her own time** 그녀 시대의 더 나은 이해를 얻다	자기 재량으로, 우리 시대의
25	**pick up** [pik ʌp]	**gather, collect, amass, assemble** He **picks up** a money on the street. 그는 길에서 돈을 모았다.	~을 모으다, 수집하다
26	**pile up***** [pail ʌp]	**collect, gather, accumulate, together, heap up, save up** ↔ **scatter, get rid of, disperse, waste** **pile up** money 돈을 축적하다	~을 모으다, 쌓다, 저축하다

DAY 10

#	Term	Definition / Example	Korean
27	**respond to** [rispánd tu]	react (to) **respond to** a charity drive 자선 운동에 응하다	~에 대응하다
28	**scoop out*** [sku:p aut]	gather **scoop out** small pieces of oyster and shell 작은 조각의 굴과 조개껍데기를 모으다	~을 퍼내다, 긁어모으다
29	**send out** [sent aut]	distribute **send out** a warning 경고를 발하다	~을 배포하다, 발하다
30	**(be) skilled at*** [skild æt]	proficient in **skilled at** working with such harder materials as stone and metals 돌과 금속 같은 딱딱한 재료로 작업하는 데 능숙한	~에 능숙한, 숙달한
31	**spell out** [spel aut]	detail, expatiate, expound **spell out** procedures of fermented rice wine 발효 막걸리의 공정을 자세히 말하다	~을 자세히 말하다, ~을 자세히 설명하다
32	**spread out** [spred aut]	radiate, diffuse, proliferate, rediate **Spread out** the map. 지도를 펴시오.	번지다, 퍼지다
33	**be subject to*** [bi sʌbdʒikt tu]	susceptible to The plan **is subject to** your approval. 이 계획은 귀하의 승인을 요합니다.	(~을) 받기 위한, 지배를 받는, ~을 필요로 하는
34	**susceptible to*** [səséptəbl tu]	subject to, be vulnerable to very **susceptible to** injury 매우 상처받기 쉬운 **susceptible to** various interpretations 여러가지 해석이 가능한	~하기 쉬운, (~의) 영향을 받기 쉬운
35	**take-off** [teik ɔ:f]	launching, depart, take wing The aeroplane **took off** at 7:55 a.m. 비행기는 오전 7시 55분에 이륙했다.	출발, 이륙, 초기 단계
36	**take into account**** [teik intu əkáunt]	consider, make allowance for, turn into advantage We must **take** his talent **into account**. 우리는 그의 재능을 고려해야 한다.	~을 이용하다, 고려하다
37	**take it for granted** [teik it fər græntid]	acknowledge, accept I **took it for granted** that he would come. 나는 그가 오는 것이 당연하다고 생각했다.	~을 당연한 일로 생각하다, 인정하다
38	**teem with** [ti:m wíð]	swarm with, be full of, abound with These water **teem with** fish. 이 근해에는 어류가 풍부하다.	~로 가득 차다, ~가 풍부하다
39	**up to** [ʌp tu]	as much as, a maximum of, as many as; dependent upon The water came **up to** his chin. 물이 그의 턱에까지 차 올랐다.	~에 이르기까지 / ~에 달려 있는
40	**wear out*** [wɛər aut]	exhaust If your shoes are **worn out** 만약 너의 신발이 닳았다면	점점 없어지다, 소모 시키다, 닳게 하다

Practice Test 10

01. A living language is subject to constant change.
    Ⓐ is affected by
    Ⓑ compresses
    Ⓒ invigorate
    Ⓓ employ

02. Disaccharides consist of two simple sugars joined together.
    Ⓐ combined
    Ⓑ differentiated
    Ⓒ separated
    Ⓓ dissolved

03. In higher animals, each important life function is carried out by a group of organs working together.
    Ⓐ disappeared
    Ⓑ broken down
    Ⓒ stopped
    Ⓓ implemented

04. Education helps people adjust to change.
    Ⓐ remove
    Ⓑ adapt to
    Ⓒ form
    Ⓓ exclude

05. Whale sharks, in spite of their enormous size, eat only plankton and small fish.
    Ⓐ despite
    Ⓑ except
    Ⓒ within
    Ⓓ outside

06. This book deals with the literature of our own time.
    Ⓐ at that wrote time
    Ⓑ contemporary to us
    Ⓒ old fashioned
    Ⓓ in time

07. The African conception of democracy does not coincide with the current American one.
    Ⓐ similar with
    Ⓑ collide with
    Ⓒ agree with
    Ⓓ was related with

08. At one end, two long flagella extend and, by beating back and forth, algae serve to propel the organism through the water.
    Ⓐ whatever
    Ⓑ zigzag
    Ⓒ separate
    Ⓓ response

09. It is up to the producer to find a suitable space for performances and rehearsals.
    Ⓐ going to
    Ⓑ related on
    Ⓒ planning to
    Ⓓ dependent upon

10. Chimpanzees live in a wide range of habitats from western to eastern Africa.
    Ⓐ a variety of
    Ⓑ a wide extent of
    Ⓒ a small region of
    Ⓓ a big land of

11. They took it for granted that Washington would be chosen as the first President.
    Ⓐ guessed
    Ⓑ neglected
    Ⓒ denied
    Ⓓ ensured

12. Bread, cereals, and potatoes furnish carbohydrates in addition to vitamins, minerals, and fiber.
    Ⓐ anymore
    Ⓑ include
    Ⓒ besides
    Ⓓ such as

13. The disintegrating supernova sent out gases that joined the existing cloud of gas.
    Ⓐ differentiated
    Ⓑ emerged
    Ⓒ expelled
    Ⓓ established

14. Many scientists, economists, and other experts fear that food production cannot keep pace with the population for much longer.
    Ⓐ grow over
    Ⓑ stay with
    Ⓒ yield to
    Ⓓ become widespread

15. Plate tectonics still provides the basic framework that accounts for the distribution of mountains across the earth's surface.
    Ⓐ reduce
    Ⓑ explain
    Ⓒ combine with
    Ⓓ list all of

16. Country music is derived from the folk music of rural whites of the Southern United States and other American traditional music.
    Ⓐ result from
    Ⓑ separated from
    Ⓒ engaged in
    Ⓓ stemmed from

17. Each day, about 0.8 percent of the body's red blood cells wear out and are destroyed.
    Ⓐ exhausted
    Ⓑ generated
    Ⓒ displayed
    Ⓓ transported

18. *Othello* and *Romeo and Juliet* differ from Shakespeare's other tragedies in that neither deals with public affairs and royalty.
    Ⓐ criticizes
    Ⓑ elevates
    Ⓒ treats with
    Ⓓ ridicules

19. Individualized reading programs take into account the wide range of reading abilities and needs.
    Ⓐ consider
    Ⓑ expand
    Ⓒ ignore
    Ⓓ provide

20. John Amos Comenius, a Czech educator, was one of the first authors who believed that children's books should entertain as well as teach.
    Ⓐ equal to
    Ⓑ as substitutes for
    Ⓒ in addition to
    Ⓓ instead of

06-10 Exercise

01. indecent language
    - Ⓐ surprising
    - Ⓑ forcible
    - Ⓒ vulgar
    - Ⓓ detailed

02. desert one's job
    - Ⓐ get
    - Ⓑ achieve
    - Ⓒ succeed
    - Ⓓ abandon

03. foster a new program
    - Ⓐ promote
    - Ⓑ object to
    - Ⓒ plan
    - Ⓓ reexamine

04. He tried to keep pace with the first runner.
    - Ⓐ set off
    - Ⓑ similar to
    - Ⓒ keep up
    - Ⓓ superior to

05. an elaborate work
    - Ⓐ coarse
    - Ⓑ difficult
    - Ⓒ invaluable
    - Ⓓ precise

06. nibble at one's nails
    - Ⓐ consider
    - Ⓑ attack
    - Ⓒ breed
    - Ⓓ bite

07. You should take these into account.
    - Ⓐ consider
    - Ⓑ engage in
    - Ⓒ accredit
    - Ⓓ perform

08. The book counts as a masterpiece.
    - Ⓐ distinctive feature
    - Ⓑ adviser
    - Ⓒ money
    - Ⓓ best work

09. silent pictures
    - Ⓐ blue
    - Ⓑ noiseless
    - Ⓒ monotonous
    - Ⓓ excellent

10. a fatal disease
    - Ⓐ defensible
    - Ⓑ frightful
    - Ⓒ curable
    - Ⓓ lethal

11. compare to his brother
    - Ⓐ prior to
    - Ⓑ similar to
    - Ⓒ contrast to
    - Ⓓ take place

12. hear distress in her voice
    - Ⓐ bliss
    - Ⓑ panic
    - Ⓒ agony
    - Ⓓ joy

13. a social and economic upheaval
    - Ⓐ district
    - Ⓑ breakthrough
    - Ⓒ boom
    - Ⓓ entrance

14. a wedge of pie
    - Ⓐ chock
    - Ⓑ darkness
    - Ⓒ preference
    - Ⓓ mass

15. a productive day
    - Ⓐ extensive
    - Ⓑ barren
    - Ⓒ fruitful
    - Ⓓ mixing

16. lag behind in an embarrassment
    - Ⓐ repent
    - Ⓑ linger
    - Ⓒ disjoin
    - Ⓓ work

17. propose a new method
    - Ⓐ consider
    - Ⓑ intent
    - Ⓒ regret
    - Ⓓ suggest

18. sensual delight
    - Ⓐ economical
    - Ⓑ sensuous
    - Ⓒ pecuniary
    - Ⓓ physical

19. monetary value
    - Ⓐ general
    - Ⓑ hormone
    - Ⓒ metal
    - Ⓓ pecuniary

20. strive after an ideal
    - Ⓐ better
    - Ⓑ banish
    - Ⓒ endeavor
    - Ⓓ forsake

Practice

01. This is not an original painting, but a reproduction.
    - Ⓐ critical
    - Ⓑ eminent
    - Ⓒ genuine
    - Ⓓ multiplication

02. The Skyline Drive along the top of the Blue Ridge offers spectacular views of the Shenandoah Valley.
    - Ⓐ common
    - Ⓑ uneven
    - Ⓒ magnificent
    - Ⓓ accidental

03. In 843, Kenneth MacAlpine, a king of the Scots, united his realm with that of the Picts.
    - Ⓐ planet
    - Ⓑ kingdom
    - Ⓒ farmland
    - Ⓓ house

04. Many crew members of whaling ships deserted their ships to search for gold.
    - Ⓐ went
    - Ⓑ tried
    - Ⓒ remained
    - Ⓓ abandoned

05. Modern science has barely begun to consider the question of how we perceive the passage of time.
    - Ⓐ always
    - Ⓑ just
    - Ⓒ naturally
    - Ⓓ accidentally

06. During a synodic month, we can see the moon 'change' from a slim crescent to a full circle and back again.
    - Ⓐ beautiful
    - Ⓑ thin
    - Ⓒ healthy
    - Ⓓ energetic

07. Neuroscientists have tried to come up with for a way to fix brain injury or brain disorders for decades.
    - Ⓐ daunted
    - Ⓑ apportioned
    - Ⓒ proposed
    - Ⓓ abetted

08. Ticks and Mites were less susceptible to insecticide than miticides.
    - Ⓐ vulnerable
    - Ⓑ rugged
    - Ⓒ firm
    - Ⓓ emotional

09. Good health enables people to enjoy life and have the opportunity to achieve their goals.
    - Ⓐ chance
    - Ⓑ desire
    - Ⓒ ability
    - Ⓓ money

10. Mechanization has helped miners to become more productive.
    - Ⓐ feasible
    - Ⓑ lucrative
    - Ⓒ practicable
    - Ⓓ powerful

11. The cytoplasm is filled with structures called myofibrils and are closely associated with the mitochondria.
    Ⓐ includes
    Ⓑ separates
    Ⓒ is full of
    Ⓓ is exempted from

12. Living things can sense and respond to changes in their surroundings.
    Ⓐ agree to
    Ⓑ stimulate
    Ⓒ in addition to
    Ⓓ adapt to

13. Over a period of 4,000 years, Indian sculptors created powerful works characterized by spiritual content and technical brilliance.
    Ⓐ overestimated
    Ⓑ represented
    Ⓒ preserved
    Ⓓ misunderstood

14. Atomic weight is the gravity of an atom in comparison with the gravity of an atom of carbon-12.
    Ⓐ dealt with
    Ⓑ equal to
    Ⓒ contrast with
    Ⓓ conflict with

15. The people of the pueblos hunted and farmed, growing such crops as maize (corn), beans, and squash.
    Ⓐ fertile soils
    Ⓑ manufacturing plants
    Ⓒ harvestable plants
    Ⓓ cultivation

16. Country radio programs provided free entertainment and helped lighten the burden of hard times.
    Ⓐ length
    Ⓑ demand
    Ⓒ load
    Ⓓ remain

17. Recently, success in hospitality and travel industry has been caused by increasing of customer demand, coupled with a greater supply.
    Ⓐ on account of
    Ⓑ combined
    Ⓒ ruled
    Ⓓ leagued

18. An important clue to the origin of the galaxy comes from the striking correlation between the type and local density of the galaxy.
    Ⓐ excites
    Ⓑ pulls out
    Ⓒ is analogized from
    Ⓓ makes

19. Solitary predators generally stalk their prey by slinking and hiding, while many of these hunters have coats that blend in with their surroundings.
    Ⓐ mix
    Ⓑ dissolve
    Ⓒ transfer
    Ⓓ reduce

20. Nations that form a free trade area have no tariffs among themselves, but each member may set its own tariffs on goods produced by nonmembers.
    Ⓐ prescribe
    Ⓑ exhibit
    Ⓒ situate
    Ⓓ decide

Intensive Practice

01. Most nutrients undergo a chemical change as they are used.
    Ⓐ go through
    Ⓑ digest
    Ⓒ convert
    Ⓓ nourish

02. As the fighting intensified, hopes of reconciliation with the United Kingdom faded.
    Ⓐ ceasefire
    Ⓑ pacification
    Ⓒ covenant
    Ⓓ abstruse

03. Scientists divide the characteristics of substances into physical properties and chemical properties.
    Ⓐ moral nature
    Ⓑ integral part
    Ⓒ distinguishing features
    Ⓓ mental abilities

04. The use of tractors and other modern farm machines has sharply reduced the need for farm labor.
    Ⓐ constantly
    Ⓑ roughly
    Ⓒ steeply
    Ⓓ grimly

05. Cells are modified according to the functions they perform; some cells live for a few days whereas others live for many years.
    Ⓐ demanded
    Ⓑ changed
    Ⓒ ruled
    Ⓓ leagued

06. In primitive societies, the people who produced food, or owned it, often deliberately handed over the best portions to others.
    Ⓐ intentionally
    Ⓑ independently
    Ⓒ repeatedly
    Ⓓ conveniently

07. Automobiles are the chief cause of traffic congestion in urban areas, and their exhaust fumes contribute heavily to urban air pollution.
    Ⓐ germs
    Ⓑ debris
    Ⓒ chemicals
    Ⓓ gases

08. While the earth travels through space around the sun, it also spins on its own axis.
    Ⓐ still
    Ⓑ hops
    Ⓒ removes
    Ⓓ turns

09. Pollutants that seep into the ground result of contaminated surface water, leaks from sewer pipes and septic tanks, and chemical spills.
    Ⓐ popularized
    Ⓑ contact
    Ⓒ polluted
    Ⓓ industrialized

10. The orbit of comets are often steeply inclined to that of the earth's.
    Ⓐ horizon   Ⓑ vertical
    Ⓒ droved   Ⓓ rushed

11. In general, the earlier prophets, such as Jeremiah and Isaiah, called on people to repent for their sins and renew their faith in God.
    Ⓐ regret
    Ⓑ change
    Ⓒ return
    Ⓓ determine

12. Global warming could radically alter coral reefs as well as their dependent communities.
    Ⓐ apparently
    Ⓑ fundamentally
    Ⓒ admittedly
    Ⓓ tragically

13. Despite the rapid accumulation of ultrastructural and immunological data on cell division, many theories still abound in the literature.
    Ⓐ recover
    Ⓑ pile up
    Ⓒ analysis
    Ⓓ treatment

14. Most sharks eat their prey whole, or they tear off large chunks of flesh, while others scoop out small pieces of flesh from large fish.
    Ⓐ throw away
    Ⓑ distribute
    Ⓒ complete
    Ⓓ gather

15. African do not feel themselves to be confronted with the danger of domination from any other quarter.
    Ⓐ clashed with
    Ⓑ faced with
    Ⓒ struggled with
    Ⓓ accede with

16. Animals and plants lived when the rocks were formed, were buried and preserved when the layers of rocks piled up.
    Ⓐ connected
    Ⓑ stack on
    Ⓒ coagulated
    Ⓓ popped up

17. Prehistoric animals with long legs were probably fast runners, just like animals that have long legs today, whereas animals with short, stout legs moved more slowly.
    Ⓐ straight
    Ⓑ curved
    Ⓒ fat
    Ⓓ skinny

18. The portraits by Houdon show his ability to capture the personalities of his subjects and his genius at working with a wide variety of materials.
    Ⓐ brilliance
    Ⓑ talking
    Ⓒ gesture
    Ⓓ skill

19. To make it coincide with Halloween, the young actor-director Orson Welles dramatized the novel for his weekly radio program "Mercury Theatre on the Air."
    Ⓐ relate with
    Ⓑ collide with
    Ⓒ occur at the same time
    Ⓓ equalize with

20. As the proteins are made, they detach from the ribosomes and move through the ER cisternae into the smooth ER, where they may subsequently be modified.
    Ⓐ saturate
    Ⓑ secrete
    Ⓒ assemble
    Ⓓ separate

Related Words 06-10

발전	- breakthrough, advance, development, discovery
경향	- inclination, tendency, trend, preference
속도	- velocity, speed, pace, rapidity, celerity
위반	- infringement, violation, contravention, breach
결론	- conclusion, end, result, outcome, consequence
대변동	- upheaval, breakthrough, violent disturbance
윤곽선	- silhouette, outline, form, profile, shape
전문가	- expert, specialist, authority, master, veteran
추측	- speculation, guess, supposition, conjecture, surmise
절약하는	- frugal, economical, thrifty
해로운	- detrimental, damaging, destructive, harmful, averse, pernicious, prejudicial
사소한	- trivial, unimportant, little, small, minor, slight
드문, 진기한	- rare, scarce, infrequent, exceptional, uncommon, extraordinary
치명적인	- fatal, deadly, mortal, lethal, disastrous
불완전한	- imperfect, flawed, damaged, defective, impaired
추상적인	- abstract, theoretical, unpracticed,
논쟁하다	- argue, debate, discuss, dispute, disagree
꾸물거리다	- linger, lag, delay, trail, diminish, decrease
의도적으로	- deliberately, intentionally, consciously, on purpose
게다가	- as well as, in addition to, moreover, besides, couple with, further, furthermore

Knowledge based Vocabulary 06-10

CAMOUFLAGE

Camouflage is the concealment of animals, or objects of military interest by any combination of methods that helps them to remain ❶ <u>unnoticed</u> with its environment. This includes the use of high-contrast ❷ <u>disruptive</u> patterns as used on military uniforms, but anything that delays recognition can be used as camouflage. Camouflage involves ❸ <u>deception</u>, whether by looking like the background or by resembling something else, which may be plainly visible to observers. The leopard's spotted coat, the battledress of a modern soldier, and the leaf- ❹ <u>mimic</u> katydid's wings were the examples. Motion ❺ <u>dazzle</u>, confuses the observer with a ❻ <u>conspicuous</u> pattern, making the object visible but ❼ <u>momentarily</u> harder to ❽ <u>locate</u> may be another approach.

The majority of camouflage methods are either by making animals or objects hard to see (crypsis), often through a general resemblance to the background, high contrast disruptive coloration, ❾ <u>eliminating</u> shadow, and countershading. In the open ocean, where there is no background, the principal methods of camouflage are ❿ <u>transparency</u>, silvering, and countershading, while the ability to produce light is among other things used for counter-illumination on the undersides of cephalopods such as squid. Some animals, such as chameleons and octopuses, are capable of actively changing their skin pattern and colours, whether for camouflage or for signalling.

What is closest meaning to left word?

1. unnoticed	Ⓐ skimmed	Ⓑ scanned	Ⓒ observed	Ⓓ overlooked
2. disruptive	Ⓐ clear-cut	Ⓑ disturbing	Ⓒ discriminative	Ⓓ different
3. deception	Ⓐ deceit	Ⓑ honesty	Ⓒ vanity	Ⓓ boastful
4. mimic	Ⓐ produce	Ⓑ resemble	Ⓒ fake	Ⓓ nibbled
5. dazzle	Ⓐ hasitate	Ⓑ shrewd	Ⓒ daze	Ⓓ brilliance
6. conspicuous	Ⓐ hidden	Ⓑ imperceptible	Ⓒ apparent	Ⓓ unknown
7. momentarily	Ⓐ consistently	Ⓑ regularly	Ⓒ everywhere	Ⓓ temporarily
8. locate	Ⓐ cover	Ⓑ confine	Ⓒ find a site	Ⓓ deliver
9. eliminating	Ⓐ eradicating	Ⓑ veiling	Ⓒ transforming	Ⓓ quivering
10. transparency	Ⓐ unclearness	Ⓑ vagueness	Ⓒ vanishing	Ⓓ translucence

위장

위장은 동물이나 군사적인 이해대상의 물체를 그들의 환경과 섞임으로 해서 알아채지 못하도록 돕는^(helps them to remain unnoticed) 어떤 방법들의 조합으로 은폐시키는 것이다. 이러한 것에는 군인들의 제복^(military uniforms)에 사용되는 고(명암)대비 교란시키는 무늬의 사용^(the use of high-contrast disruptive patterns)을 포함하고 있으나 인지를 늦추는 무엇이든^(anything that delays recognition) 간에 위장처럼 사용할 수 있다. 위장은 어떤 것과 닮게 하거나 배경과 같이 보이게 하거나^(by looking like the background)함으로써 속이는 것과 관련이 있는데^(involves deception) 관찰자의 눈에는 꾸밈없이 보일 수 있다^(may be plainly visible to observers). 표범의 반점이 있는 털이나, 현대 군인의 전투복, 잎 모양을 닮은 여치의 날개^(the leaf-mimic katydid's wings)와 같은 것들이 이러한 예이다. 분명해 보이는 무늬로 관찰자를 혼란을 주는^(confuses the observer with a conspicuous pattern) 움직임의 현혹^(motion dazzle)은 물체를 보이게 하지만 순간적으로 위치를 찾기가 힘들도록^(momentarily harder to locate) 만드는 것인데, 이 역시 하나의 방법이 될 것이다.

대다수의 위장 방법은 동물들이나 물체를 보기 힘들도록 (보호색으로) 만드는 것이지만, 종종 일반적으로 배경을 닮거나, 고대비 교란색을 갖거나, 그림자를 제거하고 역그늘현상(몸체가 햇빛에 노출된 부분은 어둡고 그늘진 부분은 밝은 색이 되는 현상)을 통해서 하기도 한다. 배경색이 없는 넓은 바다에서는 위장의 중요한 방법^(the principal methods of camouflage)으로 투명화^(transparency), 은화(체색이 은색으로 변하는 현상)와 역그늘 현상이 있는데, 빛을 만드는 능력 역시^(while the ability to produce light) 그러한 방법 중 하나로, 이는 오징어와 같은 두족류 동물의 밑면에서 역조명^(counter-illumination)하는 것에 사용된다 카멜레온과 문어와 같은 어떤 동물들은 위장을 위해서거나 신호전달을 위해서거나 간에 그들 피부의 문양과 색상을 적극적으로 바꾸는 능력을 가지고 있다^(are capable of actively changing).

1. Ⓓ	2. Ⓑ	3. Ⓐ	4. Ⓑ	5. Ⓒ
6. Ⓒ	7. Ⓓ	8. Ⓒ	9. Ⓐ	10. Ⓓ

DAY 11 Daily Checkup

01. **survive** the shipwreck
    - Ⓐ alternate
    - Ⓑ supplant
    - Ⓒ remain alive
    - Ⓓ contract

02. **squander** one's fortune
    - Ⓐ review
    - Ⓑ replace
    - Ⓒ lavish
    - Ⓓ enclose

03. a devout **pious** Christian
    - Ⓐ religious
    - Ⓑ shrewd
    - Ⓒ cunning
    - Ⓓ consistent

04. **alien** to our way of life
    - Ⓐ accede
    - Ⓑ strange
    - Ⓒ neglect
    - Ⓓ waste

05. **comply** with a request
    - Ⓐ diminish
    - Ⓑ remain
    - Ⓒ consent
    - Ⓓ compress

06. an act of **despair**
    - Ⓐ discouragement
    - Ⓑ rival
    - Ⓒ lavishness
    - Ⓓ shriveling

07. a **voluntary** contribution
    - Ⓐ vibrant
    - Ⓑ limited
    - Ⓒ harmonious
    - Ⓓ spontaneous

08. **maladroit** opinions
    - Ⓐ cunning
    - Ⓑ current
    - Ⓒ rigorous
    - Ⓓ inept

09. **shrink** the size of the project
    - Ⓐ disregard
    - Ⓑ supersede
    - Ⓒ diminish
    - Ⓓ study

10. a **proponent** of women's rights
    - Ⓐ violation
    - Ⓑ stream
    - Ⓒ supporter
    - Ⓓ competitor

11. convenience foods for **lazy** cooks
    - Ⓐ dauntless
    - Ⓑ bold
    - Ⓒ indolent
    - Ⓓ packed

12. sharply **fluctuate** from day to day
    - Ⓐ transgress
    - Ⓑ order
    - Ⓒ alternate
    - Ⓓ increase

13. **disregard** public opinion
    - Ⓐ ignore
    - Ⓑ influence
    - Ⓒ instruct
    - Ⓓ substitute

14. **instruct** the young
    - Ⓐ replace
    - Ⓑ teach
    - Ⓒ diminish
    - Ⓓ absorb

15. a new graphic to **replace** the old symbol
    - Ⓐ dominant
    - Ⓑ substitute
    - Ⓒ waste
    - Ⓓ neglect

16. made **lavish** preparations
    - Ⓐ hasty
    - Ⓑ careful
    - Ⓒ extravagant
    - Ⓓ stingy

17. accept the **consequence** of one's actions
    - Ⓐ result
    - Ⓑ spontaneousness
    - Ⓒ idleness
    - Ⓓ opponent

18. The soil is **compacted** by the winter snow.
    - Ⓐ neglected
    - Ⓑ packed
    - Ⓒ substituted
    - Ⓓ fluctuated

19. a **conscious** smile
    - Ⓐ shrewd
    - Ⓑ intentional
    - Ⓒ brutal
    - Ⓓ fictitious

20. biological processes continue function **independently**
    - Ⓐ practically
    - Ⓑ consistently
    - Ⓒ roughly
    - Ⓓ separately

11

표제어	품사	동의어와 예문	한글 뜻
1 **alien**** [éiljən]	a	strange, foreign, exotic, bizarre Such an attitude is **alien** to most students. 그런 태도는 대부분 학생들에게 낯설다.	외래의, 낯선
2 **almost**** [ɔ́:lmoust]	ad	nearly, practically, approximately, around, roughly Breakfast is **almost** ready. 아침식사 준비가 거의 다 되었다.	거의, 대개
3 **brave** [breiv]	a	courageous, audacious, intrepid, dauntless ↔ cowardly a **brave** new world 훌륭한 신세계	용감한, 훌륭한
4 **climate*** [kláimit]	n	weather conditions walk to the path in balmy **climate** 온화한 날씨에 오솔길을 걷다	날씨
5 **compact**** [kəmpǽkt]	a	tight, packed, compressed, succinct my **compact** office 내 작은 사무실	응축된, 아담한
6 **comply** [kəmplái]	v	acquiesce, conform, consent, accede **comply** with the order 명령을 따르다	순응하다, 동의하다
7 **confine*** [kənfáin]	v	limit, restrict, enclose, imprison **confine** the dog in the yard 개를 울타리 안에 가두다	제한하다, 가두다, 감금하다
8 **conscious** [kánʃəs]	a	① aware, awake, alert, alive, sensible ↔ unconscious **conscious** and breathing after accident 사고 후 의식이 있고 숨을 쉬는 ② purposeful, intentional to make a **conscious** decision 의도적인 결정을 내리다	① 의식[인식]하고 있는, ② 의도적인
9 **consequence**** [kánsəkwèns]	n	effect, result, importance, outcome people of **consequence** 중요 인물, 유력자	중요성, 결과, 결말
10 **consistent** [kənsístənt]	a	① similar, compatible, harmonious **consistent** with the policy of the school 학교 정책에 동의하는 ② constant, steady, unchanging ↔ inconsistent, discrepant be **consistent** in one's follies 하는 짓이 시종 어리석다	① 동의하는 ② 지속적인
11 **despair** [dispέər]	n	discouragement, disheartenment an act of **despair** 자포자기 행위	낙담, 절망
12 **disregard*** [dìsrigá:rd]	v	ignore, neglect, overlook **disregard** one's ideas 누구의 생각을 무시하다	무시하다, 간과하다
13 **exclamation** [èksklǝméiʃən]	n	call, interjection, shout, outcry the note of **exclamation** 감탄 부호	외침, 감탄사

DAY 11

14	**exterior** [ikstíəriər]	a	outer, outside, external an **exterior** policy 대외 정책	외부의
15	**fluctuate**** [flʌ́ktʃuèit]	v	alternate, move up and down, shift Price **fluctuate** very widely. 가격 변동이 심하다.	동요하다
16	**independently**** [ìndipéndəntli]	ad	separately, alone, autonomously react **independently** 따로따로 반응하다	독립적으로
17	**instruct** [instrʌ́kt]	v	teach, coach, train, educate, enlighten **instruct** the young 젊은 사람들을 가르치다	가르치다
18	**lavish** [lǽviʃ]	a	waste, expend, squander, extravagant **lavish** in kindness 친절을 아끼지 않는	낭비하는, 아끼지 않는
19	**lazy*** [léizi]	a	idle, indolent, slothful, sluggish ↔ industrious, active a **lazy** correspondent 편지를 잘 안 쓰는 사람	게으른, 나태한
20	**maladroit***** [mæ̀lədrɔ́it]	a	unskillful, awkward, clumsy, inept ↔ dexterous, adroit too **maladroit** a performer to respond convincingly 너무 서투른 연기자가 설득력 없게 반응하다	어색한, 서투른
21	**mandate*** [mǽndeit]	n	command, commission a democratic **mandate** 민주적인 통치	통치, 지휘, 지배
22	**mythical*** [míθikəl]	a	fictitious, legendary describe the **mythical** history of Gaya 가야의 전설적인 역사를 기술하다	전설적인
23	**pious** [páiəs]	a	devout, reverent, religious **pious** fraud 선의의 속임수	신앙심 깊은, 경건한
24	**prevail*** [privéil]	v	be prevalent in, predominate, dominate The flu **prevails** throughout the country. 독감이 전국적으로 유행하고 있다.	우세하다, 만연하다
25	**proponent** [prəpóunənt]	n	supporter, booster, advocate a **proponent** of women's rights 여권 지지자	지지자, 찬성자
26	**replace*** [ripléis]	v	substitute, supersede, supplant **replace** a sum of money borrowed 빌린 금액을 갚다	대체하다, 바꾸다, 교환하다
27	**review** [rivjúː]	n	survey, reexamination write a **review** for the articles 논문에 논평을 쓰다	재검토, 논평
		v	study, reconsider, revise, examine **review** a paper by two journal editors 두 명의 학회지 편집자가 논문을 살펴보다	정밀하게 살피다, 논평하다
28	**rival** [ráivəl]	n	competitor, contestant, antagonist, opponent without a **rival** 무적으로	경쟁자, 적수
29	**self-esteem** [self istíːm]	n	pride, self-respect, honor build the **self-esteem** of Korean children 한국의 아이들의 자부심을 세우다	자부심

30	**severe***** [sivíər]	a	① harsh, rough, tough, rigid, brutal, stern, strict **severe** reading problems 심각한 독해 문제들 ② formidable, rigorous a **severe** examination for the entrance of university 대학입학을 위한 호된 입시시험	① 맹렬한, 격렬한, 심한 ② 호된, 엄한
31	**shrink*** [ʃriŋk]	v	contract, shrivel, diminish, dwindle ↔ expand, increase **shrink** back(away) from a person ~을 피하다, 꺼리다, 겁내다	오그라들다, 감소하다
32	**sip*** [sip]	v	absorb, drink, taste **sip** soup 국을 마시다	홀짝이다
33	**squander**** [skwándər]	v	waste, lavish, misuse **squander** a fortune on gambling 도박으로 재산을 낭비하다	낭비하다
34	**stream** [stri:m]	n	current, run, flow the **stream** of water 물의 흐름 tidal **stream** 조류	흐름, 조류
35	**survive**** [sərváiv]	v	remain alive, endure They cannot **survive** the winter. 그들은 겨울에 살아남지 못한다.	살아남다
36	**vibrant*** [váibrənt]	a	shaking, oscillating, quivering; energetic, dynamic a city **vibrant** with life 활기 넘치는 도시	진동하는, 떨리는 / 활기찬
37	**violation** [vàiəléiʃən]	n	infringement, breach, transgression commit a traffic **violation** 교통위반을 범하다	위반, 방해자
38	**voluntary***** [váləntèri]	a	spontaneous, free, unforced provide the blood annually from **voluntary** donors 자발적인 기증자들로부터 피를 매년 제공받다	자발적인, 임의의
39	**wildlife*** [waildlaif]	n	not tamed or domesticated animals, animals **wildlife** preservation 야생동물의 보호	야생 생물
40	**wily** [wáili]	a	shrewd, cunning, crafty a **wily** trader 교활한 장사꾼	간사한, 교활한

Practice

01. Desert wildlife in California includes coyotes, lizards, and rattlesnakes.
    Ⓐ weather
    Ⓑ untamed animals
    Ⓒ region
    Ⓓ effectiveness

02. The apparatus was made according to the instructions given by the professor.
    Ⓐ teaching
    Ⓑ directions
    Ⓒ tutorials
    Ⓓ manuscripts

03. Warriors fought for glory and often tattooed their bodies with symbols of brave deeds.
    Ⓐ brilliant
    Ⓑ hearty
    Ⓒ curious
    Ⓓ courageous

04. As sediments are buried more deeply into the earth over geological time, they become increasingly compacted.
    Ⓐ broken down
    Ⓑ embedded
    Ⓒ compiled
    Ⓓ compressed

05. The blue colors of some aquamarine and topaz stones look almost identical.
    Ⓐ absolutely
    Ⓑ basically
    Ⓒ nearly
    Ⓓ simultaneously

06. Writing is a skill that requires consistent practice.
    Ⓐ conservative
    Ⓑ considerable
    Ⓒ customary
    Ⓓ constant

07. For more than 200 years, no theme in late medieval sculpture could rival the popularity of Virgin Mary.
    Ⓐ compete
    Ⓑ spur
    Ⓒ stylistic
    Ⓓ conflict

08. During an earthquake, tall buildings may vibrate uncontrollably and knock into each other.
    Ⓐ shock
    Ⓑ shake
    Ⓒ secure
    Ⓓ support

09. Deductive reasoning is used to explore the necessary consequences of certain assumptions.
    Ⓐ explanations
    Ⓑ analysis
    Ⓒ results
    Ⓓ relevance

10. A mild heart attack may force a person to lead a less active life, while a severe attack may cause death.
    Ⓐ disconnected
    Ⓑ unpleasant
    Ⓒ unexpected
    Ⓓ harsh

11. In Greek mythology, there are many mythical beings including gods and goddesses who resemble humans and animals.
    - Ⓐ legendary
    - Ⓑ magical
    - Ⓒ frightening
    - Ⓓ perplexing

12. Most harmful acts that cause injury to another person are considered violations of the civil law.
    - Ⓐ riots
    - Ⓑ judges
    - Ⓒ infringement
    - Ⓓ blunders

13. The climate along the coast of northern and central California is mild, but this region is generally cooler than the southern coast.
    - Ⓐ biological balance
    - Ⓑ circulation
    - Ⓒ weather conditions
    - Ⓓ geography

14. The feelings that teenagers may have about themselves may fluctuate, especially during early adolescence.
    - Ⓐ change rapidly
    - Ⓑ move quickly
    - Ⓒ diminish
    - Ⓓ improve

15. A character in the tragic play King Lear cries out in despair, "As flies to wanton boys are we to the gods."
    - Ⓐ happiness
    - Ⓑ misery
    - Ⓒ thrill
    - Ⓓ hesitation

16. Supporters of Afro-centrism believe the approach builds self-esteem amongst African American children and also improves their success rate in school.
    - Ⓐ loyalty
    - Ⓑ liberty
    - Ⓒ selfishness
    - Ⓓ pride

17. Most large wild mammals are now few in number and are confined to parks, which in some cases provide little protection or insufficient living space.
    - Ⓐ compared
    - Ⓑ attached
    - Ⓒ limited
    - Ⓓ engaged

18. The most elements of the atoms can bond to other atoms, while most of those cannot exist independently.
    - Ⓐ commonly
    - Ⓑ separately
    - Ⓒ undoubtedly
    - Ⓓ unsuitably

19. Warmth from higher global temperatures that have prevailed for at least 10,000 years since the end of the Ice Age has been slowly heating the ice sheets.
    - Ⓐ dominated
    - Ⓑ transformed
    - Ⓒ rebuilt
    - Ⓓ generalized

20. In addition to reporting the news, the Tribune published book reviews and poetry and ran editorials opposing slavery and supporting women's rights.
    - Ⓐ commentary
    - Ⓑ censors
    - Ⓒ articles
    - Ⓓ abstracts

DAY 12 Daily Checkup

01. pray for pardon
    - Ⓐ mercy
    - Ⓑ scatter
    - Ⓒ beg
    - Ⓓ undermine

02. unwilling consent
    - Ⓐ disinclined
    - Ⓑ agitate
    - Ⓒ declined
    - Ⓓ releasing

03. a quaint person
    - Ⓐ opaque
    - Ⓑ loathe
    - Ⓒ strange
    - Ⓓ producing

04. the melancholy days of autumn
    - Ⓐ learned
    - Ⓑ wavering
    - Ⓒ dismal
    - Ⓓ reserving

05. try to console the grieving child
    - Ⓐ entail
    - Ⓑ question
    - Ⓒ blood
    - Ⓓ soothe

06. the scoff of the world
    - Ⓐ learning
    - Ⓑ precipitous
    - Ⓒ forgiving
    - Ⓓ mock

07. wear camouflage
    - Ⓐ impurity
    - Ⓑ unusually
    - Ⓒ cover
    - Ⓓ relatively

08. heated discussions ensued.
    - Ⓐ pervaded
    - Ⓑ happened
    - Ⓒ sneer
    - Ⓓ released

09. extol a person's virtue
    - Ⓐ praise
    - Ⓑ punish
    - Ⓒ shake
    - Ⓓ fabricate

10. shake a bottle of champagne
    - Ⓐ scoff
    - Ⓑ obliterate
    - Ⓒ comfort
    - Ⓓ wave

11. a rigid point of view
    - Ⓐ strict
    - Ⓑ valiant
    - Ⓒ malevolent
    - Ⓓ depressed

12. annihilate a law
    - Ⓐ upright
    - Ⓑ implore
    - Ⓒ nullify
    - Ⓓ shudder

13. grudge the time
    - Ⓐ resent
    - Ⓑ change
    - Ⓒ save
    - Ⓓ define

14. learn how to fabricate steel
    - Ⓐ hide
    - Ⓑ transform
    - Ⓒ make
    - Ⓓ agitate

15. disseminate false reports
    - Ⓐ disperse
    - Ⓑ go through
    - Ⓒ shudder
    - Ⓓ sneer

16. a fair decision
    - Ⓐ rigid
    - Ⓑ inactive
    - Ⓒ unbiased
    - Ⓓ inequitable

17. explain rules
    - Ⓐ mix
    - Ⓑ elucidate
    - Ⓒ solve
    - Ⓓ resolve

18. entail a huge political risk
    - Ⓐ comfortable
    - Ⓑ despondent
    - Ⓒ uncommon
    - Ⓓ involve

19. a dwarf tree
    - Ⓐ pure
    - Ⓑ pygmy
    - Ⓒ inflexible
    - Ⓓ subordinate

20. a gallant sight
    - Ⓐ odd
    - Ⓑ splendid
    - Ⓒ pricking
    - Ⓓ severe

DAY 12 Voca Bank

표제어	품사	동의어와 예문	한글 뜻
1 **annihilate**** [ənáiəlèit]	v	abolish, remove, liquidate, exterminate, eradicate **annihilate** the enemy forces 적군을 전멸시키다	파멸시키다, 제거하다
2 **astronomical***** [æstrənámikəl]	a	celestial, heavenly; a large number of **astronomical** figures 천문학적 수	천체의 / 천문학적인 (수의)
3 **auxiliary**** [ɔːgzíljəri]	a	subsidiary, subordinate, reserved, additional an **auxiliary** engine 보조기관	보조의, 부가적인
4 **camouflage*** [kǽməflɑ̀ːʒ]	v	conceal, disguise, hide, bury, cover **camouflage** the hat with beautiful feather and leaves 아름다운 깃털과 나뭇잎으로 모자를 위장하다	위장하다
5 **component** [kəmpóunənt]	n	constitute, part, element, ingredient **component** parts 구성요소, 성분	구성요소, 성분
6 **concern**** [kənsə́ːrn]	v	relate to; worry, bother Most training is **concerned** with technique. 대부분의 훈련은 기술과 관련된다.	~에 관계하다 / 걱정하다
	n	importance, business a matter of **concern** 관심사	중요성, 관심, 업무
7 **console** [kənsóul]	v	comfort, solace, soothe **console** one's grief 누구의 슬픔을 달래다	위로하다
8 **continent** [kántənənt]	n	large land on the European **Continent** 유럽대륙에서는	대륙
9 **convert** [kənvə́ːrt]	v	change, transform **convert** cotton into cloth 면사를 천으로 만들다	변환하다, 변형시키다
10 **cozy** [kóuzi]	a	① comfortable, soft, snug ↔ uncomfortable a **cozy** chair 편안한 의자 ② intimate, familiar ↔ strange, unfamiliar **cozy** setting for a party 파티를 위해 친근하게 차려진	① 편안한 ② 친근한
11 **disseminate** [disémənèit]	v	spread, disperse, scatter, dissipate, distribute **disseminate** the seed 씨앗을 흩뿌리다	흩뿌리다
12 **dwarf** [dwɔːrf]	n	pygmy, gnome, midget found a **dwarf** human in an island of Indonesia 인도네시아의 한 섬에서 난쟁이를 발견하다	난쟁이
	a	miniature, small, diminutive ↔ giant, huge become a white **dwarf** star 백색 왜성이 되다	자그마한, 소형의
13 **ensue** [insúː]	v	follow, succeed, happen later **ensue** the conflict between two Parties 두 정당 간의 갈등이 계속되다	연속되다

#	Word	PoS	Definition / Example	Korean
14	**entail** [intéil]	v	**involve, implicate** His way of living **entails** great expense. 그의 생활 방식에는 큰 비용이 든다.	끌어들이다
15	**explain**** [ikspléin]	v	① **describe, define, eulcidate**, explicate, clarify ② **solve, decipher, decode**, resolve try to **explain** the puzzle 퍼즐을 풀려고 노력하다	① 설명하다, ② 명확히 하다, 해결하다
16	**extol** [ikstóul]	v	**praise, acclaim, eulogize, applaud** **extol** one's heroic deeds ~의 영웅적 업적을 칭찬하다	칭찬하다
17	**fabricate*** [fǽbrikèit]	v	**make, build, produce, construct** **fabricate** a product 제품을 만들다	가공하다, 날조하다
18	**fair**** [fɛər]	a	① **just unbiased, right, honest, truthful** ↔ **unfair** a **fair** verdict 공정한 평결 **fair** wages 적정한 임금 ② **sunny, light** ↔ **rainy, dark** **fair** weather 갠 날씨 ③ **beautiful, handsome** ↔ **ugly** a **fair** lady 아름다운 금발의 여성	① 공정한 ② 맑은, 밝은 ③ 아름다운, 금발의
		n	**exhibition, gathering, exposition,** festival, carnival a job **fair** 취업 박람회	전시회, 박람회
	fairly** [fɛ́ərli]	ad	**relatively, somewhat** **fairly** close to the surface 표면에 상당히 가까운	꽤, 아주, 상당히
19	**filth** [filθ]	n	**dirt, obscenity, impurity** talk **filth** 추담	쓰레기
20	**gallant** [gǽlənt]	a	**brave, valiant, intrepid,** chivalrous, dashing, valorous; splendid **gallant** warriors 용감한 전사들	용감한 / 훌륭한
21	**game**** [geim]	n	**hunting, sport, match,** wild animals, pastime, scheme the most important **game** animals 가장 중요한 사냥감 동물들	놀이, 경기, 사냥감
22	**grudge** [grʌdʒ]	n	**malice, spite,** malevolence hold a **grudge** against them 그들에게 악의를 품고 있다	불평, 악의
		v	**resent,** complain, envy **grudge** the books to give the others 그 책을 다른 사람들에게 주는데 아까워하다	아까워하다
23	**inquiry*** [inkwáiəri]	n	**investigation, scrutiny, research,** question a writ of **inquiry** 조사 명령서	질문, 조사
24	**melancholy** [mélənkàli]	a	**depressed, gloomy,** despondent, dismal in a **melancholy** mood 울적한 기분으로	우울한, 침울한
25	**mutate** [mjú:teit]	v	**change, transform,** evolve **mutate** from the larva to the butterfly 애벌레에서 나비로 변화하다	변화하다
26	**myriad*** [míriəd]	a	**many, army, numerous** a **myriad** of stars 무수한 별	많은, 무수한
27	**outcome** [áutkʌm]	n	**result, consequence** The **outcome** is doubtfully. 결과가 어찌 될지 모른다.	결과, 성과

DAY 12

28	**penetrate*** [pénətrèit]	v	go through, pierce, perforate, permeate, pervade **penetrate** a mystery 비밀을 간파하다 (꿰뚫어보다)	꿰뚫다, 감동시키다
29	**pray** [prei]	v	entreat, supplicate, beg, beseech **pray** to God for help 신의 도움을 빌다	빌다, 기도하다
30	**quaint** [kweint]	a	strange, odd, unusual, extraordinary, uncommon ↔ ordinary a **quaint** person 괴짜	기이한, 기묘한
31	**quarantine*** [kwɔ́:rəntì:n]	v	isolate, separate, keep apart, sequester in **quarantine** 검역 중인	검역하다, 격리시키다
32	**rigid** [rídʒid]	a	① stiff, firm, hard, inflexible ↔ flexible become **rigid** method in the ways of learning 배움의 길에 있어서 확고한(고정된) 방법이 되다 ② strict, severe, stern, rigorous **rigid** opinions 융통성 없는 의견	① 단단한, 딱딱한 ② 엄격한, 엄숙한
33	**scholarly** [skálərli]	a	academic, learned a **scholarly** journal 학술잡지	학문적인
34	**scoff** [skɔ:f]	v	mock, scorn, jeer, sneer, ridicule **scoff** at their beliefs 그들의 믿음을 비웃다	비웃다, 조롱하다
35	**sedentary** [sédntèri]	a	inactive, seated, torpid live terribly **sedentary** in the office and home 사무실과 집에서 심하게 앉아서 일하며 살아간다	앉아서 일하는
36	**shake*** [ʃeik]	v	quake, tremble, agitate, shudder, sway, shiver **shake** with fear 두려움에 떨다 **shake** the bottle of juice 주스 병을 흔든다	흔들리다, 진동하다
37	**sheer*** [ʃiər]	a	① thin, fine, transparent, diaphanous **sheer** cloth 얇은 옷 ② absolute, complete speak in a **sheer** folly 완전히 어리석은 말하다 ③ pure, utter, clear **sheer** delight 큰 기쁨 ④ abrupt, perpendicular, very steep, precipitous fall a 10 meter **sheer** 수직 아래로 10미터 떨어지다	① 얇은 ② 완전한 ③ 섞인 것이 없는, 순수한 ④ 깎아지른 듯한
38	**spare** [spεər]	v a	save, reserve **spare** your country's flag 당신 나라의 국기를 구하다 extra, reserve, surplus, supplemental **spare** enough time to play 경기하기에 충분한 여분의 시간	절약하다, 구하다 여분의
39	**unwilling*** [ʌnwíliŋ]	a	reluctant, averse, opposed, loath willing or **unwilling** 좋든 싫든 간에	마음 내키지 않은
40	**vein** [vein]	n	① blood vessel constantly running in a **vein** 정맥에서 지속적으로 흐르는 ② mood, style, note, temper say in a humorous **vein** 반농담조로(희롱삼아) 말하다	① 정맥 ② 기질, 성질

Practice

01. Raiders had little effect on the outcome of the Civil War.
    - Ⓐ success
    - Ⓑ consequence
    - Ⓒ failure
    - Ⓓ destruction

02. When a star becomes a white dwarf, it has entered into its final stage of its existence.
    - Ⓐ small and dull star
    - Ⓑ supernova
    - Ⓒ sun
    - Ⓓ planet

03. Phospholipids are important components of all membranes found in living organisms.
    - Ⓐ parts
    - Ⓑ varieties
    - Ⓒ changes
    - Ⓓ environments

04. Because cells are so minute, the numbers occurring in full-grown organisms are astronomical.
    - Ⓐ economical
    - Ⓑ dimensional
    - Ⓒ exposable
    - Ⓓ innumerable

05. The United Kingdom and France were unwilling to risk another war so soon after World War I.
    - Ⓐ reluctant
    - Ⓑ ready
    - Ⓒ compliant
    - Ⓓ feeble

06. A number of electric power plants have gas turbines or diesel engines to drive auxiliary generators.
    - Ⓐ main
    - Ⓑ useless
    - Ⓒ effective
    - Ⓓ supplementary

07. The glaciers created Yosemite Valley's sheer granite cliffs.
    - Ⓐ steep
    - Ⓑ splendid
    - Ⓒ even
    - Ⓓ glitter

08. Sanitation is important because many germs that cause disease breed in filth.
    - Ⓐ cleanness
    - Ⓑ garage
    - Ⓒ contamination
    - Ⓓ purity

09. Both carpets and rugs help create a warm, cozy atmosphere.
    - Ⓐ light
    - Ⓑ roomy
    - Ⓒ cluttered
    - Ⓓ comfortable

10. A third-degree burn penetrates all the layers of the skin and also affects the tissues underneath.
    - Ⓐ pumps
    - Ⓑ perceives
    - Ⓒ pierces
    - Ⓓ produces

11. Research or scholarly dictionaries may cover earlier vocabulary of a language, such as in the case of Old English and Late Latin.
    Ⓐ learned
    Ⓑ concise
    Ⓒ popular
    Ⓓ contemporary

12. The dermis contains the arteries and veins that supply the skin with blood.
    Ⓐ hair
    Ⓑ blood vessels
    Ⓒ oxygen
    Ⓓ stripe

13. Geographers often consider Europe and Asia as one continent and call it Eurasia.
    Ⓐ country
    Ⓑ race
    Ⓒ very large area of land
    Ⓓ united nations

14. Public health officers may quarantine any person who has a contagious disease.
    Ⓐ limit under protection
    Ⓑ interview on television
    Ⓒ contaminate with germs
    Ⓓ isolate for medical reasons

15. The theory of continental drifting helps explain the presence of coral reef fossils in Wisconsin and also that of tropical plant fossils in areas north of the Arctic Circle.
    Ⓐ wipe out
    Ⓑ employ
    Ⓒ account for
    Ⓓ obscure

16. Philosophic inquiry can be made in any subject, because philosophy deals with all things in the world as well as all knowledge.
    Ⓐ gossip
    Ⓑ requisition
    Ⓒ investigation
    Ⓓ recording

17. When a pioneer family arrived at a place where they intended to settle down, they could not spare time right away to build a permanent house.
    Ⓐ exceed
    Ⓑ waste
    Ⓒ give
    Ⓓ sure

18. On land, the air provides plants and animals with a fairly constant mixture of life – giving 210 milliliters of gas per liter. In the sea, oxygen enters only at or near the surface.
    Ⓐ naturally
    Ⓑ pretty
    Ⓒ relatively
    Ⓓ almost

19. Microscopy, whether it is light, electron, or video, reveals the cell as a unit composed of a myriad of "sub-cellular" structures (organelles).
    Ⓐ short
    Ⓑ numerous
    Ⓒ a bit of
    Ⓓ a few

20. Recent concerns about global warming and the effects of man-made greenhouse gases have only heightened the need to understand the basic natural processes that cause the climate to change.
    Ⓐ analysis   Ⓑ research
    Ⓒ rises   Ⓓ worries

DAY 13 Daily Checkup

01. skip in reading
    - Ⓐ unrestrained
    - Ⓑ carve
    - Ⓒ jump
    - Ⓓ forestall

02. smart for one's impudence
    - Ⓐ clever
    - Ⓑ suffer
    - Ⓒ hard
    - Ⓓ luminous

03. make every endeavor
    - Ⓐ nature
    - Ⓑ prejudice
    - Ⓒ alliance
    - Ⓓ effort

04. scurry off to bed
    - Ⓐ scamper
    - Ⓑ fly
    - Ⓒ run
    - Ⓓ trudge

05. The dove represents peace.
    - Ⓐ prevents
    - Ⓑ increases
    - Ⓒ symbolizes
    - Ⓓ mitigates

06. forestall an argument
    - Ⓐ ally
    - Ⓑ prevent
    - Ⓒ investigate
    - Ⓓ ordain

07. an incised wound
    - Ⓐ futile
    - Ⓑ trivial
    - Ⓒ carved
    - Ⓓ suitable

08. prescribe by law
    - Ⓐ dictate
    - Ⓑ inspect
    - Ⓒ attempt
    - Ⓓ differ

09. The necklace is very becoming to her.
    - Ⓐ imprudent
    - Ⓑ certain
    - Ⓒ fixed
    - Ⓓ appropriate

10. gratify one's curiosity
    - Ⓐ develop
    - Ⓑ explore
    - Ⓒ satisfy
    - Ⓓ express

11. habits that impair one's health
    - Ⓐ piece
    - Ⓑ deteriorate
    - Ⓒ slow
    - Ⓓ moderate

12. bias in the news media
    - Ⓐ prejudice
    - Ⓑ note
    - Ⓒ exertion
    - Ⓓ innovation

13. examine our mistakes
    - Ⓐ prevent
    - Ⓑ increase
    - Ⓒ investigate
    - Ⓓ formulate

14. The improvident students do not study.
    - Ⓐ unwary
    - Ⓑ unrestrained
    - Ⓒ garrulous
    - Ⓓ unavailing

15. packed the books in a sturdy box
    - Ⓐ unavailing
    - Ⓑ hard
    - Ⓒ odd
    - Ⓓ soften

16. the disadvantage of smart phone
    - Ⓐ prejudice
    - Ⓑ drawback
    - Ⓒ attempt
    - Ⓓ part

17. the association between the two companies
    - Ⓐ blockade
    - Ⓑ alliance
    - Ⓒ expansion
    - Ⓓ effort

18. lead to a discord
    - Ⓐ prejudice
    - Ⓑ disposition
    - Ⓒ portray
    - Ⓓ confusion

19. a hysterical temperament
    - Ⓐ disposition
    - Ⓑ incensement
    - Ⓒ fluctuating
    - Ⓓ blockade

20. take up one's station
    - Ⓐ disadvantage
    - Ⓑ animosity
    - Ⓒ rank
    - Ⓓ probe

DAY 13 Voca Bank

표제어	품사	동의어와 예문	한글 뜻
1 **ascend*** [əsénd]	v	**move up, climb,** go up **ascend** the mountain 산을 오르다	오르다
2 **association** [əsòusiéiʃən]	n	**alliance,** club **association** of ideas 관념연합, 연상	동맹, 연합
3 **becoming** [bikʌ́miŋ]	a	**appropriate, attractive, comely,** suitable The necklace is very **becoming** to her. 그 목걸이는 그녀에게 썩 잘 어울린다.	어울리는, 적당한
4 **bias**** [báiəs]	n	**prejudice, inclination,** slant racial **bias** by a biased decision 편향된 결정에 의한 인종차별	편견, 차별
5 **bizarre**** [bizá:r]	a	**exotic, strange, odd,** alien, foreign It was a **bizarre** scene. 그것은 낯선 장면이었다.	이상한, 낯선
6 **constant**** [kánstənt]	a	**invariable, consistent, uniform,** stable, unchanging a **constant** source of energy 무한한 에너지 자원	지속적인, 끊임없는
7 **despite***** [dispáit]	prep	**regardless of, even though** **despite** the high temperature 고온에도 불구하고	불구하고
8 **differ** [dífər]	v	**be dissimilar, contradict, disagree** **differ** in opinion 견해를 달리하다	다르다
9 **disadvantage***** [dìsədvǽntidʒ]	n	**drawback, harm, damage, injury, handicap, obstacle** **disadvantage** of postage stamp 우표의 단점	불이익, 피해, 부상, 단점
10 **discern** [disə́:rn]	v	**perceive, notice, discriminate, distinguish,** detect **discern** good from evil 선악을 구별하다	구별하다, 인식하다
11 **discord** [dískɔ:rd]	v	**disharmony, animosity, disagreement, confusion** lead to a **discord** 불일치를 초래하다	불일치, 불화, 혼란
12 **draft** [dræft]	v	**formulate, draw up** **draft** men into the army 남자들을 군대로 선발하다	조직하다, 선발하다
	n	**note** prepare a first **draft** for spaceship 우주선에 대한 초안을 준비하다	설계도, 도안
13 **endeavor**** [indévər]	n	**strive, struggle, effort, labor,** exertion, attempt scientific **endeavor** in history 역사에서의 과학적 노력	노력, 투쟁
14 **examine** [igzǽmin]	v	**inspect, probe, investigate,** explore **examine** one's health 신체검사를 하다	검사하다, 조사하다

15	**fast** [fæst]	a	① **quick, fleet, swift,** speedy ↔ **slow, sluggish,** tardy a **fast** swimmer 빨리 헤엄치는 사람 a **fast** operator (돈벌이에) 재빠른 사람 ② **sudden, instant; adherent, attached,** immovable make a boat **fast** 배를 꽉 잡다	① 빠른 ② 갑작스런 / 고정된
		ad	**rapidly, swiftly; suddenly,** instantly; **tightly** walk **fast** 빨리 걸어라 Hold **fast** to the rope. 밧줄을 꽉 잡아라.	빨리 / 갑자기 / 단단하게
		v	**fix, attach,** affix Please **fasten** your seat belt for safety. 안전을 위하여 좌석벨트를 매주세요.	묶다, 고정시키다
16	**firm** [fə:rm]	a	① **stable, steadfast,** determined, reliable ↔ **fluctuating, wavering** a **firm** decision 확고한 결정 **firm** friendship 굳은 우정 ② **hard, solid** ↔ **soft** **firm** muscles 단단한 근육	① 확고한 ② 단단한
17	**forestall** [fɔ:rstɔ:l]	v	**prevent,** stop **forestall** the market 매점하다	방해하다
18	**fragment** [frǽgmənt]	n	**piece, part,** bit burst into **fragments** 터져서 산산조각이 나다	조각
19	**gratify** [grǽtəfài]	v	satisfy, content **gratify** one's curiosity 궁금증을 풀다	만족시키다
20	**growth** [grouθ]	n	**advancement, expansion, development,** increase reach one's **growth** 완전히 성장하다	발전, 성장
21	**impair**** [impéər]	v	**injure, deteriorate** seriously **impairs** the functioning 기능이 심각하게 손상되다	손상시키다
22	**improvident*** [imprávədənt]	a	**thoughtless, careless, imprudent,** unwary The **improvident** worker saved no money. 낭비가 심한 그 일꾼은 저축을 하지 않았다.	생각 없는, 경솔한
23	**incandescent*** [inkəndésnt]	a	**luminous** a **incandescent** light with bright golden 밝은 금 색깔의 백열등	백열의
24	**incised*** [insáizd]	a	**carved, cut,** embed the design **incised** into a transparent square plastic 투명한 사각 플라스틱 안에 새겨진 도안	깊이 새겨넣은
25	**innovation** [ìnəvéiʃən]	n	**modernization, alteration,** change technological **innovation** 기술 혁신	혁신, 쇄신
26	**prescribe*** [priskráib]	v	**dictate, ordain, direct, decree** **prescribe** complete test 시험을 마치도록 규정하다	규정하다, 명령하다
27	**remote** [rimóut]	a	**secluded, distant,** removed live **remote** 벽촌에 살다	멀리 떨어진
28	**represent***** [rèprizént]	v	**symbolize, depict, express, portray** **represent** significant differences 중요한 차이를 나타내다	나타내다, 표현하다

DAY 13

29	scurry [skə́:ri]	v	hurry, dash, dart **scurry** around the school to find a child 아이를 찾기 위하여 학교를 허둥지둥 돌아다니다	허둥지둥하다
30	siege [si:dʒ]	n	blockade, besieging, surrounded attack **siege** warfare 포위 공격전	포위, 공격
31	skip* [skip]	v	① miss, omit, disregard ↔ include **skip** a word 단어를 빠뜨리다 ② spring, jump, leap, bound, hop **skip** along 계속 뛰다	① 빠뜨리다 ② 뛰어다니다, 뛰놀다
32	smart [sma:rt]	a	intelligent, bright, sharp, clever, adroit a **smart** child 영리한 아이	영리한, 기민한
33	soften [sɔ́:fən]	v	assuage, moderate, mitigate, soothe, alleviate **soften** water 물을 연수로 만들다	부드럽게 하다
34	station [stéiʃən]	n	① place, location, situation, stage take up one's **station** 부서에 자리잡다 ② stop, terminal, depot a train **station** 기차역	① 위치, 장소 ② 역, 정거장
35	sturdy* [stə́:rdi]	a	strong, robust, stalwart, muscular, stout ↔ fragile a **sturdy** device 튼튼한 장비	억센, 튼튼한
36	talkative** [tɔ́:kətiv]	a	garrulous, wordy, verbose a **talkative** person 말이 많은 사람	이야기를 좋아하는, 말 많은
37	temperament [témpərəmənt]	n	disposition, temper, nature a hysterical **temperament** 히스테리성 기질	기질, 성미
38	unrestrained [ʌnristréind]	a	unchecked **unrestrained** joy 구속되지 않은 즐거움	억제되지 않은
39	vain [vein]	a	useless, worthless, trifling, trivial, futile a **vain** hope 헛된 희망	공허한, 실속 없는
40	vile [vail]	a	wicked **vile** weather 험한 날씨	몹시 나쁜, 비열한

Practice Test 13

01. The physical science examines the nature of the universe.
    A watch
    B search
    C survey
    D study

02. Amateur astronomers have their own associations and local and regional clubs.
    A difference
    B union
    C temple
    D church

03. The king represents the country at important diplomatic and ceremonial affairs.
    A outlines
    B symbolizes
    C coordinates
    D illusions

04. The human eye is capable of discerning an object no smaller than 0.1 mm.
    A can seeing
    B able to handling
    C knows searching
    D divided into others

05. Some schools give certificates after the completion of a prescribed program.
    A set
    B certain
    C altered
    D popular

06. People born under the star sign Gemini are supposedly talkative and witty.
    A audacious
    B serene
    C humorous
    D loquacious

07. When ships enter into a port of another country, the goods were inspected for diseases.
    A scheduled
    B overlooked
    C examined
    D glazed

08. The Publish Company just received the first draft of the article about pronunciation from the English Research Institutes.
    A a piece of writing
    B tuition
    C draw up
    D masterpiece

09. The restriction endonuclease will actually attack sites that are easily breakable and cut the DNA molecule into smaller DNA fragments.
    A families
    B skeletons
    C pieces
    D relief

10. After the direct attacks failed, he began a siege on the city.
    A retreat
    B surrounded attack
    C invade
    D attack

11. Many of the generalizations made about the future of Africa are based upon insufficient knowledge and therefore valueless.
    A worthless
    B important
    C immeasurable
    D invaluable

12. Space vehicles require a heat shield which can resist high temperatures and a sturdy structure to endure crushing acceleration forces.
    A weak
    B strong
    C short
    D long

13. Carmen was a beautiful Gypsy who was dedicated to a life of unrestrained freedom.
    A unavoidable
    B unexpected
    C unchecked
    D unnecessary

14. Although the novel contains many historical facts, the author also included fantasy, extraordinary characters, bizarre events, suspense, and unusual humor.
    A divided
    B imaginative
    C strange
    D strong

15. Despite of the efforts to return Cuban refugees to their homeland, the United States admits thousands of them each year.
    A Nevertheless
    B Certain
    C Desperate
    D In spite of

16. As the warm air ascends, its temperature drops, relative humidity increases, and clouds and perhaps precipitation form.
    A arises
    B retreats
    C moves down
    D standstills

17. Book consists of written or printed sheets of paper or some other material fastened together along one edge so it can be opened at any point.
    A affixed
    B polished
    C tanned
    D dyed

18. A person should carefully choose between incandescent and fluorescent lights because color schemes appear different under each type of illumination.
    A dark
    B tainted
    C luminous
    D colorless

19. Scientists say that once the temperature rises at the base of an ice sheet, the ice is likely to soften, causing it to flow faster and as a result leading to its catastrophic collapse.
    A melt
    B evaporate
    C easy to melt
    D disappear

20. The first law of thermodynamics states that energy is constant – it cannot be increased or diminished – but it can be converted from one form to another.
    A instant   B conserved
    C controlled   D accidental

DAY 14 Daily Checkup

01. the legal limit of alcohol
    - Ⓐ incident
    - Ⓑ vague
    - Ⓒ restriction
    - Ⓓ hollow

02. perform surgery
    - Ⓐ comment
    - Ⓑ charge
    - Ⓒ purify
    - Ⓓ execute

03. refined distinctions
    - Ⓐ clarified
    - Ⓑ solid
    - Ⓒ authentic
    - Ⓓ maneuvered

04. a hollow tree
    - Ⓐ indented
    - Ⓑ vacant
    - Ⓒ stable
    - Ⓓ trivial

05. neglected the growing plants
    - Ⓐ harassed
    - Ⓑ threatened
    - Ⓒ disregarded
    - Ⓓ distilled

06. liberate the country
    - Ⓐ free
    - Ⓑ misdirect
    - Ⓒ discharge
    - Ⓓ afflict

07. tormented by jealousy
    - Ⓐ compensate
    - Ⓑ free
    - Ⓒ anguish
    - Ⓓ utter

08. The fever has abated.
    - Ⓐ ignored
    - Ⓑ decreased
    - Ⓒ uttered
    - Ⓓ hindered

09. A good newspaper should herald the truth.
    - Ⓐ nuisance
    - Ⓑ firm
    - Ⓒ indicate
    - Ⓓ confine

10. hail an old friend
    - Ⓐ disengage
    - Ⓑ stay
    - Ⓒ mislead
    - Ⓓ applaud

11. misleading information about the law
    - Ⓐ comment
    - Ⓑ stable
    - Ⓒ misdirect
    - Ⓓ strong

12. menace (a person's) right to live
    - Ⓐ fulfill
    - Ⓑ doubt
    - Ⓒ threaten
    - Ⓓ encroach

13. full of whims and fancies
    - Ⓐ caprices
    - Ⓑ delineations
    - Ⓒ lineages
    - Ⓓ comments

14. be defeated in one's purpose
    - Ⓐ annoyed
    - Ⓑ expressed
    - Ⓒ conquered
    - Ⓓ plotted

15. make a vague answer
    - Ⓐ clarified
    - Ⓑ obscure
    - Ⓒ restrict
    - Ⓓ hindering

16. Somebody denounced him to the police as a spy.
    - Ⓐ accused
    - Ⓑ excavated
    - Ⓒ trespassed
    - Ⓓ encroached

17. compensate a person for his work
    - Ⓐ reimburse
    - Ⓑ misguide
    - Ⓒ hinder
    - Ⓓ cheer

18. African descent
    - Ⓐ outstanding
    - Ⓑ function
    - Ⓒ whimsy
    - Ⓓ origin

19. expertise in computer science
    - Ⓐ origin
    - Ⓑ proficiency
    - Ⓒ concurrence
    - Ⓓ treat

20. maneuver a car into the garage
    - Ⓐ liberate
    - Ⓑ decay
    - Ⓒ move
    - Ⓓ accelerate

DAY 14 Voca Bank

	표제어	품사	동의어와 예문	한글 뜻
1	**abate*** [əbéit]	v	reduce, decrease, diminish, lessen The fever has **abated**. 열이 내렸다.	줄이다, 감소하다
2	**accelerate*** [æksélərèit]	v	speed up, increase, hurry, expedite, hasten **accelerate** speed 속력을 가하다	촉진하다
3	**belong to** [bilɔ́:ŋ tu]	v	be owned by, are members of He **belongs to** Seoul. 그는 서울 사람이다.	~에 속하다
4	**compensate*** [kámpənsèit]	v	reimburse, atone, indemnify **compensate** (a person) for loss 손해를 보상하다	보상하다
5	**continuously** [kəntínjuəsli]	ad	without interruption a **continuous** stream of telephone calls 계속되는 전화 소리	계속하여, 끊임없이
6	**contour*** [kántuər]	v	outline, curve, delineation, figuration the **contour** of one's face 얼굴의 윤곽	윤곽, 곡선
7	**corpse** [kɔ:rps]	n	dead body, carcass a living **corpse** 산 송장	시체
8	**decline**** [dikláin]	v	① refuse, reject **decline** with thanks 좋은 말로 [고맙다고 하며] 거절하다 ② decrease, weaken, deteriorate, diminish, dwindle **decline** great number of species in many parts of the world 세상의 많은 곳에서 수많은 종들의 수가 감소하다 ③ sink The building has **declined** steadily. 그 건물은 꾸준히 조금씩 기울었다.	① 거절하다 ② 약하게 하다, 쇠퇴하다 ③ 기울다, 가라앉다
9	**defeat** [difí:t]	v	conquer, overwhelm, subdue, overcome **defeat** an enemy 적을 패배시키다	패배시키다
10	**denote*** [dinóut]	v	signify A red light **denotes** 'Danger,' 빨간 등불은 '위험'을 표시한다.	표시하다
11	**denounce** [dináuns]	v	condemn, accuse, reproach, scold, blame, indict, charge, decry **denounce** the government for maladministration 정부의 실정을 규탄하다	비난하다
12	**descent*** [disént]	n	① falling, descending ↔ ascent The airplane going to begin the **descent** for Incheon Int'l airport. 비행기가 인천국제공항을 향해 하강을 시작하고 있다. ② origin, ancestry, genesis, lineage, pedigree in direct **descent** from ~부터의 직계로	① 하강 ② 가계, 유래, 기원, 혈통

#	Word	PoS	Synonyms / Example	Meaning
13	**emancipate*** [imǽnsəpèit]	v	liberate, free **emancipate** slaves 노예를 해방하다	(노예) 해방하다
14	**encircle** [insə́:rkl]	v	surround, encompass, enclose be **encircled** by cell membrane 세포막으로 둘러싸이다	둘러싸다
15	**erect** [irékt]	a	construct, straight, upright standing, vertical stand **erect** 똑바로 서다	직립의
16	**event** [ivént]	n	occurrence, happening, incident, occasion a main **event** 주요 시합	발생, 사건
17	**expertise** [èkspərtí:z]	n	skill, adroitness, mastery, proficiency bring customers **expertise** 고객들에게 전문적 조언을 주다 gain **expertise** 전문적 지식을 얻다	기술, 전문적 지식
18	**fierce*** [fiərs]	a	ferocious, wild, savage, cruel, brutal a **fierce** tiger 맹호	사나운, 잔인한
19	**hail** [heil]	v	acclaim, applaud, exalt, glorify, eulogize, extol **Hail** to you! 만세!	환호하다
20	**hamper*** [hǽmpər]	v	impede, hinder, prevent, obstruct be **hampered** in one's plans 계획을 방해하다	방해하다
21	**herald** [hérəld]	v	indicate, announce A good newspaper should **herald** the truth. 좋은 신문은 진실을 알려야 한다.	알리다, 예고하다
22	**hollow** [hálou]	a	① empty, vacant, excavate a **hollow** tree 속이 빈 나무 ② false, insincere, hypocritical, deceptive **hollow** promises 거짓 약속 ③ useless, fruitless, profitless, worthless **hollow** action 무의미한 행동	① 빈, 움푹 패인 ② 거짓의 ③ 무의미한
23	**idiotic** [ìdiátik]	a	ridiculous, foolish, stupid, fatuous What an **idiotic** thing to say! 말하기에 얼마나 어리석은 일이냐!	어리석은
24	**intrude** [intrú:d]	v	① trespass, encroach, violate **intrude** in someone else's business 다른 사람들의 일에 간섭하다 ② invade, infringe **intrude** on one's privacy 프라이버시를 침해하다	① 간섭하다 ② 침입하다
25	**liberate** [líbərèit]	v	free, release, disengage, deliver **liberate** a slave 노예를 해방하다	해방하다, 자유롭게 하다
26	**limit** [límit]	n v	bound, boundary, border, perimeter ① bound, confine, restrict, curb, prohibit ② determine, specify, fix **limit** the area that can be used 사용할 구역을 정하다	한계, 경계 ① 제한하다 ② 정하다
27	**maneuver**** [mənú:vər]	v	scheme, plot, design, move **maneuver** a car into the garage 차를 몰아 차고에 넣다	계획하다, 움직이다
28	**menace** [ménis]	v	threaten, frighten **menace** (a person's) right to live 생존권을 위협하다	위협하다

DAY 14

#	Word	PoS	Synonyms / Example	Meaning
29	**mislead** [misli:d]	v	misguide, misdirect **mislead** the enemy 적들을 속이다	잘못 인도하다, 오도하다
30	**monumental*** [mànjuméntl]	a	outstanding a **monumental** work 불후의 작품	기념비의, 불후의
31	**neglect*** [niglékt]	v	disregard, ignore, overlook **neglect** a person's advice 남의 충고를 무시하다	무시하다, 간과하다
32	**perform** [pərfɔ́:rm]	v	carry out, execute, serve, discharge, fulfill **perform** the work 작업을 수행하다	실행하다, 이행하다
33	**refined*** [rifáind]	a	purified, clarified, distilled Crude oil could be **refined** into many products. 원유는 많은 제품으로 가공된다.	정제된, 세련된
34	**remark*** [rimá:rk]	n	comment, statement, utterance, saying, commentary pass a **remark** 의견을 말하다	의견
		v	say, express, utter **remark** on her appearance 용모에 대하여 말하다	의견을 말하다
35	**resistance** [rizístəns]	n	fight, battle, defiance the end of **resistance** 저항의 끝	저항
36	**solid** [sálid]	v	firm, substantial, stable, strong, sound **solid** surface 단단한 표면	단단한
37	**torment** [tɔ:rmént]	v	harass, annoy, vex suffer **torment**(s) 괴로워하다	괴롭히다
		n	anguish be a real **torment** to a teacher by asking silly question of students 학생들의 바보 같은 질문이 선생님에게는 진정 고통이 되다	고통
38	**true*** [tru:]	a	① real, authentic, genuine, actual ↔ fake a **true** diamond 진짜 다이아몬드	① 진짜의
			② correct, accurate, confirmable ↔ false a **true** statement 진실	② 정확한
			③ honest, upright, faithful, trustworthy ↔ unfaithful a **true** love 참된 사랑	③ 정직한
39	**vague*** [veig]	a	imprecise, indefinite, unspecified, obscure ↔ obvious a **vague** air of mystery 자못 신비스러운 분위기	막연한, 모호한
40	**whim** [hwim]	n	caprice, whimsy as one's **whim** dictates 기분에 따라서	변덕
	whimsical* [hwímzikəl]	a	capricious, impulsive, fanciful **whimsical** sense of humor 기발한 유머감각	변덕스러운, 마음이 잘 변하는, 기발한

Practice Test 14

01. Minerals are the most common solid material found on the earth.
    Ⓐ gaseous
    Ⓑ liquid
    Ⓒ float
    Ⓓ hard

02. Malnutrition lowers the body's resistance to disease.
    Ⓐ opportunity
    Ⓑ feasibility
    Ⓒ susceptibility
    Ⓓ fight

03. Most crude oil is refined into gasoline, heating oil, and other fuels.
    Ⓐ purified
    Ⓑ transmitted
    Ⓒ concocted
    Ⓓ reproduced

04. The food we eat supplies the energy for every action we perform, from reading a book to running a race.
    Ⓐ serve
    Ⓑ execute
    Ⓒ masquerade
    Ⓓ pose

05. After the 200 B.C., Greek drama declined and leadership in the art passed on to Rome.
    Ⓐ repeated
    Ⓑ analyzed
    Ⓒ described
    Ⓓ faded

06. Gravity gives weight to everything on earth and accelerates the downward movement of free-falling objects downward.
    Ⓐ turn around
    Ⓑ destroy
    Ⓒ speed up
    Ⓓ change

07. In September, Lincoln issued a preliminary order to emancipate the slaves.
    Ⓐ loot
    Ⓑ free
    Ⓒ despoil
    Ⓓ appraise

08. Many people try to foretell future events by analyzing the relationships among the planets and the stars.
    Ⓐ incidents
    Ⓑ contests
    Ⓒ memorials
    Ⓓ predictions

09. Large-scale sculptures are often called monumental because of their size.
    Ⓐ archaic
    Ⓑ degrading
    Ⓒ colossal
    Ⓓ entire

10. More than 7 million people of Asian descent live in the United States.
    Ⓐ indigence
    Ⓑ opulence
    Ⓒ offspring
    Ⓓ precursor

11. Parabolic dish systems have reflectors arrayed along the contour of a bowl-shaped structure called a dish.
    A) outline
    B) pattern
    C) shade
    D) tone

12. By November 1941, the Germans had surrounded Leningrad and had begun to encircle Moscow.
    A) infiltrate
    B) circulate
    C) encompass
    D) shift

13. The arrow of time denotes an asymmetry of the world with time, not an asymmetry or flux of time.
    A) signifies
    B) predicts
    C) contrasts
    D) examines

14. Antarctica originally belonged to a land mass that included Africa, Australia, India, and South America.
    A) engaged in
    B) excluded
    C) was part of
    D) included

15. Any disease that hampers the heart's ability to deliver blood to the body may cause this condition.
    A) evades
    B) overlooks
    C) hinders
    D) perplex

16. Television stations erect their antennas on high buildings or towers so that the signal can reach as far as possible.
    A) plan
    B) level
    C) enlarge
    D) raise

17. The knowledge of the anatomy was greatly advanced by Galen who dissected animal corpses for study.
    A) hides
    B) corrupts flesh
    C) dead body
    D) herds

18. The rising demand for sugar in European helped create fierce competition over slaves and for new sugar colonies.
    A) energetic
    B) violent
    C) vigorous
    D) critic

19. Some historians believe that New York's nickname 'the Empire State' came from a remark made by George Washington.
    A) comment
    B) joke
    C) brag
    D) explain

20. The court based its decision in part on the principle that the U.S. Constitutional Bill of Rights created a "zone of privacy" into which a state could not intrude.
    A) forbid
    B) eliminate
    C) amend
    D) interrupt

DAY 15 Daily Checkup

01. a precise description
    - Ⓐ strict
    - Ⓑ coarse
    - Ⓒ induced
    - Ⓓ subvert

02. smash a window
    - Ⓐ cover
    - Ⓑ eradicate
    - Ⓒ shatter
    - Ⓓ convey

03. unrefined taste
    - Ⓐ accurate
    - Ⓑ foolish
    - Ⓒ irrational
    - Ⓓ crude

04. cheat in gambling
    - Ⓐ deplore
    - Ⓑ delude
    - Ⓒ upset
    - Ⓓ subdue

05. designate the scholarship winners
    - Ⓐ entitle
    - Ⓑ smash
    - Ⓒ delude
    - Ⓓ demolish

06. stamp out noxious insects
    - Ⓐ damp
    - Ⓑ deploring
    - Ⓒ fortune
    - Ⓓ harmful

07. mourn over the election results
    - Ⓐ float
    - Ⓑ conceal
    - Ⓒ grieve
    - Ⓓ assign

08. steadily losing weight
    - Ⓐ preposterously
    - Ⓑ afterward
    - Ⓒ intelligently
    - Ⓓ consistently

09. allot shares to persons
    - Ⓐ allure
    - Ⓑ distribute
    - Ⓒ convey
    - Ⓓ decoy

10. an impartial decision
    - Ⓐ unbiased
    - Ⓑ lasting
    - Ⓒ hasty
    - Ⓓ prejudiced

11. make a futile attempt
    - Ⓐ observed
    - Ⓑ definite
    - Ⓒ vain
    - Ⓓ continuous

12. an absurd project
    - Ⓐ accurate
    - Ⓑ allured
    - Ⓒ ridiculous
    - Ⓓ unbiased

13. overthrow a government
    - Ⓐ subvert
    - Ⓑ abide
    - Ⓒ persuade
    - Ⓓ coagulate

14. fulfill your duties
    - Ⓐ recover
    - Ⓑ finish
    - Ⓒ settle
    - Ⓓ pound

15. The offer tempted me.
    - Ⓐ uncovered
    - Ⓑ amended
    - Ⓒ conquered
    - Ⓓ seduced

16. eradicate a disease
    - Ⓐ heal
    - Ⓑ eliminate
    - Ⓒ entitle
    - Ⓓ swindle

17. on the authority of
    - Ⓐ attraction
    - Ⓑ outlet
    - Ⓒ power
    - Ⓓ strike

18. an outlet for internal industry
    - Ⓐ erosion
    - Ⓑ authority
    - Ⓒ market
    - Ⓓ abundance

19. apathetic students
    - Ⓐ uninterested
    - Ⓑ ineffective
    - Ⓒ disinterested
    - Ⓓ senseless

20. Teachers assign homework to their students.
    - Ⓐ divide
    - Ⓑ deceive
    - Ⓒ persuade
    - Ⓓ deliver

DAY 15 Voca Bank

표제어	품사	동의어와 예문	한글 뜻
1 **absurd*** [æbsə́:rd]	a	ridiculous, foolish, stupid ↔ rational, reasonable an **absurd** project 어처구니없는 계획	터무니없는
2 **allot** [əlát]	v	divide, distribute, assign, allocate **allot** a part of the work 분담시키다	할당하다, 배당하다
3 **apathetic** [æpəθétik]	a	uninvolved, impassive, phlegmatic an **apathetic** person 패기 없는 사람	냉담한
4 **assign** [əsáin]	v	distribute, allocate, divide **assign** work to each man 각자에게 작업을 할당하다	할당하다, 배정하다
5 **authority**** [əθɔ́:rəti]	n	power, supremacy on one's own **authority** 자기 혼자 의견으로, 독단으로	권위
authorize** [əθɔ́:rəraiz]	v	empower, mandate, permit, approve, allow **authorize** a person to fly a plane 누구에게 비행할 수 있게 허가하다	권한을 부여하다, 허가하다
6 **cheat** [tʃi:t]	v	deceive, defraud, trick, delude **cheat** in gambling 도박에서 사기 치다	속이다, 사기 치다
7 **coagulate** [kouǽgjulèit]	v	clot, congeal **coagulate** the protein molecule 단백질 분자를 응고시키다	응고시키다
8 **conceal*** [kənsí:l]	v	cover, hide, bury, mask ↔ divulge, uncover, reveal He **concealed** the fugitive. 그는 도망자를 숨겨주었다.	숨기다
9 **contemporary**** [kəntémpərèri]	a	existing, modern, coexisting Shakespeare and his **contemporary** writers 셰익스피어와 그의 동시대의 작가들	동시대의, 현대의
10 **designate** [dézignèit]	v	name, appoint, entitle **designate** the boundaries of a country 국경을 명시하다	가리키다, 지정하다
11 **eradicate** [irǽdəkèit]	v	eliminate, completely destroy, root out **eradicate** tuberculosis 결핵을 박멸하다	근절하다
12 **erosion** [iróuʒən]	n	deterioration, abrasion, destruction **erosion**-resistance 침식에 잘 견디는	부식
13 **float** [flout]	v	drift along, sail Leafy plants **float** on the surface of water. 잎이 무성한 식물은 물의 표면에 뜬다.	뜨다
14 **fulfill*** [fulfíl]	v	① complete, finish **fulfill** a dream 꿈을 실현하다 ② satisfy, realize, accomplish, achieve **fulfill** the requirements for graduation 졸업 이수학점을 채우다	① 마치다 ② 이행하다, 채우다

15	**futile*** [fjúːtl]	a	useless, ineffective, vain a **futile** effort 헛된 노력	(노력이) 헛된
16	**glue** [gluː]	v	adhere, cement, gum **glue** one's eyes to the TV screen 텔레비전에 시선을 집중하다	접착하다, 집중하다
17	**heal** [hiːl]	v	remedy, amend, cure **heal** the soul 영혼을 맑게 하다	고치다, 치료하다
18	**homogeneous** [hòumədʒíːniəs]	a	analogous, uniform, akin ↔ heterogeneous a **homogeneous** equation 동차 방정식	동종의
19	**humid** [hjúːmid]	a	damp, moist, wet, soaked ↔ dry **humid** air 눅눅한 공기	습기 찬
20	**impartial**** [impáːrʃəl]	a	unbiased, just, fair, disinterested an **impartial** judge 공명정대한 재판	정당한, 공평한
21	**inhabit**** [inhǽbit]	v	abide, dwell, occupy, reside, live in largest animals ever to **inhabit** the Earth 지구에 사는 가장 큰 동물	거주하다
22	**mourn** [mɔːrn]	v	grieve, lament, deplore **mourn** for one's failure 실패를 한탄하다	슬퍼하다, 한탄하다
23	**murder** [məːrdər]	n	slaying, assassination, killing, homicide, massacre **Murder** will out. (속담) 나쁜 짓은 반드시 탄로나는 법이다.	암살
		v	kill, slaughter, butcher, exterminate was **murdered** the numerous Koreans impressed by Japan's army 일본군에 의해 강제 징용된 많은 한국인들이 죽임을 당했다	죽이다
24	**notice*** [nóutis]	v	observe, detect, discern, distinguish **notice** a stop signal 정지신호를 알아채다	알아채다
25	**noxious** [nákʃəs]	a	harmful, deadly, destructive The rice plant is infested with **noxious** insects. 벼에 해충이 들끓는다.	몸에 해로운, 유독한
26	**outlet** [áutlet]	n	release, channel, duct, market; socket an **outlet** for internal industry 국내산업의 판로	출구, 판로 / 콘센트
27	**overthrow** [óuvərθróu]	v	upset, overturn, capsize **overthrow** a government 정부를 넘어뜨리다	뒤엎다, 전복시키다
28	**philanthropic** [fìlənθrápik]	a	humanitarian, humane as a religious and **philanthropic** society 양심적이고 인도주의적인 사회로서	인도주의의
29	**precise*** [prisáis]	a	accurate, definite, correct, strict the **precise** meaning 정확한 의미	정확한, 정밀한
30	**smash*** [smæʃ]	v	shatter, crush, crash, compress, demolish ↔ repair **smash** a window 창을 부수다	박살내다, 산산이 부수다

DAY 15

31	**steadily** [stédili]	ad	continuously, consistently **steadily** losing weight 꾸준히 살이 빠지다	착실하게, 끊임없이
32	**strike** [straik]	v	hit, knock, beat, pound, slap **strike** at the roof of ~을 뿌리째 흔들려고 하다, ~이 파멸될 듯하다	치다, 때리다
33	**stupid** [stjú:pid]	a	dull, senseless, foolish, absurd, uneducated ↔ reasonable a **stupid** joke 바보 같은 농담	바보 같은
34	**subsequently***** [sʌbsikwəntli]	ad	later, afterwards The parasite itself **subsequently** ceases to grow. 기생충 스스로 그 후에 성장을 멈추다.	그 후에
35	**tactics**** [tæktiks]	n	strategy, maneuver change one's **tactics** 작전을 바꾸다	전술, 병법
36	**tempt** [tempt]	v	induce, persuade, entice, allure, seduce, attract **tempt** one's frailty 약한 마음을 이용해 유혹하다	유혹하다, 부추기다
37	**transport** [trænspɔ́:rt]	v	carry, convey, deliver **transport** the mail by air 항공으로 우편물을 나르다	수송하다, 운송하다
38	**unreasonable**** [ʌnríːzənəbl]	a	irrational, senseless, foolish, silly, preposterous, idiotic an **unreasonable** demand 부당한 요구	타당치 않는
39	**unrefined**** [ʌnrifáind]	a	coarse, crude, unpolished, vulgar **unrefined** customs 야비한 풍습	세련되지 못한
40	**wealth*** [welθ]	n	abundance, profusion, riches, treasure, affluence ↔ poverty man of **wealth** 재산가, 부자	부유, 풍부

Practice

01. All the animal and plant populations that inhabit the area make up a community.
    - Ⓐ occupy
    - Ⓑ surround
    - Ⓒ threat
    - Ⓓ govern

02. As humid air sweeps up the slopes of a mountain range, the air cools, and clouds form.
    - Ⓐ damp
    - Ⓑ hot
    - Ⓒ coastal
    - Ⓓ tropical

03. Even within a homogeneous community differences of opinion arise.
    - Ⓐ different race
    - Ⓑ identical
    - Ⓒ advanced
    - Ⓓ broaden

04. The desire to gain wealth was the motivating force behind nearly all the efforts to establish empires.
    - Ⓐ power
    - Ⓑ admiration
    - Ⓒ affluence
    - Ⓓ success

05. One of the state's greatest problems is how to transport water from rainy areas to the dry places where it is needed.
    - Ⓐ convoke
    - Ⓑ inundate
    - Ⓒ bring
    - Ⓓ trespass

06. The ozone molecule (O_3) is created when an ultraviolet light strikes an oxygen molecule (O_2).
    - Ⓐ chemical converts
    - Ⓑ filters through
    - Ⓒ divide into
    - Ⓓ hit up

07. European heroic dramas of medieval times may seem absurd today, but they were popular in their time.
    - Ⓐ desperate
    - Ⓑ congruous
    - Ⓒ ridiculous
    - Ⓓ vanish

08. After the New Deal was made, the government's role in banking and public welfare steadily grew.
    - Ⓐ discreetly
    - Ⓑ consistently
    - Ⓒ automatically
    - Ⓓ disproportionately

09. Lithium is the lightest of the solid elements, can float when it is in its pure form.
    - Ⓐ drift
    - Ⓑ condense
    - Ⓒ bunch together
    - Ⓓ proliferate

10. Electronic flash units operate on batteries or on electric currents that come from an outlet.
    - Ⓐ lease
    - Ⓑ release
    - Ⓒ socket
    - Ⓓ flow

11. The ghost of Hamlet's father appears in front of the prince and tells him that he was murdered by Claudius.
    A accused
    B slandered
    C killed
    D alarmed

12. Plateau Indians believed shamans could heal people and have some control over the spirit world.
    A upgrade
    B cure
    C divide
    D order

13. Workers in contemporary civilization are not so interested in their everyday work as were primitive people.
    A informative
    B controversial
    C modern
    D faultfinding

14. Prehistoric people probably noticed that the seasons changed every year when certain groups of stars reached certain positions in the night sky.
    A observed
    B announced
    C corrected
    D predicted

15. If people were to lack free will, it would seem unreasonable to hold them responsible for their decisions and actions.
    A moderate
    B impeccable
    C senseless
    D reliable

16. Washington probably prepared for his new duties by reading books on military drills and tactics.
    A traditions
    B rules
    C observances
    D strategies

17. Computerized controls will probably do more and more tasks in future cars because of their low cost and precise functioning.
    A logical
    B independent
    C accurate
    D technical

18. Farmers can reduce soil erosion by planting trees and leaving patches of natural vegetation between their fields and other unplowed areas.
    A fertilization
    B deterioration
    C hardness
    D draining

19. After proteins have been eaten, hydrochloric acid, which most people have in their stomach, causes the protein molecules to coagulate.
    A thicken and clump together
    B circulate
    C digest
    D distribute nutrients

20. Each element, such as hydrogen and nitrogen, has a designated symbol, often driving from its Latin name.
    A labeled
    B transferred
    C acquired
    D unified

11-15

01. **violation** of human rights
    - Ⓐ infringement
    - Ⓑ slug
    - Ⓒ enemy
    - Ⓓ minimum

02. build fence to **confine** and protect the livestock
    - Ⓐ converge
    - Ⓑ discard
    - Ⓒ limit
    - Ⓓ embelish

03. **prevailed** a graffiti art in that village
    - Ⓐ influenced
    - Ⓑ dominanted
    - Ⓒ enlarged
    - Ⓓ absorbed

04. a **cozy** room
    - Ⓐ small
    - Ⓑ familiar
    - Ⓒ commending
    - Ⓓ assembling

05. **scholarly** monographs
    - Ⓐ important
    - Ⓑ academic
    - Ⓒ unusual
    - Ⓓ quarantining

06. to be **quarantined** for six months
    - Ⓐ exposed
    - Ⓑ constituted
    - Ⓒ isolated
    - Ⓓ transformed

07. turn on the **auxiliary** motor
    - Ⓐ additional
    - Ⓑ following
    - Ⓒ permeating
    - Ⓓ thin

08. unable to **penetrate** the surface
    - Ⓐ mutate
    - Ⓑ explicate
    - Ⓒ convert
    - Ⓓ pierce

09. Please **fasten** your seat belt.
    - Ⓐ stout
    - Ⓑ uncheck
    - Ⓒ depict
    - Ⓓ fix

10. The path **ascends** here.
    - Ⓐ goes up
    - Ⓑ fluctuates
    - Ⓒ strives
    - Ⓓ satisfies

11. **unrestrained** joy
    - Ⓐ directed
    - Ⓑ bright
    - Ⓒ unchecked
    - Ⓓ stout

12. **hamper** your progress
    - Ⓐ delineation
    - Ⓑ reject
    - Ⓒ hinder
    - Ⓓ dwindle

13. **intrude** on private property
    - Ⓐ trespass
    - Ⓑ overwhelm
    - Ⓒ express
    - Ⓓ overlook

14. stand **erect**
    - Ⓐ unsettled
    - Ⓑ glorifying
    - Ⓒ vertical
    - Ⓓ strong

15. **accelerate** our pace
    - Ⓐ design
    - Ⓑ speed up
    - Ⓒ abate
    - Ⓓ reimburse

16. **transport** them to Europe
    - Ⓐ conceal
    - Ⓑ uniform
    - Ⓒ eliminate
    - Ⓓ carry

17. **inhabit** a forest
    - Ⓐ clot
    - Ⓑ improve
    - Ⓒ shatter
    - Ⓓ reside

18. the **precise** meaning
    - Ⓐ fatuous
    - Ⓑ accurate
    - Ⓒ crashed
    - Ⓓ unpolished

19. an **unreasonable** demand
    - Ⓐ enticed
    - Ⓑ coexisting
    - Ⓒ defraud
    - Ⓓ irrational

20. **contemporary** writers
    - Ⓐ coexisting
    - Ⓑ silly
    - Ⓒ disinterested
    - Ⓓ mourning

Practice

01. Readers can skip items that do not interest them.
    - Ⓐ eliminate
    - Ⓑ augment
    - Ⓒ pass over
    - Ⓓ glare

02. Powerful earthquakes can shake the firm ground violently for great distances.
    - Ⓐ spine
    - Ⓑ vibrate
    - Ⓒ shock
    - Ⓓ shift

03. The answers given by the volunteers were wrong.
    - Ⓐ frontiers
    - Ⓑ developers
    - Ⓒ candidates
    - Ⓓ attendants

04. An excess of bile, can supposedly make a person melancholy.
    - Ⓐ upset
    - Ⓑ sad
    - Ⓒ voracious
    - Ⓓ satiated

05. Socrates wanted to replace vague opinions with clear ideas.
    - Ⓐ imprecise
    - Ⓑ diffuse
    - Ⓒ unpolished
    - Ⓓ elementary

06. The United Kingdom had just defeated France in the French and Indian War (1754-1763).
    - Ⓐ scattered
    - Ⓑ starved
    - Ⓒ wounded
    - Ⓓ conquered

07. Some psychologists believed that the chief purpose of psychology was to describe, analyze, and explain conscious experience, and particular feelings and sensations.
    - Ⓐ clever
    - Ⓑ humorous
    - Ⓒ intentional
    - Ⓓ cognizant

08. The rock climber is stuck fast on the rocks.
    - Ⓐ rapid
    - Ⓑ heavy
    - Ⓒ sluggish
    - Ⓓ tight

09. California has a great variety of climates.
    - Ⓐ biological balance
    - Ⓑ weather conditions
    - Ⓒ rotation
    - Ⓓ geography

10. Plants grow by taking in simple molecules and chemically converting them into complex plant materials.
    - Ⓐ assembling
    - Ⓑ changing
    - Ⓒ promoting
    - Ⓓ dissolving

11. In many parts of the world, diseases and poor living conditions are a severe problem.
    Ⓐ harsh
    Ⓑ alarming
    Ⓒ disunited
    Ⓓ pleasant

12. Engineers have developed plastics that are as rigid as steel or as soft as cotton.
    Ⓐ pliant
    Ⓑ adaptable
    Ⓒ firm
    Ⓓ cool

13. The discovery of cells is associated with the development of the microscope in the seventeenth century.
    Ⓐ accompanied by
    Ⓑ influenced on
    Ⓒ informed about
    Ⓓ acquainted with

14. In many species, the color of the hair blends in with the surroundings to help conceal the animal from enemies.
    Ⓐ highlight
    Ⓑ cover
    Ⓒ transform
    Ⓓ contaminate

15. The large arteries of people who died from alcoholic liver cirrhosis were remarkably free of atherosclerosis
    Ⓐ definitely
    Ⓑ commendably
    Ⓒ surprisingly
    Ⓓ exaggeratedly

16. The continent was part of a land mass called Gondwanaland, which included Africa, Australia, India, and South America.
    Ⓐ Earth's surface
    Ⓑ very large area
    Ⓒ integrated tribes
    Ⓓ biological distinction

17. Many schools in the United States teach French as a second language and provide special instruction for children who speak two languages.
    Ⓐ teaching
    Ⓑ friendship
    Ⓒ contact
    Ⓓ speech

18. The function of the nuclear gene is to produce the ribosomal RNA molecule that eventually becomes a part of the ribosome.
    Ⓐ ultimately
    Ⓑ actually
    Ⓒ definitely
    Ⓓ officially

19. About 96% of protoplasm is composed of the elements carbon, hydrogen, oxygen, and nitrogen; 3% consists of phosphorus, potassium, and sulphur.
    Ⓐ is made up of
    Ⓑ determines by
    Ⓒ free of
    Ⓓ reserves for

20. During World War II (1939-1945), George fulfilled his duties conscientiously, and people much admired his conduct during the air raids in London.
    Ⓐ performed
    Ⓑ concluded
    Ⓒ leaved
    Ⓓ attained

Intensive Practice

01. Many young people in each country disregard traditional marriage patterns.
    Ⓐ ignore
    Ⓑ deplore
    Ⓒ explore
    Ⓓ implore

02. Several modern English translations of the Bible have tried to replace the out-of-date language of the older versions.
    Ⓐ translate
    Ⓑ substitute
    Ⓒ rehearse
    Ⓓ converse

03. For the past one or two centuries, mountain glaciers have been shrinking, so that the water released into the streams and rivers has been adding to the sea.
    Ⓐ cold
    Ⓑ fading
    Ⓒ unraveling
    Ⓓ decreasing

04. If a particle and its antiparticle collide, they annihilate each other, releasing gamma rays and other energy.
    Ⓐ help
    Ⓑ advise
    Ⓒ destroy
    Ⓓ teach

05. Kublai Khan had a somewhat milder temperament than his predecessors and actually encouraged contact with Europeans.
    Ⓐ cruelty
    Ⓑ crook
    Ⓒ indulgence
    Ⓓ nature

06. Some patients lose their capacity to perform simple, everyday tasks and show impairments in intellectual abilities such as planning.
    Ⓐ damages
    Ⓑ improvements
    Ⓒ strengths
    Ⓓ flaws

07. Admiral Lee SoonShin's successful maneuverings at Myeongrang and Noryang naval battles embarrassed the Japanese navy.
    Ⓐ speeches
    Ⓑ duties
    Ⓒ marches
    Ⓓ moves

08. Some people call tsunamis tidal waves, but scientists think the term is misleading because the waves are not caused by the tide.
    Ⓐ abuse
    Ⓑ ambiguous
    Ⓒ conspicous
    Ⓓ regretful

09. Many elegies mourn the death of a famous person or a close friend.
    Ⓐ covet
    Ⓑ secret
    Ⓒ fright
    Ⓓ sorrow

10. In the United States, the federal policy of land allotment to individual Native Americans remained in effect during the early 1900's.
    Ⓐ donation
    Ⓑ distribution
    Ⓒ trespass
    Ⓓ minimization

11. Most Indian wars were little more than futile attempts by desperate, poorly equipped Indians to keep their land and their way of life.
    A useless
    B necessary
    C helpful
    D unpleasant

12. General Henri Petain who had organized the defense of Verdun was hailed a hero by France.
    A inaugurated
    B categorized
    C acclaimed
    D promoted

13. Some vitamins are produced in food and pills in an inactive form.
    A strenuous
    B valueless
    C inoperative
    D insignificant

14. The object of anthropologist is to understand the way in which cultures change and differentiate.
    A combine
    B constrain
    C accustom
    D distinguish

15. Everyone has the right to be secure against unreasonable searches or seizures.
    A mistrusted
    B illegal
    C unfair
    D awkward

16. Despite the many statistical ideas and methods of analysis developed in the late 1800's, there remained unrefined until the 1920's.
    A ameliorated
    B mysterious
    C unprocessed
    D established

17. In October 1777, in the Second Battle of Freeman's Farm, Arnold showed gallant courage against Burgoyne and was again seriously wounded.
    A brave
    B pertinent
    C obedient
    D violent

18. Women who filled jobs in offices and factories after the men went to war, were reluctant to give up their newly found independence.
    A palpable
    B unwilling
    C negligent
    D obdurate

19. Although the play ends happily for everyone except the revengeful Shylock, it is not a light-hearted comedy.
    A dangerous
    B blithe
    C critical
    D serious

20. Scientists measure the relative tilt of a planet at the right angle of the orbital plane, an imaginary surface that touches all points of the orbit.
    A unexpected
    B uncommon
    C unusual
    D unreal

Related

오르내리다	- fluctuate, alternate, move up and down, shift
빠뜨리다, 건너뛰다	- skip, miss out, omit, disregard, leave out, jump over, skim
위장하다	- camouflage, conceal, disguise, hide, bury, cover
비난하다	- denounce, condemn, accuse, reproach, scold, blame, indict, charge, decry
박살내다	- smash, shatter, crush, crash, compress, demolish
보상하다	- compensate, reimburse, indemnify, atone, make a good loss
어색한, 서투른	- maladroit, unskillful, awkward, clumsy, inept
신앙심이 깊은	- pious, devout, reverent, religious, devoted, saintly
자발적인	- voluntary, spontaneous, free, unforced
마음이 내키지 않는	- unwilling, reluctant, averse, opposed, loath
사나운, 잔인한	- fierce, ferocious, wild, savage, cruel, brutal
용감한	- brave, courageous, audacious, intrepid, dauntless
천체의	- astronomical, celestial, heavenly
공정한	- fair, just unbiased, right, honest, truthful
확고한	- firm, stable, steadfast, determined, reliable
우울한	- melancholy, depressed, gloomy, despondent, dismal
냉담한	- apathetic, uninvolved, impassive, phlegmatic
습기 찬	- wet, humid, damp, moist, soaked, saturated, soggy, watery
노력	- endeavor, struggle, effort, labor, exertion, attempt
거의	- almost, nearly, practically, approximately, around, roughly

Knowledge based

ROCKS AND LAYERS

Earth's history has been studied by examining the record of past ❶ events that is preserved in the rocks. Most of the rocks exposed at the surface of Earth are formed sedimentary from particles of older rocks that have been ❷ broken apart by water or wind and settled down to the bottom in rivers, lakes, and oceans with gravel, sand, and mud. These sedimentary particles may bury together with living and dead organisms including animals and plants on the lake or sea bottom.

Sedimentary particles more ❸ accumulated by layers over time and sometimes ❹ undergo chemical changes. The sediments at the bottom of the pile finally become rock: gravel becomes a rock called conglomerate, sand becomes sandstone, mud becomes mudstone or shale, and the animal ❺ skeletons and plant ❻ pieces can become ❼ fossils.

The most ❽ obvious feature of sedimentary rocks is layering, or bedding. Sedimentary rocks are formed particle by particle and bed by bed, and the layers are piled one on top of the other. Thus, a given bed in any sequence of layered rocks must be older than any bed on top of it. This Law of Superposition is ❾ fundamental to the ❿ interpretation of Earth history, because at any one location it indicates the relative ages of rock layers and the fossils in them. Rock layer is also called stratum (pl. strata).

What is closest meaning to left word?

1. events — Ⓐ incident Ⓑ investigation Ⓒ location Ⓓ recording
2. broken apart — Ⓐ piled up Ⓑ classified into Ⓒ assembly by Ⓓ fallen apart
3. accumulated — Ⓐ piled up Ⓑ preserved Ⓒ shattered Ⓓ oppressed
4. undergo — Ⓐ undertake Ⓑ dig Ⓒ suffer Ⓓ surpass
5. skeletons — Ⓐ slither Ⓑ protection Ⓒ remnant Ⓓ backbone

6. pieces — Ⓐ serenity Ⓑ part Ⓒ entire Ⓓ debris
7. fossils — Ⓐ recordings Ⓑ fireworks Ⓒ remains Ⓓ trivialness
8. obvious — Ⓐ oblique Ⓑ obscure Ⓒ necessary Ⓓ apparent
9. fundamental — Ⓐ manifest Ⓑ secondary Ⓒ essential Ⓓ unimportant
10. interpretation — Ⓐ encoding Ⓑ elucidation Ⓒ conversion Ⓓ transformation

암석rocks과 지층layers

지구의 역사Earth's history는 암석에 보존된preserved 과거 사건past events의 기록을 조사하면서by examining 연구되어왔다. 지구의 표층the surface of Earth에 노출된exposed 대부분의 암석들은 오래된 암석의 입자들의 침전작용sedimentary을 통해 형성되었는데, 이 오래된 암석들은 물이나 바람에 의해 부서져 떨어지고broken apart 강과 호수, 바다의 바닥에 자갈, 모래, 진흙gravel, sand and mud과 함께 가라앉았던settled down 것들이다. 이러한 침전입자들은 호수나 해저에 동물과 식물을 포함한 살아 있거나 죽은 유기체organisms와 함께 묻힐 수bury together with 있다.

침적입자sedimentary particle들은 시간이 지나갈수록over time 더욱 층층으로 축적되고accumulated by layers, 때때로 화학적 변화를 겪는다undergo changes. 더미의 바닥에 쌓인 침전물sediments은 마침내 암석이 되는데become rock, 자갈은 역암conglomerate이라 부르는 암석이 되고 모래는 사암sandstone, 진흙은 이암mudstone 또는 아판암shale이 되고, 동물의 뼈skeletons와 식물의 조각pieces은 화석fossils이 될 수 있다.

퇴적암sedimentary rock의 가장 분명한 특징obvious feature은 층layering 또는 성층bedding이 있다는 것이다. 퇴적암은 입자에 입자가, 층위에 층이 형성되는 것으로 그 층들은 한 층이 다른 층의 위에 쌓이는 것이다are piled one on top of the other. 그러므로 층이 형성된 암석들 내의 순서에 상관없이in any sequence 일정한 층given bed은 그것의 위에 쌓인 어떠한 층보다도 오래되었다는must be older than 것이다. 이 지층 누중의 법칙(중첩의 법칙)law of superposition은 어떠한 한 장소에서 암석층과 그 속에 있는 화석의 상대적 나이relative ages를 암시하기indicates 때문에 지구의 역사를 해석interpretation하는 데 필수적이다fundamental. 암석층rock layer은 또한 지층stratum이라고도 부른다.

1. Ⓐ 2. Ⓓ 3. Ⓐ 4. Ⓒ 5. Ⓓ
6. Ⓑ 7. Ⓒ 8. Ⓓ 9. Ⓒ 10. Ⓑ

DAY 16　Daily Checkup

01. neat attire
    - Ⓐ lord
    - Ⓑ allowance
    - Ⓒ measurement
    - Ⓓ clothing

02. beyond compare
    - Ⓐ dissimilarly
    - Ⓑ impartially
    - Ⓒ above
    - Ⓓ universally

03. wander lonely as a cloud
    - Ⓐ roar
    - Ⓑ stray
    - Ⓒ flow
    - Ⓓ float

04. a remedy for all diseases
    - Ⓐ treatment
    - Ⓑ deposit
    - Ⓒ pension
    - Ⓓ traitor

05. the rebel army
    - Ⓐ roved
    - Ⓑ retired
    - Ⓒ co-existed
    - Ⓓ insurgent

06. roar for mercy
    - Ⓐ cry
    - Ⓑ specify
    - Ⓒ estimate
    - Ⓓ accord

07. withdraw an offer
    - Ⓐ retract
    - Ⓑ appraise
    - Ⓒ custom
    - Ⓓ garment

08. drive into catastrophe
    - Ⓐ dimension
    - Ⓑ calamity
    - Ⓒ confinement
    - Ⓓ deposit

09. sinuous movements
    - Ⓐ winding
    - Ⓑ co-existed
    - Ⓒ stated
    - Ⓓ embraced

10. live on one's pension
    - Ⓐ misfortune
    - Ⓑ allowance
    - Ⓒ gauge
    - Ⓓ correctness

11. assess the value of the coin collection
    - Ⓐ appraise
    - Ⓑ increase
    - Ⓒ reduce
    - Ⓓ elucidate

12. illustrate the point
    - Ⓐ enclose
    - Ⓑ represent
    - Ⓒ correct
    - Ⓓ withdraw

13. operate a machine
    - Ⓐ contain
    - Ⓑ bellow
    - Ⓒ manage
    - Ⓓ produce

14. godly thoughts
    - Ⓐ cautious
    - Ⓑ pious
    - Ⓒ relative
    - Ⓓ happy

15. reluctant assistants
    - Ⓐ lofty
    - Ⓑ elucidated
    - Ⓒ unwilling
    - Ⓓ principal

16. meditate on the meaning of life
    - Ⓐ deviate
    - Ⓑ depict
    - Ⓒ ponder
    - Ⓓ rule

17. one book include four novels
    - Ⓐ perform
    - Ⓑ define
    - Ⓒ treat
    - Ⓓ contain

18. specifies the size of apple
    - Ⓐ states
    - Ⓑ corrects
    - Ⓒ retreat
    - Ⓓ attempt

19. the lordly, lovely Han River
    - Ⓐ curiously
    - Ⓑ merrily
    - Ⓒ tenderly
    - Ⓓ majestic

20. an easygoing way of thinking
    - Ⓐ relaxed
    - Ⓑ depicted
    - Ⓒ indirect
    - Ⓓ measured

DAY 16 Voca Bank

	표제어	품사	동의어와 예문	한글 뜻
1	**adjacent*** [ədʒéisnt]	a	nearby, near, neighboring a park **adjacent** to the castle 성에 인접한 공원	이웃의, 인접한
2	**assess**** [əsés]	v	estimate, appraise, calculate, evaluate **assess** the effectiveness of insecticidal activity 살충제 활성의 효과를 검정하다 **assess** a tax on a person 누구에게 세금을 부과하다	평가하다, 부과하다
3	**attire**** [ətáiər]	n	clothing, apparel, custom, garment neat **attire** 단정한 복장으로	의류, 의복
4	**beyond**** [bijánd]	prep	outside, exceeding, surpassing the back of **beyond** 머나먼 곳, 세상 끝	~을 넘어서
5	**calamity*** [kəlǽməti]	n	disaster, catastrophe, tragedy, cataclysm a **calamity** howler 비관론자	재난, 참사, 불행
6	**catastrophe**** [kətǽstrəfi]	n	disaster, mishap, misfortune, calamity financial **catastrophe** 재정적 파탄	재난, 파국
7	**coexist** [kòuigzíst]	v	accord, be concurrent hope that all people can **coexist** without religions and races 종교와 인종 없이 모든 사람이 공존할 수 있다는 희망	공존하다
8	**consume** [kənsúːm]	v	eat, exhaust, expend ↔ produce **consume** large amount of fuels by cars 자동차에 의해 많은 양의 연료를 소비하다	소비하다
9	**dissimilar** [dissímələr]	a	different, disparate They are brothers, but quite **dissimilar** in character. 그들은 형제지만 성격은 아주 딴판이다.	공통점이 없는
10	**dominant*** [dámənənt]	a	ruling, prevailing, prevalent **dominant** artistic trends 지배적인 예술적 성향	지배적인, 우세한
11	**easygoing** [íːzigóuiŋ]	a	relaxed, calm, serene, easy, tranquil, placid an **easygoing** manner 안이한 당식	안이한
12	**embrace*** [imbréis]	v	include, take up **embrace** one's beloved 애인을 껴안다	포옹하다
13	**foresight** [fɔ́ːrsait]	n	forethought, precaution Purpose supposes **foresight**. 목적은 선견을 전제로 한다.	선견지명

14	**general** [dʒénərəl]	a	① **common, universal, conventional, prevalent, popular** **general** opinion 일반적인 의견 as a **general** rule 일반적으로, 보통은 ② **vague, indefinite, abstract** ↔ specific a **general** explanation of how it works 어떻게 작동하는지의 일반적인 설명	① 일반적인 ② 막연한
	generally** [dʒénərəli]	ad	**usually, as a rule, by and large** be **generally** accurate 대개 정확하다	대개
15	**godly** [gádli]	a	**pious, saintly, devout,** holy **godly** thoughts 사념 없는 마음	신을 충성하는, 경건한
16	**illustrate**** [íləstrèit]	v	① **draw, picture portray, depict** **illustrate** the flowers 꽃을 설명하다 ② **represent, demonstrate, show, elucidate** **illustrate** how the heart works 어떻게 심장이 작동하는지 보여주다	① 설명하다 ② 표현하다, 나타내다
17	**incarcerate** [inkáːrsərèit]	v	**imprison,** confine **incarcerate** a person by unknown reason 알 수 없는 이유로 한 남자를 투옥시키다	투옥하다
18	**include** [inklúːd]	v	**contain, enclose, comprise,** embrace **include** all charges for accommodation and registration fee 숙박과 등록비의 모든 것을 포함하다	포함하다
19	**lordly** [lɔ́ːrdli]	a	**grand, magnificent, majestic,** lofty act in a **lordly** manner 교만하게 굴다	귀족다운, 당당한
20	**measure*** [méʒər]	n	**means, indication, gauge, rule,** extent, dimension take **measures** to preserve the environment 환경을 보호하려는 대책을 세우다	측정, 계량, 대책
		v	**rule, appraise, estimate** **measure** the intensity of light 빛의 세기를 측정하다	측정하다, 평가하다
21	**meditate***** [médətèit]	v	**think deeply, contemplate, reflect, ponder** **meditate** the muse 시상에 잠기다	명상하다, 숙고하다
22	**neural** [njúərəl]	a	**nerve, nervous, neuronal** control the cockroaches connecting **neural** circuit 신경회로를 연결해서 바퀴벌레를 통제하다	신경의
23	**operate**** [ápərèit]	v	① **work, manage, direct,** perform Several causes **operated** to begin the war. 여러 가지 원인으로 전쟁이 일어났다. ② **cut, open up** be **operated** on for lung cancer 폐암으로 수술 받다	① 움직이다, 수행하다 ② 수술하다
24	**pension** [pénʃən]	n	**allowance, annuity,** benefit live on one's **pension** 연금으로 생활하다	연금, 보조금
25	**prime**** [praim]	a	**primary, chief, leading, principal,** peak, zenith the **prime** time of movies program 영화 프로그램의 황금 시간대	첫째의, 최고의
26	**rebel** [rebə́l]	n	**insurgent, traitor** the **rebel** army inhabiting far away island 멀리 떨어진 섬에 거주하는 반란군	반역자

DAY 16

27	**reluctant**** [rilʌ́ktənt]	a	unwilling, disinclined, loath, averse **reluctant** to expel students 학생을 제적할 마음이 내키지 않는	마음이 내키지 않는
28	**remedy** [rémədi]	v	correct, cure, treat **remedy** a fault 허물을 고치다	치료하다
29	**revoke** [rivóuk]	v	cancel, recall, withdraw, abolish **revoke** a license 면허를 취소하다	취소하다
30	**roar** [rɔ:r]	v	cry, bellow, shout, yell **roar** with laughter 크게 웃다	으르렁 거리다, 울부짖다
31	**secret**** [sí:krit]	v	discharge, hide, conceal **secret** oneself 자취를 감추다, 숨다	비밀로 하다, 숨기다
	secrete*** [sí:krí:t]	v	emanate, give off, emit, exude Bees-wax is **secreted** by bees. 밀랍은 벌에 의해 분비된다.	분비하다
32	**sediment** [sédəmənt]	n	dregs, deposit accumulate more **sediment** due to the erosion of soil 토양의 침식으로 인해 더 많은 퇴적물이 축적되다 **sedimentary** rocks 퇴적암	침전물, 퇴적물
33	**shore** [ʃɔ:r]	n	coast, beach, seashore inhabit along the **shores** of the East Sea 동해의 바닷가를 따라서 거주하다	물가, 바닷가
34	**sinuous*** [sínjuəs]	a	winding, curving, crooked a **sinuous** line 꾸불꾸불한 줄	꼬불꼬불한, 굴곡이 많은
35	**specify*** [spésəfài]	v	state, define, detail **specify** in a contract note 계약서에 명기하다	제시하다, 정의하다
36	**unbiased** [ʌnbáiəst]	a	impartial, unprejudiced, disinterested, fair an **unbiased** opinion 정당한 의견	편견이 없는, 정당한
37	**undertake*** [ʌ̀ndərteik]	v	assume, attempt, wage, take on, embark, initiate **undertake** an experiment 실험에 착수하다	시작하다, 떠맡다
38	**wander*** [wándər]	v	roam, stray, ramble, rove, stroll, deviate The car **wandered** all over the road. 소들이 들판을 돌아다닌다.	헤매다, 방랑하다
39	**wary** [wέəri]	a	alert, careful, cautious be **wary** of advice to get a job as soon as possible 가능한 빨리 직장을 구하라는 충고를 신중하게 받아들이다	주의 깊은, 세심한
40	**withdraw*** [wiðdrɔ́:]	v	quit, retire, retreat, retract, secede **withdraw** an offer 신청을 철회하다	철회하다, 후퇴하다

Practice

01. Mathematical statements can be illustrated in everyday language.
  A) rated
  B) listed
  C) verified
  D) represented

02. Scientists measure the amount of heat produced using an instrument called a calorimeter.
  A) believe
  B) indicate
  C) calculate
  D) necessary

03. The Romantics tended to rebel against traditional social and political institutions.
  A) support
  B) perceive
  C) allow
  D) resist

04. Public universities in California operate many fine medical facilities and research laboratories.
  A) investigate
  B) manage
  C) support
  D) behave

05. The grade level rating of a book in the bibliographies is intended merely as a general guide.
  A) regular
  B) common
  C) rare
  D) never

06. Famine, plagues, and other calamities caused a radical decline in population.
  A) catastrophes
  B) foresights
  C) seditions
  D) affinities

07. In the past, most of the world's economic leaders have been the dominant political and military powers.
  A) governing
  B) influential
  C) disregarded
  D) commanded

08. A supersonic transport plane (SST) can roar through the air at about 1,350mph (2,180kph).
  A) pass
  B) fly
  C) blast
  D) soar

09. Fish as well as amphibians, have glands that secrete a slimy substance onto their skin.
  A) hide
  B) warm
  C) exude
  D) absorb

10. Jackson's allies won control of the Senate, and revoked the resolution.
  A) reconsidered
  B) exorcised
  C) cancelled
  D) investigated

DAY 16

125

11. Astronomers think that many stars beyond our solar system may have planets on which life could exist.
    Ⓐ on
    Ⓑ outside
    Ⓒ toward
    Ⓓ beside

12. In quantum physics, all particles and fields are divided into extremely dissimilar types: fermions and bosons.
    Ⓐ inestimable
    Ⓑ comparable
    Ⓒ different
    Ⓓ confusable

13. Copyright infringers may be liable for actual damages and profits or for damages specified by the law.
    Ⓐ stated
    Ⓑ singular
    Ⓒ particular
    Ⓓ peculiar

14. In the autumn, General James Wilkinson and General Wade Hampton undertook a campaign against Montreal.
    Ⓐ embarked
    Ⓑ underestimated
    Ⓒ took down
    Ⓓ underplayed

15. A mammal wanders around its home range during it's daily activities of feeding, drinking, and seeking shelter.
    Ⓐ transfers
    Ⓑ roams
    Ⓒ forages
    Ⓓ digress

16. Between 30 to 40 million years ago, the Himalaya Mountains and the adjacent Tibetan plateau of southern Asia began to rise.
    Ⓐ similar
    Ⓑ nearby
    Ⓒ indigenous
    Ⓓ colonial

17. Because racial discrimination, high crime rates, and excessive land prices can make investors wary of committing to such projects, urban renewal often requires the help of the government.
    Ⓐ bellicose
    Ⓑ exhaust
    Ⓒ cautious
    Ⓓ severe

18. Some goods, like new bread, fresh cream and strawberries, must be consumed very soon after they are produced, and this restricts their sale to local markets.
    Ⓐ expand
    Ⓑ discovered
    Ⓒ supplied
    Ⓓ eaten up

19. Yet the Roman and the Chinese Empire had co-existed on the face of the same planet for two centuries with scarcely any direct intercourse, either it being political or economic.
    Ⓐ contend each other
    Ⓑ worked
    Ⓒ stand
    Ⓓ been concurrent

20. During the late Paleozoic Era, a great variety of amphibians inhabited the shores of lakes and rivers, dividing their lives between land and water.
    Ⓐ coasts   Ⓑ cliffs
    Ⓒ rivers   Ⓓ pools

DAY 17 Daily Checkup

01. wide gap between the two views
    - Ⓐ difference
    - Ⓑ understanding
    - Ⓒ surprise
    - Ⓓ precaution

02. feel nervous about new job
    - Ⓐ clear
    - Ⓑ comfortable
    - Ⓒ light
    - Ⓓ excitable

03. have a rough time
    - Ⓐ difficult
    - Ⓑ pleasant
    - Ⓒ unlawful
    - Ⓓ attentive

04. a dubious answer
    - Ⓐ unprejudiced
    - Ⓑ different
    - Ⓒ foresight
    - Ⓓ doubtful

05. in some odd corner
    - Ⓐ thrifty
    - Ⓑ miserly
    - Ⓒ unusual
    - Ⓓ alter

06. be overcome with grief
    - Ⓐ suitable
    - Ⓑ exotic
    - Ⓒ defeated
    - Ⓓ insane

07. held an impromptu concert
    - Ⓐ violent
    - Ⓑ cleaned
    - Ⓒ improvised
    - Ⓓ decorated

08. the harmony of colors
    - Ⓐ disorder
    - Ⓑ unbalance
    - Ⓒ concord
    - Ⓓ various

09. Students packed into the ground.
    - Ⓐ crowded
    - Ⓑ canned
    - Ⓒ wandered
    - Ⓓ scattered

10. The storm subsides.
    - Ⓐ stays
    - Ⓑ subdues
    - Ⓒ stimulates
    - Ⓓ provoke

11. puncture the bag with an ice pick
    - Ⓐ subside
    - Ⓑ pierce
    - Ⓒ combine
    - Ⓓ judge

12. confused by his capricious behavior
    - Ⓐ warrantable
    - Ⓑ sagacious
    - Ⓒ unpredictable
    - Ⓓ miserly

13. revise the schedule
    - Ⓐ change
    - Ⓑ excite
    - Ⓒ separate
    - Ⓓ connect

14. Some birds migrate to warmer countries in winter.
    - Ⓐ conform
    - Ⓑ reside
    - Ⓒ live
    - Ⓓ move

15. a benevolent feeling toward all their neighbors
    - Ⓐ gainful
    - Ⓑ kind
    - Ⓒ coarse
    - Ⓓ irregular

16. a stingy income
    - Ⓐ parsimonious
    - Ⓑ subsided
    - Ⓒ unpredictable
    - Ⓓ unearned

17. fuse the rhythms of jazz
    - Ⓐ combine
    - Ⓑ think
    - Ⓒ beat
    - Ⓓ surmount

18. green vegetables in season
    - Ⓐ a particular time of year
    - Ⓑ periodically
    - Ⓒ reside in
    - Ⓓ stand for

19. put to nurse
    - Ⓐ tend
    - Ⓑ study
    - Ⓒ course
    - Ⓓ rise

20. vigilant soldiers
    - Ⓐ unprejudiced
    - Ⓑ watchful
    - Ⓒ foot
    - Ⓓ artillery

DAY 17 Voca Bank

표제어	품사	동의어와 예문	한글 뜻
1 **adapt*** [ədǽpt]	v	suit, adjust, fit, modify, conform **adapt** oneself to the new life 새로운 삶에 적응하다	적응하다
2 **benevolent**** [bənévələnt]	a	kind, altruistic, benign **benevolent** neutrality 호의적 중립	호의적인
3 **capricious** [kəpríʃəs]	a	unpredictable, changeable, variable ↔ consistent, inflexible, firm behave **capriciously** 변덕을 부리다	변덕스러운
4 **crazy** [kréizi]	a	insane, lunatic, mad like a **crazy** (구어) 맹렬하게, 무지무지하게	제정신이 아닌, 미친
5 **dubious** [djú:biəs]	a	doubtful a **dubious** answer 모호한 답변	의심스러운
6 **dwell (in)**** [dwel]	v	reside (in), live, inhabit, stay, abide **dwell** at home 국내에 거주하다	거주하다
7 **fuse** [fju:z]	v	combine **fuse** the rhythms of jazz 재즈 리듬을 혼합하다	융합하다
8 **gap**** [gæp]	n	opening, a space, difference fill a **gap** of continental crust 대륙 지각의 틈을 채우다	사이, 틈, 차이, 간격
9 **harmony*** [háːrməni]	n	agreement, concord, unity the **harmony** of colors 색채의 조화	조화
10 **hectic*** [héktik]	a	frantic, chaotic, frenetic **hectic** fever (폐결핵 환자 등의) 소모열	열광적인, 격앙된
11 **illegal**** [ilí:gəl]	a	unlawful, illegitimate, illicit ↔ authorized **illegal** drug deals 불법 마약 거래	불법적인
12 **impromptu**** [imprámptju:]	a	improvised, unprepared held an **impromptu** concert 즉석 공연을 열다	즉석의
13 **in season**** [in síːzn]	n	a particular time of year outbreak of an insect **in season** of summer 여름 한철에 한 곤충의 출현	제철이 된, 특정한 때에
14 **intermittent*** [intərmítnt]	a	periodical, irregular, occasional, sporadic an **intermittent** spring 간헐천	간헐적인
15 **lucrative** [lúːkrətiv]	a	profitable, gainful, productive, fruitful a **lucrative** game of paid services on the smart phone 스마트폰상의 유료서비스 중에서 수익이 나는 게임	이익이 되는

16	**mean**** [miːn]	v	signify, imply, express, intend This **means** that the difference between winner and loser. 이것은 승자와 패자간의 차이를 의미한다.	의미하다, 의도하다, 나타내다
		a	unkind, cruel, heartless, aggressive, bad-tempered **mean** words spilled out by the mean guys 비열한 자식들이 내뱉은 비열한 말들	잔인한, 비열한
17	**melody** [mélədi]	n	tune, music a beautiful **melody** 아름다운 멜로디	선율, 멜로디
18	**migrate***** [máigreit]	v	move from one place to another, immigrate, emigrate, move People **migrate** to cities in search of job. 사람들은 직업을 찾기 위해 도시로 이동한다.	이주하다
19	**nervous** [nə́ːrvəs]	a	excitable, uneasy, neural **nervous** tension 신경성 긴장	신경성의, 흥분하기 쉬운
20	**nurse*** [nəːrs]	v	tend, attend **nurse** a bad cold by going to bed 잠으로써 독감을 고치려고 하다	치료하다, 돌보다, 보살피다
21	**odd*** [ad]	a	unusual, weird, bizarre, strange, queer ↔ ordinary in some **odd** corner 어떤 외진 곳에서	이상한, 기묘한
22	**overcome*** [òuvərkÁm]	v	conquer, defeat, surmount, subdue, crush We are **overcome** by numbers. 중과부적이다.	정복하다
23	**pack** [pæk]	n	package, bundle, parcel; band, gang, group carry the **pack** 짐을 나르다 a **pack** of wolves 늑대 무리	꾸러미, 보따리 / 무리
		v	load, stuff, store, stow, compress **pack** the backpack with warm clothes and the foods 따뜻한 옷과 식량으로 배낭을 꽉 채우다	꽉 채우다
24	**puncture** [pÁŋktʃər]	v	pierce, bore **puncture** a tire by an nail 못에 의해 타이어가 구멍 나다	구멍 내다, 뚫뚫다
25	**reform*** [rifɔ́ːrm]	v	rectify, correct, amend, ameliorate, mend, improve, repair **reform** the shape 모양을 수정하다	개정하다, 수정하다
26	**relief***** [rilíːf]	n	① deliverance, alleviation, help, assistance, aid send **relief** to the victims 희생자에게 구제 물자를 보내다	① 구제, 구원, 경감
			② ease, comfort a feeling of **relief** 편안한 느낌	② 편안함
27	**reshape** [riːʃeip]	v	change the character of, recreate, remake **reshape** the buildings and the roads after the end of war 전쟁이 끝난 후에 건물과 도로의 모습을 고치다	모습을 고치다, 새 형태를 만들다
28	**revise*** [riváiz]	v	change, modify, amend, alter, correct **revise** a manuscript 원고를 교정하다	교정하다, 수정하다

DAY 17

29	**rough*** [rʌf]	a	① coarse, uneven, irregular, rugged, violent, wild ↔ smooth a **rough** texture 거친 천 ② rude, harsh, impolite; stormy ↔ polite, calm **rough** manners 무례한 방법 **rough** weather 거친 날씨 ③ hard, difficult, tough ↔ easy a **rough** test 거친 시험	① 난폭한, 격렬한 ② 무례한 / 폭풍의 ③ 거친
30	**rouse** [rauz]	v	stir, excite, stimulate, awaken, provoke **rouse** up one's child 누구의 아이를 깨우다	깨우다, 눈뜨게 하다
31	**scour** [skauər]	v	search, beat, hunt He **scoured** the library for the book. 그는 책을 찾으려고 온 서고 안을 돌아다녔다.	바쁘게 찾아다니다
32	**seething** [síːðiŋ]	a	overflowing, furious, boiled **seething** with life 굴곡이 심한 삶	소용돌이치는, 들끓는
33	**sensation** [senséiʃən]	n	feeling, excitement, stimulation, agitation keen **sensation** 예리한 감각	감각, 대사건, 자극, 흥분
34	**split*** [split]	v	cleave, separate, share, divide, rend ↔ connect, join **split** a log 통나무를 자르다 **split** into a several group 여러 그룹으로 나누다	분리하다, 쪼개다
		n	crack, fissure, breach cause a **split** in the cabinet by corruption 부정부패로 내각이 분열되다	분열
35	**stingy** [stíndʒi]	a	parsimonious, miserly, mean, frugal, thrifty a **stingy** income 적은 수입	인색한
36	**subside*** [səbsáid]	v	die down, sink, submerge, dip, collapse, subdue **subside** the tumult while raining 비가 오는 동안에 소동이 가라앉다	가라앉다
37	**tenable** [ténəbl]	a	warrantable no longer **tenable** by a new facts 새로운 사실들로 더 이상 주장할 수 없는	주장할 수 있는
38	**vigilant** [vídʒələnt]	a	attentive, wary, alert, awake, watchful **vigilant** soldiers 불침번 병사	자지 않고 지키는, 방심하지 않는
39	**wise** [waiz]	a	judicious, sensible, sagacious, rational, sage ↔ ignorant a **wise** decision 현명한 결정	현명한, 이성적인
40	**wonder*** [wʌndər]	n	surprise, astonishment, amazement, awe for a **wonder** 이상하게도	놀라움, 기적
		v	think, ponder, meditate, speculate, marvel **wonder** about the natural events such as lightening 번개와 같은 자연현상에 대해 경탄하다	~이 아닐까 생각하다, 경탄하다

Practice Test 17

01. To survive, living things must adapt to long-term changes in the environment.
    - Ⓐ adjust
    - Ⓑ escape
    - Ⓒ run
    - Ⓓ be sensitive

02. From the often terrestrially biased perspective of people, marine organisms can seem odd.
    - Ⓐ trouble
    - Ⓑ disagree
    - Ⓒ strange
    - Ⓓ minority

03. After Alexander's death in 323 B.C., his empire was split into smaller kingdoms.
    - Ⓐ divide
    - Ⓑ emulate
    - Ⓒ haggle
    - Ⓓ impugn

04. Children's literature introduces the readers to the wonders of science and the beauty of art.
    - Ⓐ marvelous
    - Ⓑ curiosities
    - Ⓒ knowledge
    - Ⓓ information

05. During the 1700's, the Bourbon rulers of Spain carried out many government reforms.
    - Ⓐ unifications
    - Ⓑ creations
    - Ⓒ revivals
    - Ⓓ betterments

06. As Election Day approaches, the pace of the campaign becomes hectic.
    - Ⓐ loose
    - Ⓑ vigorous
    - Ⓒ frenetic
    - Ⓓ unenergetic

07. Magma (liquefied rock) rises from the asthenosphere, filling the gap between the separating plates.
    - Ⓐ debris
    - Ⓑ crevices
    - Ⓒ buildings
    - Ⓓ electric lines

08. Some mammals such as monkeys and elephants dwell in tropical regions.
    - Ⓐ reside in
    - Ⓑ feed on
    - Ⓒ rest
    - Ⓓ mature

09. In 1402, an intermittent war raged between Scotland and England.
    - Ⓐ steady
    - Ⓑ abundant
    - Ⓒ sporadic
    - Ⓓ daily

10. Africa had been an earlier source of slaves for the lucrative slave trade in the Americas.
    - Ⓐ profitable
    - Ⓑ safe
    - Ⓒ easy
    - Ⓓ extensive

11. Members of the Homo erectus eventually migrated from Africa to Asia and Europe.
    A felt death is near
    B obtained secured places
    C search for food and water
    D moved from one place to another

12. To make wise decisions, students must acquire full and accurate information about themselves and their world.
    A unaware
    B serious
    C sensible
    D light

13. Tremendous changes reshaped the economy following the Civil War.
    A challenged
    B criticized
    C interviewed
    D recreated

14. Even after a cell stops working, its electrolyte continues to eat away at the container and thus may puncture it.
    A fill
    B reshape
    C bore
    D construct

15. At first, rock music generally followed a 4/4 beat and used only two or three chords in its melody.
    A beat
    B piano
    C tune
    D opera

16. In Africa, the main cause of the decline in the number of elephants is illegal hunting.
    A all over
    B intrepid
    C illicit
    D valid

17. Rescue crews had scoured an area of 10 kilo meters.
    A searched
    B reflected
    C fluctuated
    D moved

18. Country music is often played by memory or by improvising an existing song.
    A spontaneously vary
    B not supported by fact
    C all out of proportion
    D tongue in cheek

19. In Hehe agriculture, beer is used as a means of paying the people who help with the annual hoeing of the ground.
    A wealth
    B mediums
    C systems
    D assistants

20. In his speech and writings after 1932, Churchill tried to rouse his nation's and the world's attention to the dangers of Nazi Germany.
    A strengthen
    B remove
    C prevent
    D awaken

DAY 18 Daily Checkup

01. adhere to neutrality
    - Ⓐ approve
    - Ⓑ watch
    - Ⓒ stick
    - Ⓓ determine

02. a lively discussion
    - Ⓐ active
    - Ⓑ ardent
    - Ⓒ dull
    - Ⓓ conspicuous

03. subscribe a contract
    - Ⓐ approve
    - Ⓑ help
    - Ⓒ incarcerate
    - Ⓓ consent

04. lose favor with a person
    - Ⓐ mariner
    - Ⓑ vigorousness
    - Ⓒ kindness
    - Ⓓ privilege

05. Sugar is ubiquitous in the food.
    - Ⓐ omnipresent
    - Ⓑ conspicuous
    - Ⓒ unvaried
    - Ⓓ prosaic

06. Catholic doctrines
    - Ⓐ imprints
    - Ⓑ abstinences
    - Ⓒ respects
    - Ⓓ principles

07. crude petroleum
    - Ⓐ unlawful
    - Ⓑ unfair
    - Ⓒ unrefined
    - Ⓓ real

08. gain knowledge
    - Ⓐ surround
    - Ⓑ secure
    - Ⓒ undergo
    - Ⓓ seize

09. It is economical to buy in large quantities.
    - Ⓐ suitable
    - Ⓑ stubborn
    - Ⓒ obstinate
    - Ⓓ frugal

10. the omnipresent God
    - Ⓐ positive
    - Ⓑ love
    - Ⓒ ubiquitous
    - Ⓓ forgiveness

11. disappeared trace
    - Ⓐ mark
    - Ⓑ vase
    - Ⓒ foot
    - Ⓓ finger

12. house commanding a fine view
    - Ⓐ supporting
    - Ⓑ superior
    - Ⓒ overlooking
    - Ⓓ pursuing

13. fix a poster to a wall
    - Ⓐ push
    - Ⓑ drive
    - Ⓒ attach
    - Ⓓ present

14. the privileges of birth
    - Ⓐ royal
    - Ⓑ lowness
    - Ⓒ prerogative
    - Ⓓ slave

15. an unlawful union
    - Ⓐ illicit
    - Ⓑ prosaic
    - Ⓒ widespread
    - Ⓓ respectable

16. ready to dare any danger
    - Ⓐ assent
    - Ⓑ maybe
    - Ⓒ prefer
    - Ⓓ venture

17. accuse him of being disloyal
    - Ⓐ unfaithful
    - Ⓑ heart
    - Ⓒ piracy
    - Ⓓ spoliation

18. seek a quarrel with
    - Ⓐ privilege
    - Ⓑ dispute
    - Ⓒ prerogative
    - Ⓓ monotonous

19. write an outstanding composition
    - Ⓐ unrefined
    - Ⓑ excellent
    - Ⓒ unfaithful
    - Ⓓ technical

20. a fervent follower of
    - Ⓐ unintelligent
    - Ⓑ ardent
    - Ⓒ abstruse
    - Ⓓ humble

DAY 18 Voca Bank

#	표제어	품사	동의어와 예문	한글 뜻
1	**adhere (to)**** [ædhíər]	v	stick, cling (to), cleave **adhere to** neutrality 중립을 지키다	달라붙다, 집착하다
2	**advantage***** [ædvǽntidʒ]	n	profit, benefit, behalf take **advantage** of 이용하다	이익
3	**affect** [əfékt]	v	influence, impress, stir; pretend, feign, assume Care **affects** the health. 근심 걱정은 건강을 해친다.	영향을 끼치다 / 가장하다
4	**alternate***** [ɔ́:ltərnèit]	v	interchange, change, take turn, occur successively **alternate** a flat tire with new one 바람 빠진 타이어를 새것으로 교체하다	교체하다
		a	every other, every second, rotating in a condition of **alternate** high and low temperature 고온과 저온이 번갈아 일어나는 조건에서	번갈아 하는
5	**assembly** [əsémbli]	n	gathering, group; congress, legislature, parliament set a moving **assembly** line in his factory 그의 공장에 이동식 조립라인을 설치하다	집회, 조립 / 국회, 의회
6	**bid** [bid]	v	command, order, direct Do as you are **bid**. 시키는 대로 해라.	명령하다, 지시하다
7	**bonanza** [bənǽnzə]	n	boom, jackpot, windfall, boon, good fortune a **bonanza** in hot summer during vacation season 휴가철 동안의 뜨거운 여름의 대성공	대성공, 노다지
8	**commanding** [kəmǽndiŋ]	a	forceful, superior **commanding** officer 사령관, 지휘관	당당한, 지휘하는 입장에 있는, (장소가) 전망이 좋은
9	**concentrate**** [kánsəntrèit]	v	① focus (on), intensify, think **Concentrate** on your homework. 숙제하는 데 집중하라.	① 집중하다
			② collect, gather, consolidate ↔ disperse, distribute **concentrate** the information in one place 한 곳에 정보를 모으다	② 모으다
			③ condense, reduce, contract ↔ dilute thin **Concentrate** the juice by removing the water. 물기를 없애서 주스를 농축하다.	③ 압축하다, 농축하다
10	**crude*** [kru:d]	a	roughly made, unrefined, unprocessed, coarse, raw **crude** pottery bowls and dishes 조잡한 물병과 그릇들	조잡한, 세련되지 못한
11	**dare** [dɛər]	v	venture, risk, challenge, defy ready to **dare** any danger 어떠한 위험도 감수할 준비가 되다	모험하다, 무릅쓰다

12	**diet*** [dáiət]	n	nutritional plan, abstinence a vegetable **diet** 채식	식단, 자제, 절제
13	**disloyal** [dislɔ́iəl]	a	unfaithful ↔ reliable accuse him of being **disloyal** 충성스럽지 못한 그를 비난하다	충성스럽지 못한
14	**doctrine** [dáktrin]	n	dogma, theory, principle, tenet Catholic **doctrines** 가톨릭 교리	교리, 원리, (집합적) 가르침
15	**economical***** [èkənámikəl]	a	saving, thrifty, frugal **economical** method to fight the cold night 추운 밤과 싸울 수 있는 경제적인 방법	경제적인, 절약하는
16	**favor*** [féivər]	n	kindness, benefit, help, good-will; regard, esteem, respect Will you do me a **favor**? 무엇을 도와드릴까요?	호의, 친절함 / 존경
		v	prefer, approve **favor** a proposal of project 프로젝트의 제안을 찬성하다	편들다, 찬성하다
17	**fervent*** [fə́:rvənt]	a	ardent, passionate, earnest, heated, zealous deliver a **fervent** speech 열변을 토하다	열렬한
18	**fix**** [fiks]	v	① fasten, attach, secure, determine, set, prepare **Fix** the picture to the wall. 벽에 그림을 고정시켜라.	① 고정시키다
			② restore, mend, repair, improve, heal, cure, remedy ↔ break, destroy Let's **fix** the car. 차를 고치자. The doctor will **fix** the broken bone. 의사가 부러진 뼈를 치료할 것이다.	② 고치다, 개선하다
19	**gain**** [gein]	v	secure, procure, earn, win, achieve, acquire, attain, obtain, profit **gain** understanding from the experience 경험으로 이해하다 **gain** knowledge 지식을 얻다 **gain** strength 강해지다	획득하다
20	**graze** [greiz]	v	feed (on), pasture, crop, range a cow **grazes** 소가 풀을 뜯어먹다	풀을 뜯어먹다
21	**halt** [hɔ:lt]	v	stop, cease, pause, terminate, quell ↔ proceed **halt** at the border 국경선 앞에서 멈추다 **halt** the abuse 남용을 막다 **halt** for lunch 점심을 먹으려고 멈추다	멈추다, 정지하다
22	**lively** [láivli]	a	busy, energetic, active, vigorous, brisk ↔ dull, sluggish a **lively** discussion 활발한 토론	생기 넘치는, 명랑한
23	**mariner** [mǽrənər]	n	sailor, seaman a master **mariner** 선장	선원
24	**monotonous*** [mənátənəs]	a	unvarying, tedious, dull, unvaried **monotonous** work 단조로운 일	단조로운, 지루한

25	**omnipresent***** [àmnipréznt]	a	ubiquitous, universal, widespread the **omnipresent** God 어디에나 존재하는 신	어디에나 있는
26	**outstanding***** [autstǽndiŋ]	a	① excellent, notable, prominent, distinguish an **outstanding** performance 눈에 띄는 연극 ② remarkable, noticeable, conspicuous, striking an **outstanding** student 뛰어난 학생 an **outstanding** debt 두드러진 인물	① 눈에 띄는 ② 현저한
27	**privilege*** [prívəlidʒ]	n	prerogative the **privilege** of equality 평등권	특권, 특전
28	**proliferation** [prəlìfəréiʃən]	n	expansion, increase, multiplication nuclear **proliferation** 핵 확산	증식, 급증, 확산
29	**pure**** [pjuər]	a	① clear, immaculate, unadulterated, spotless, clean ↔ polluted **pure** gold 순금 live a **pure** life 순결한 삶을 살다 ② innocent, guiltless, virtuous, chaste ↔ immoral, corrupt	① 순수한, 깨끗한 ② 결백한
30	**quarrel** [kwɔ́:rəl]	n	dispute, argument, controversy, fight make up a **quarrel** 화해하다, 사과하다	말다툼
31	**semblance** [sémbləns]	n	appearance, likeness, air, figure, mask in **semblance** 겉보기에는	외관
32	**sin** [sin]	n	violation, crime, transgression, trespass, offense commit a **sin** 죄악을 범하다	죄, 죄악, 잘못
33	**submit**** [səbmít]	v	yield, surrender, obey; present **submit** to the warrior 그 전사를 따르다 **Submit** your best photograph. 제일 잘 나온 사진을 제출하세요.	복종시키다 / 제출하다
34	**subscribe** [səbskráib]	v	agree, assent, consent **subscribe** a contract 계약서에 서명하다	서명하다, 찬성하다
35	**tedious**** [tí:diəs]	a	irksome, wearisome, tiresome, monotonous, boring a **tedious** speech 지루한 강연	지루한, 지겨운
36	**trace**** [treis]	n	very small, bit; residue, imprint, mark, trail, track, sign, footprint in **trace** quantities 미량으로 disappear **trace** 종적이 사라지다	소량 / 흔적, 자취
37	**ubiquitous**** [ju:bíkwətəs]	a	universal, widespread, omnipresent Sugar is **ubiquitous** in the food. 당분은 어떤 음식에나 있다.	어디에나 있는, 보편적인
38	**uncompromising**** [ʌnkámprəmàiziŋ]	a	unyielding, inflexible, rigid, firm, obstinate Naturalist have been the most **uncompromising** realists. 자연주의자들은 가장 비타협적인 현실주의자가 되었다.	양보하지 않은, 타협 없는
39	**unlawful** [ʌnlɔ́:fəl]	a	illegal, illicit, illegitimate **unlawful** entry 불법 침입	불법적인
40	**wretched** [rétʃid]	a	dejected, miserable, pitiable, distressed, pitiful a **wretched** poet 서투른 시인	비참한, 낙담한

Practice Test 18

01. Periods of low rainfall alternate with periods of high rainfall from year to year and from place to place.
    Ⓐ change
    Ⓑ linger
    Ⓒ continue
    Ⓓ maintain

02. The Proclamation of 1763 halted westward expansion for only a short time.
    Ⓐ intensified
    Ⓑ recessed
    Ⓒ stopped
    Ⓓ excited

03. Some scientists believe the core of Mars consists of pure iron sulfide, the compound of sulfur and iron.
    Ⓐ unrefined
    Ⓑ unadulterated
    Ⓒ unclear
    Ⓓ stable

04. During the late 1940's, engineers worked to improve the crude jet engines built during World War II.
    Ⓐ discarded
    Ⓑ misused
    Ⓒ destroyed
    Ⓓ roughly made

05. The prices obtainable in one part of the market affect the prices paid in other parts.
    Ⓐ concern
    Ⓑ respect
    Ⓒ fond
    Ⓓ relate to

06. Many social critics studied life in the slums and reported on the wretched living conditions there.
    Ⓐ convenient
    Ⓑ miserable
    Ⓒ happy
    Ⓓ humble

07. When two oppositely charged ions are in contact with each other, they are said to be bound by an ionic bond.
    Ⓐ trouble
    Ⓑ release
    Ⓒ touch
    Ⓓ rush

08. Republicans condemned the Democrats as disloyal to the Union during the Civil War.
    Ⓐ adherent
    Ⓑ unfaithful
    Ⓒ opposite
    Ⓓ dependent

09. Chemicals taken from some marine organisms are used in medicines to fight cancer and other diseases.
    Ⓐ plant-eating
    Ⓑ fur-covered
    Ⓒ sea-dwelling
    Ⓓ warm-blooded

10. Jefferson lost his bid for the presidency in 1796 but became Vice-President under President John Adams.
    Ⓐ election
    Ⓑ proposal
    Ⓒ achievement
    Ⓓ attempt

11. Cattle ranchers let their herds graze on the open range, so they needed just a few buildings and no fences.
    Ⓐ live
    Ⓑ play
    Ⓒ feed
    Ⓓ run

12. The hero of Don Quixote is a Spanish landowner who enlivens his monotonous life by reading old fictional tales about knights of the past, which he believes to be true and accurate.
    Ⓐ tedious
    Ⓑ complicated
    Ⓒ destitute
    Ⓓ luxurious

13. Assembling prototypes often reveals design problems that can be corrected to make the final assembly of the car more efficient.
    Ⓐ protest
    Ⓑ manufacture
    Ⓒ responsibility
    Ⓓ liability

14. Each religion has its own stories that can be used to convey its teachings and to illustrate a moral doctrine.
    Ⓐ paradox
    Ⓑ advice
    Ⓒ demeanor
    Ⓓ principle

15. Many scholars have concentrated on the study of Shakespeare's earlier texts in order to bring critics closer to what the playwright actually wrote.
    Ⓐ contracted
    Ⓑ absorbed
    Ⓒ converged
    Ⓓ focused

16. The great advantage of the alphabetic system is the relatively small number of symbols needed, which makes universal literacy possible.
    Ⓐ employment
    Ⓑ benefit
    Ⓒ art
    Ⓓ complex

17. In humans, as well as wildlife populations, infectious diseases emerge or become more prevalent as features of the landscape change in ways that favor the proliferation of disease-causing organisms.
    Ⓐ trauma
    Ⓑ saturation
    Ⓒ naive
    Ⓓ reproduction

18. The personal identification numbers (PIN's) that people use to gain access to Automated Teller Machines (ATM's) are an example of a numerical verification system.
    Ⓐ procure
    Ⓑ fund
    Ⓒ campaign
    Ⓓ oppose

19. Many scientists believe that energy from the earth, sun, wind, and ocean can be used more extensively to produce economical electric power in the future.
    Ⓐ very dear
    Ⓑ costly
    Ⓒ efficient
    Ⓓ successful

20. Today, computer techniques have replaced the tedious tasks of hand-inking, painting, and photographing.
    Ⓐ a curious   Ⓑ a tiresome
    Ⓒ a challenging   Ⓓ an overwhelming

DAY 19 Daily Checkup

01. a rural community
    - A urban
    - B foreign
    - C rustic
    - D new

02. artificial ice
    - A scattered
    - B impenetrable
    - C man-made
    - D dreadful

03. banish a person for treason
    - A promulgate
    - B expel
    - C deport
    - D exploit

04. an isolated district
    - A exiled
    - B nurtured
    - C commandeered
    - D separated

05. sequester oneself
    - A seclude
    - B settle
    - C set free
    - D strip

06. proclaim war
    - A provoke
    - B settle
    - C perform
    - D announce

07. outline a strategy
    - A sketch
    - B source
    - C origin
    - D fiction

08. the solar apex
    - A cargo
    - B top
    - C indignity
    - D likelihood

09. suffer an indignity
    - A insult
    - B shelter
    - C seclusion
    - D pioneer

10. the lap of a valley
    - A spot
    - B feat
    - C hollow
    - D accomplishment

11. blame something upon a person
    - A disapprove
    - B scorn
    - C nurture
    - D seclude

12. War is looming ahead.
    - A dashing
    - B approaching
    - C enlarging
    - D declaring

13. Their income is pitiful.
    - A incorrect
    - B plumb
    - C pathetic
    - D unreal

14. detect the smell of smoke
    - A scorn
    - B expel
    - C scatter
    - D discover

15. exploit the mineral deposits
    - A settle
    - B develop
    - C unaided
    - D postpone

16. bear afflictions with patience
    - A shield
    - B fiction
    - C outline
    - D endurance

17. inaccurate information
    - A appalling
    - B ensure
    - C erroneous
    - D unreal

18. terrible sufferings
    - A unbridled
    - B riotous
    - C awful
    - D conduct

19. put on a screen of indifference
    - A shield
    - B chasm
    - C trouble
    - D cargo

20. abhor all forms of violence
    - A declare
    - B hate
    - C sequester
    - D magnify

DAY 19 Voca Bank

표제어	품사	동의어와 예문	한글 뜻
1 **abhor*** [æbhɔ́:r]	v	hate, detest, loathe Nature **abhors** a vacuum. 자연은 아무것도 없는 것을 싫어한다.	증오하다, 싫어하다
2 **adjourn*** [ədʒə́:rn]	v	suspend, postpone, defer, delay **adjourn** the session 다음 회기까지 회의를 연기하다	연기하다
3 **amplify**** [ǽmpləfài]	v	enlarge, expand, magnify He **amplified** the matter by illustrations. 그는 예를 들며 그것을 부연설명했다.	확대하다, 자세히 진술하다
4 **announce*** [ənáuns]	v	proclaim, publish, declare **announce** the winner 승자를 알리다	발표하다, 공표하다
5 **apex** [éipeks]	n	summit, zenith, acme, climax, tip, top the **apex** of a triangle 삼각형의 정점	최고 정점, 정상
6 **artificial**** [à:rtəfíʃəl]	a	synthetic, manmade, unreal, counterfeit, fake ↔ genuine **artificial** daylight 인공 일광	인공의
7 **banish** [bǽniʃ]	v	expel, exile, deport **banish** a person for treason 누구를 반역죄로 추방하다	추방하다, 쫓아내다
8 **behave**** [bihéiv]	v	conduct The children didn't **behave**. 어린이들은 예의 바르게 행동하지 못했다.	행동하다, 예의 바르게 행동하다
9 **blame** [bleim]	v	reproach, censure, condemn, disapprove **blame** a dog 개를 나무라다	비난하다, 못마땅해하다
10 **detect**** [ditékt]	v	find, discover the presence of, uncover, spot, discern **detect** the battleship by radar 레이더로 전함을 감지하다	감지하다, 찾아내다
11 **dot** [dat]	v	scattered across Numerous stars are **dotting** beautifully in the sky. 수많은 별들이 하늘에 아름답게 흩어져 있다.	흩어져 있다, 산재하다
12 **drastically**** [drǽstikəli]	ad	severely, radically **drastically** reduced overnight 밤새 급격하게 떨어진	급격하게
13 **ensure** [inʃúər]	v	guarantee It will **ensure** your success. 그것으로 너의 성공은 확실하다.	안전하게 하다, 확실히 하다
14 **exploit** [ikspl3it]	n	feat, accomplishment acclaim for his last **exploit** 그의 마지막 공적에 대해서 찬사하다	성취, 공적
	v	utilize, take advantage of **exploit** a mine 광산을 개발하다	개발하다, 이용하다

15	**freight** [freit]	n	cargo, shipment, load **freight** free 운임 무료	화물
16	**inaccurate**** [inǽkjərit]	a	incorrect, erroneous ↔ correct an **inaccurate** account 부정확한 보고	부정확한
17	**indignity** [indígnəti]	n	humiliation, insult, scorn suffer an **indignity** 모욕을 견디다	모욕, 굴욕
18	**insoluble** [insáljubl]	a	inexplicable, baffling, impenetrable **insoluble** salts 불용성 염류	녹지 않은
19	**isolated**** [áisəlèitid]	a	remote, solitary, quarantine an **isolated** district 고립된 지방	격리시킨
20	**likelihood*** [láiklihùd]	n	predictability There is little **likelihood** of his returning today. 오늘 그가 돌아올 가능성은 거의 없다.	가능성
21	**loom*** [lu:m]	v	emerge, appear **loom** on the horizon 수평선에 어렴풋이 나타나다	어렴풋이 나타나다
22	**master** [mǽstər]	n	commander, chief, head a **master** at carpentry 목수의 장인	주인, 지배자, 대가, 거장
23	**naked** [néikid]	a	bare, unaided, nude, stripped a **naked** electric wire 벗긴 전선	벌거벗은
24	**nourish** [nə́:riʃ]	v	nurture, breed, feed **nourishes** their hopes 희망을 키우다	기르다
25	**outline**** [autlain]	n	contour, silhouette, sketch, draft, rough outline give an **outline** of ~의 개요를 말하다	윤곽, 약도
26	**patience** [péiʃəns]	n	endurance, tolerance, fortitude, perseverance Keep **patience**! 참으시오, 진정하시오!	인내, 참을성
27	**pitiful** [pítifəl]	a	pitiable, pathetic, piteous a **pitiful** story 가여운 이야기	가엾은
28	**proclaim** [proukléim]	v	announce, declare, promulgate **proclaim** war 선전포고하다	선언하다, 발표하다
29	**rural** [rúərəl]	a	rustic, country ↔ urban **rural** life 전원 생활	시골의, 지방의
30	**screen** [skri:n]	n	shelter, protect, veil, defense, cover, shield handle on the bathroom **screen** rattled 덜컹거리는 욕실 칸막이를 손보다	칸막이, 보호물
31	**sequester*** [sikwéstər]	v	seclude, isolate **sequester** himself from the world 세상으로부터 은둔하다	격리하다
32	**source*** [sɔ:rs]	n	origin, beginning a news **source** 뉴스의 출처	근원, 출처
33	**tale** [teil]	n	story, narrative, account, fiction a **tale** of a tub 터무니없는 이야기	이야기, 설화

34	**terrible**** [térəbl]	a	**dreadful, awful, frightful,** appalling, horrible **terrible** sufferings 혹독한 고난	무서운, 끔찍한
35	**trailblazer** [tréilbleizər]	n	pioneer, innovator a **trailblazer** in natural science 자연과학의 선구자	개척자, 선구자
36	**transact**** [trænsǽkt]	v	**settle, perform, manage, conduct,** execute **transact** business 사업 거래하다	집행하다, 처리하다
37	**trial** [tráiəl]	n	**affliction, suffering, distress,** sorrow, trouble the **trials** of job hunters 구직자의 시련	시련, 고난
38	**uncontrolled** [ʌnkəntróuld]	a	**unrestrained, rampant, unbridled,** riotous his **uncontrolled** behavior 그의 무절제한 행동	제한되지 않은
39	**valley** [vǽli]	n	**hollow, crater, chasm,** abyss the **valley** of despair 절망의 골짜기	골짜기, 단절, 틈
40	**vertical** [və́:rtikəl]	a	**upright, erect, perpendicular,** plumb ↔ horizontal out of the **vertical** 수직에서 벗어나	수직의, 정점의

Practice Test 19

01. A moderate, well-balanced diet can help ensure good health.
    - Ⓐ guarantee
    - Ⓑ prove
    - Ⓒ teach
    - Ⓓ assume

02. The blood vessels nourish both the dermis and the epidermis.
    - Ⓐ arrange
    - Ⓑ shelter
    - Ⓒ accept
    - Ⓓ provide for

03. The Homo erectus was probably the first human being to master the use of fire.
    - Ⓐ susceptible
    - Ⓑ owner
    - Ⓒ indebt
    - Ⓓ operate

04. Many hearing-impaired people depend on electronic hearing aids to amplify the sound waves.
    - Ⓐ lower
    - Ⓑ strengthen
    - Ⓒ weaken
    - Ⓓ alter

05. Probability is the mathematical study of the likelihood of events.
    - Ⓐ probability
    - Ⓑ fallibility
    - Ⓒ desirability
    - Ⓓ deniability

06. Among primates, only humans have an almost naked skin that comes in different colors.
    - Ⓐ perfect
    - Ⓑ beautiful
    - Ⓒ smooth
    - Ⓓ unprotected

07. Many nations are working to develop other sources of energy to reduce their dependence on fossil fuels.
    - Ⓐ materials
    - Ⓑ mouth
    - Ⓒ power
    - Ⓓ beginnings

08. In the Globalization Plan, Charlie Yoon outlined his ideas for international industrialization for insect markets.
    - Ⓐ created
    - Ⓑ excepted
    - Ⓒ delineated
    - Ⓓ enriched

09. Airplanes provide the world's fastest and practical mean of transporting passengers and freight.
    - Ⓐ machinery
    - Ⓑ shipment
    - Ⓒ crew
    - Ⓓ pilot

10. Monroe finally decided to follow Adams's advice and proclaimed the Monroe Doctrine.
    - Ⓐ generated
    - Ⓑ shouted
    - Ⓒ operated
    - Ⓓ declared

11. By studying myths, we can try to understand why people behave as they do.
    Ⓐ act reasonably
    Ⓑ build strongly
    Ⓒ work hard
    Ⓓ examine deeply

12. The president may only adjourn Congress if the two houses cannot agree on an adjournment date.
    Ⓐ suspend
    Ⓑ disapprove
    Ⓒ disband
    Ⓓ approve

13. Livestock ranches, orchards, vineyards, and truck gardens dot the beautiful valleys.
    Ⓐ reach
    Ⓑ scatter across
    Ⓒ approach
    Ⓓ bordered by

14. Another government spending crisis is looming in the United States.
    Ⓐ emerging
    Ⓑ weaving
    Ⓒ invigorating
    Ⓓ enervating

15. Many Americans thought Nixon had violated federal laws and wanted him brought to trial.
    Ⓐ office
    Ⓑ attempt
    Ⓒ hearing
    Ⓓ prison

16. Vertical lines, such as those of a tower or a tall tree, may convey a sense of dignity and grandeur.
    Ⓐ Inclined
    Ⓑ Horizontal
    Ⓒ Perpendicular
    Ⓓ Curved

17. In the 1970's, OPEC raised oil prices so drastically that its members were able to increase their national income while restricting oil production.
    Ⓐ virtually
    Ⓑ dramatically
    Ⓒ primarily
    Ⓓ conveniently

18. Indian legends included stories about the world before there were people, stories of the origin of people and tribes, and the tales of tribal heroes.
    Ⓐ stories
    Ⓑ statues
    Ⓒ songs
    Ⓓ speeches

19. A quorum is the minimum number of members who that are present for the organization to transact business.
    Ⓐ ruin
    Ⓑ catalyze
    Ⓒ form
    Ⓓ carry out

20. The nation could be completely uncontrolled in its dealings with other nations while it's own citizens are made into slaves.
    Ⓐ restrained
    Ⓑ unrestrained
    Ⓒ lawless
    Ⓓ strict

DAY 20 Daily Checkup

01. **expose** a plant to sunlight
    - Ⓐ disclose
    - Ⓑ embed
    - Ⓒ adhere
    - Ⓓ adapt

02. **restrain** one's temper
    - Ⓐ provoke
    - Ⓑ assemble
    - Ⓒ integrate
    - Ⓓ suppress

03. rayon, one of the first **synthetic** fabrics
    - Ⓐ betray
    - Ⓑ artificial
    - Ⓒ embed
    - Ⓓ immersed

04. interesting scientific **phenomenon**
    - Ⓐ era
    - Ⓑ scent
    - Ⓒ occurrence
    - Ⓓ disturbance

05. **cling to** the branch
    - Ⓐ immerse
    - Ⓑ regain
    - Ⓒ repress
    - Ⓓ stick to

06. a **contemptuous** look
    - Ⓐ scornful
    - Ⓑ suitable
    - Ⓒ sharp
    - Ⓓ suppressed

07. **expend** time and effort on an experiment
    - Ⓐ hybrid
    - Ⓑ retrieve
    - Ⓒ use
    - Ⓓ scour

08. the **resilient** bough of a young tree
    - Ⓐ suitable
    - Ⓑ elastic
    - Ⓒ keen
    - Ⓓ feeble

09. **proper** for the occasion
    - Ⓐ recover
    - Ⓑ resilient
    - Ⓒ suitable
    - Ⓓ reciprocal

10. **touchdown** point
    - Ⓐ landing
    - Ⓑ susceptible
    - Ⓒ penetrating
    - Ⓓ fragrance

11. an **extraordinary** general meeting
    - Ⓐ hybrid
    - Ⓑ outstanding
    - Ⓒ appropriate
    - Ⓓ submerged

12. **urban** living
    - Ⓐ city
    - Ⓑ inappropriate
    - Ⓒ humid
    - Ⓓ elastic

13. a memorable **epoch** in my life
    - Ⓐ microorganism
    - Ⓑ era
    - Ⓒ hybrid
    - Ⓓ odor

14. **rustic** cabins in the woods
    - Ⓐ submerged
    - Ⓑ hindered
    - Ⓒ unsophisticated
    - Ⓓ remarkable

15. diverse **aspects** of human life
    - Ⓐ facets
    - Ⓑ unconnected
    - Ⓒ advances
    - Ⓓ origins

16. **circumvent** the real issue
    - Ⓐ integrate
    - Ⓑ avoid
    - Ⓒ enter
    - Ⓓ describe incorrectly

17. **corroded** by moisture
    - Ⓐ introduced
    - Ⓑ retrieved
    - Ⓒ eroded
    - Ⓓ inhibited

18. the **germ** of a book
    - Ⓐ assembly
    - Ⓑ disturbance
    - Ⓒ addition
    - Ⓓ origin

19. a **hybrid** maize seed
    - Ⓐ exceptional
    - Ⓑ humid
    - Ⓒ crossbreed
    - Ⓓ bitter

20. These wines may taste rather hard and somewhat **acid**.
    - Ⓐ bitter
    - Ⓑ feeble
    - Ⓒ rare
    - Ⓓ inappropriate

20

	표제어	품사	동의어와 예문	한글 뜻
1	**acid*** [ǽsid]	a	sour, harsh, rough, austere, bitter, acrid, severe **acid**-flavored biscuit 신맛이 나는 비스킷	맛이 신, 신랄한
2	**arrange*** [əréindʒ]	v	put together, plan, array, dispose, organize, lay out **arrange** flowers 꽃꽂이 하다	배열하다
3	**aspect** [ǽspekt]	n	appearance, look, facet, countenance a mountain with a beautiful **aspect** 경관이 아름다운 산	외관, 측면, 경관
4	**blossom** [blásəm]	n	flower, bloom, full-bloom come into **blossom** 꽃피기 시작하다	꽃, 개화
5	**circumvent*** [sə̀:rkəmvént]	v	avoid, evade, bypass, elude, sidestep **circumvent** the issue by another question 또 다른 질문으로 문제를 회피하다	우회하다, 회피하다
6	**cling (to)**** [kliŋ]	v	hold fast to, stick (to), adhere, cleave, cohere Lint often **clings to** fabric. 보풀은 종종 천에 달라붙는다. **cling** together (물건이) 서로 들러붙다, 단결하다	달라붙다, 고수하다
7	**contemptuous** [kəntémptʃuəs]	a	scornful, sneering a **contemptuous** air 업신여기는 태도	경멸하는, 비웃는
8	**corrode*** [kəróud]	v	wear away, eat away, erode, scour **corrode** the metal pipe 금속 파이프를 부식시키다	부식하다
9	**dawn** [dɔ:n]	n	daybreak, beginning before **drawn** 날이 새기(동이 트기) 전에	새벽, 여명
10	**deter*** [ditə́:r]	v	inhibit, prevent, stop, hinder, discourage The fear of punishment **deters** many people from crime. 벌받는 무서움이 많은 사람들로 하여금 범죄를 단념시킨다.	단념시키다
11	**epoch** [épək]	n	period of history, era make an **epoch** 하나의 신기원을 이루다	신기원, 새로운 시대
12	**expend*** [ikspénd]	v	use, consume, spend, exhaust **expend** my time 내 시간을 쓰다	소비하다, 쓰다
13	**expose*** [ikspóuz]	v	uncover, bare, disclose, reveal, display **expose** the wound to the air 공기 중에 상처를 노출하다 **expose** the truth 진실을 폭로하다	노출하다, 드러내다
14	**extraordinary**** [ikstrɔ́:rdənèri]	a	① exceptional, noteworthy, important recognized for one's **extraordinary** talent 누구의 비상한 재능을 발견하다 ② remarkable, outstanding; inordinate, unusual, rare an **extraordinary** event 예외적인 사건 the **extraordinary** beauty of nature 자연의 독특한 아름다움 **extraordinary** deeds 이상한 행동	① 비상한, 중요한 ② 예외적인 / 중요한

15	**flavoring** [fléivəriŋ]	a	**distinctive, seasoning** cook with **flavoring** called saffron 풍미를 더해주는 샤프란과 함께 요리하다	풍미있는, 맛내는
16	**germ** [dʒə:rm]	n	**microorganism, microbe,** bacterium; embryo, origin **germ** warfare 세균전	미생물 / 근원
17	**hybrid** [háibrid]	a	**crossbreed, amalgam,** composite a **hybrid** animal 잡종동물	혼합의, 잡종의
18	**increment** [ínkrəmənt]	n	**increase, accrual, addition,** advancement unearned **increment** (땅값 등의) 자연증가 (불노증가)	증식, 증가
19	**insert** [insə́:rt]	v	**put,** enter, embed, introduce **insert** an advertisement in ~에 광고를 내다	넣다
20	**irrelevant**** [iréləvənt]	a	**unconnected, inappropriate,** beside the point an **irrelevant** remark 딴 말	관련 없는
21	**misrepresent** [mìsreprizént]	v	**describe incorrectly** **misrepresent** the condition of the fruit trees 과실수의 상태를 잘못 전하다	잘못 전하다
22	**moist*** [mɔist]	a	**damp, humid, wet** a **moist** atmosphere 축축한 공기	축축한, 습기 있는
23	**notwithstanding*** [nɑ̀twiðstǽndiŋ]	prep	**nevertheless** **notwithstanding** his disapproval 그의 불찬성에도 불구하고	그럼에도 불구하고
24	**odor*** [óudər]	n	**smell, fragrance, scent, perfume** A regular bath or shower keeps the body free from dirt and **odor**. 규칙적인 목욕이나 샤워는 몸에서 더러움이나 악취가 없도록 유지시켜준다.	냄새, 악취
25	**phenomenon*** [finάmənὰn]	n	**occurrence** a meteoric **phnomenon** 대기 현상	현상
26	**plunge**** [plʌndʒ]	v	**immerse, submerge, dip** be **plunged** into despair 절망에 빠지다	빠지게 하다, 가라앉히다
27	**prestige** [prestí:ʒ]	n	**reputation, influence,** distinction national **prestige** 국위	명성, 평판
		a	**luxury, extravagant** a **prestige** car as Equus 에쿠스 같은 고급차	사치품의, 고급의
28	**proper**** [prάpər]	a	**appropriate, fit, suitable,** suited, adapted, correct, right the **proper** clothes 적당한 옷 the **proper** thing to do 적당한 일	적당한, 적합한
29	**recover*** [rikʌ́vər]	v	**regain, reclaim, retrieve,** restore **recover** one's weight 원래의 체중을 되찾다	되찾다, 회복하다
30	**relative to*** [rélətiv tu]	prep	**with respect to, with regard to,** concerning question **relative to** the deficit 적자와 관계 있는 질문을 하다	~와 관계 있는, 비례하는
31	**resilient** [rizíljənt]	a	**rebounding, elastic** the **resilient** bough of a young tree 어린 나무의 탄력 있는 가지	탄력성 있는, 되튀는

DAY 20

32	**restrain**** [ristréin]	v	suppress, repress, restrict, check, curb **restrain** a person of his liberty ~의 자유를 빼앗다, 제한하다	억제하다, 제지하다
33	**riot*** [ráiət]	n	uproar, disturbance, tumult, revolt run **riot** 방탕하다	폭동, 소동
34	**rustic** [rʌstik]	a	rural, awkward **rustic** simplicity 꾸밈없이 소박함	시골의, 서투른, 미숙한
35	**shrewd*** [ʃruːd]	a	clever, astute, sharp, acute, keen, penetrating a **shrewd** guess 예리한 추측	빈틈없는, 날카로운
36	**skyrocket*** [skairakit]	v	increase rapidly **skyrocket** living costs 생활 물가가 천정부지로 올라가다	갑자기 날아오르다, 급등시키다
37	**synthesize*** [sínθəsàiz]	v	integrate, assemble Chemists **synthesize** many thousands of new compounds each year. 화학자들은 매년 수천 종류의 새로운 화합물을 합성한다.	합성하다, 통합하다
38	**touchdown** [tʌtʃdaun]	n	landing **touchdown** speed 접지 속도	접지, 착지
39	**urban** [ə́ːrbən]	a	civic, city, municipal **urban** living 도시생활	도시의
40	**vulnerable to***** [vʌlnərəbl tu]	a	susceptible to, weak, feeble **vulnerable to** the disease 병에 걸리기 쉬운	상처 입기 쉬운, 병에 걸리기 쉬운

Practice

01. Legends usually relate to some aspect of history of a culture.
    - Ⓐ incident
    - Ⓑ perspective
    - Ⓒ occurrence
    - Ⓓ invention

02. When a moist lichen absorbs sunlight, the algal part produces sugar through photosynthesis.
    - Ⓐ appetizing
    - Ⓑ nutritious
    - Ⓒ damp
    - Ⓓ chewed

03. Even with protection, some species may not be able to recover.
    - Ⓐ replenish
    - Ⓑ refinish
    - Ⓒ dissolve
    - Ⓓ retrieve

04. Alloys are often easier to create than new synthetic polymers.
    - Ⓐ financed
    - Ⓑ publicized
    - Ⓒ artificial
    - Ⓓ disproved

05. In Italy, economic distress after World War I led to strikes and riots.
    - Ⓐ tumult
    - Ⓑ wrath
    - Ⓒ felon
    - Ⓓ thrifty

06. An Era is divided into periods, and a period is divided into epochs.
    - Ⓐ episodes
    - Ⓑ days
    - Ⓒ migrations
    - Ⓓ stories

07. Germs that cause diseases attack a tired person more easily than a rested one.
    - Ⓐ Medicines
    - Ⓑ Injections
    - Ⓒ Microorganisms
    - Ⓓ Materials

08. Queen Victoria inherited a throne that had already lost its power, dignity, and prestige.
    - Ⓐ initiative
    - Ⓑ reputation
    - Ⓒ capability
    - Ⓓ advantage

09. Muslims may not eat or drink between dawn and sunset during Ramadan, the ninth month of the Islamic year.
    - Ⓐ daybreak
    - Ⓑ continuation
    - Ⓒ expansion
    - Ⓓ outcome

10. Novelists can arrange incidents, describe places, and represent characters in an almost limitless variety of ways.
    - Ⓐ study
    - Ⓑ organize
    - Ⓒ imagine
    - Ⓓ explain

11. Washington brought extraordinary courage, prestige, and wisdom to the U.S. presidency.
    A exciting
    B outstanding
    C natural
    D abstract

12. Interpretations of economic and social life are often based on ideas which are irrelevant to the actual facts.
    A important
    B good
    C trivial
    D profound

13. Every spring, blue and white violets blossom along the river valleys and in the lower portions of the upland regions.
    A wilt
    B perish
    C grow
    D flower

14. In traditional photography, light is exposed to the image sensor in the camera, recording the image to the data.
    A damaged
    B changed
    C transferred
    D displayed

15. In his score, Gershwin captured the flavor of the songs sung by black people from Southeastern America.
    A aura
    B season
    C development
    D odor

16. Adolescence has always existed as a biological phenomenon in human development.
    A distinction
    B evolution
    C happening
    D history

17. Chemotherapy may dramatically decrease the number of white blood cells, leaving the patient vulnerable to infection.
    A healthy
    B susceptible
    C powerful
    D durable

18. The popularity of videocassette recorders skyrocketed in many industrial countries during the 1980's.
    A invariably continued
    B steeply inclined
    C susceptibly changed
    D increased rapidly

19. During the 1970's and 1980's, urban settlement and the location of industries along Chesapeake Bay caused pollution and some damage to plants and wildlife.
    A metropolitan
    B foreign
    C rural
    D suburb

20. If floor coverings are to be used, a person must choose between carpets, area rugs, and hard coverings, also known as resilient floors.
    A hard
    B timber
    C elastic
    D slate-tiled

16-20

01. undertake an experiment
    - Ⓐ wander
    - Ⓑ retire
    - Ⓒ exceed
    - Ⓓ take on

02. an unbiased opinion
    - Ⓐ reflected
    - Ⓑ impartial
    - Ⓒ cut
    - Ⓓ interested

03. rouse the crowd
    - Ⓐ stir
    - Ⓑ move
    - Ⓒ exhaust
    - Ⓓ compress

04. a tedious speech
    - Ⓐ extemporarily
    - Ⓑ wearisome
    - Ⓒ passionate
    - Ⓓ fluent

05. Day alternates with night.
    - Ⓐ obeys
    - Ⓑ is compared
    - Ⓒ exchanges
    - Ⓓ fluctuates

06. the blossoms of plants, shrubs and trees
    - Ⓐ blooms
    - Ⓑ looks
    - Ⓒ increase
    - Ⓓ scents

07. Boston and its adjacent suburbs
    - Ⓐ near
    - Ⓑ primary
    - Ⓒ suitable
    - Ⓓ short

08. be wary of explicit statements
    - Ⓐ fair
    - Ⓑ disparate
    - Ⓒ conventional
    - Ⓓ careful

09. establish a lucrative business
    - Ⓐ horrible
    - Ⓑ productive
    - Ⓒ sound
    - Ⓓ reliable

10. an intermittent pulse
    - Ⓐ electronic
    - Ⓑ heart
    - Ⓒ periodic
    - Ⓓ weird

11. vertical motion
    - Ⓐ upright
    - Ⓑ awful
    - Ⓒ scattered
    - Ⓓ disapproved

12. a prestige car as Rolls Loyce
    - Ⓐ corroding
    - Ⓑ reputation
    - Ⓒ elastic
    - Ⓓ luxury

13. Population tends to concentrate in large cities.
    - Ⓐ venture
    - Ⓑ gather
    - Ⓒ interchange
    - Ⓓ order

14. Milk nourishes a baby.
    - Ⓐ feeds
    - Ⓑ condemns
    - Ⓒ secludes
    - Ⓓ frights

15. ensure one's success
    - Ⓐ abhor
    - Ⓑ hate
    - Ⓒ guarantee
    - Ⓓ amplify

16. a fortress vulnerable to attacks from the sky
    - Ⓐ keen
    - Ⓑ suppressing
    - Ⓒ austere
    - Ⓓ weak

17. in all likelihood
    - Ⓐ patience
    - Ⓑ source
    - Ⓒ tale
    - Ⓓ predictability

18. adjourn a meeting
    - Ⓐ loathe
    - Ⓑ enlarge
    - Ⓒ suspend
    - Ⓓ announce

19. eliminate all irrelevant details
    - Ⓐ unconnected
    - Ⓑ astute
    - Ⓒ suitable
    - Ⓓ appropriate

20. skyrocketing living ccsts
    - Ⓐ increasing rapidly
    - Ⓑ misrepresenting
    - Ⓒ resilient
    - Ⓓ assembling rapidly

Practice Test 16-20

01. Beef cattle graze in the valley pastures.
    A scratch
    B feed
    C look
    D live

02. Sulfur has no taste or odor.
    A scent
    B tint
    C shape
    D size

03. Many unemployed workers blamed their troubles on Chinese laborers, who were willing to work for low wages.
    A appraised
    B increased
    C accused
    D dwindled

04. Advanced air forces use radar stations and satellites to detect surprise attacks by enemy bombers or missiles.
    A reveal
    B identify
    C unearth
    D disclose

05. The court has interpreted the word regulate to mean encourage, promote, protect, prohibit, or restrain.
    A withdraw
    B refuse
    C absolve
    D restrict

06. From the terrestrially biased perspective of people, marine organisms may seem odd.
    A various
    B bizarre
    C ordinary
    D working

07. Adults should consume about 23/10 quarts (2.4 liters) of water daily in the form of a beverage or water in food.
    A supply
    B catch
    C breed
    D eat

08. If the catastrophe had been severe and widespread enough, plant-eating dinosaurs would have starved to death.
    A disaster
    B event
    C phenomenon
    D explosion

09. The skeleton of all adult mammals consists of more than 200 bones, where some of these bones are fused to form a single structure.
    A added
    B united
    C coagulated
    D congregated

10. Burns should be cooled immediately by flushing the burned area with cool water or by applying cool, wet towels until the pain subsides or until professional help arrives.
    A abates
    B succeed
    C proceed
    D be dislodged

11. Whale milk is highly concentrated and much richer in fat, protein, and minerals than the milk of land mammals.
    A) engrossed
    B) condensed
    C) contracted
    D) absorbed

12. By practicing to relax, people can avoid becoming tense and nervous.
    A) cumbersome
    B) massive
    C) spruce
    D) apprehensive

13. Like all other mammals, mother whales nurse their young and are highly protective of their babies so they stay close to them for at least a year.
    A) care for
    B) protest
    C) monitor
    D) disdain

14. Neutron stars are the densest material objects known to mankind, packing slightly more than the mass of sun inside a ball just 20 kilometers in diameter.
    A) emitting
    B) expanding
    C) absorbing
    D) compressing

15. Most national parks are preserved to maintain their outstanding beauty and the scientific importance of their natural features.
    A) advanced
    B) visited
    C) protected
    D) utilized

16. The transition from a reptile to a mammal is so gradual that it is impossible to fix a point when reptiles became mammals.
    A) determine
    B) repair
    C) place
    D) connect

17. Most people of the Marginal Regions went about naked or wore only brief skin garments, even in the cold areas.
    A) inhabited
    B) concealed
    C) bare
    D) equipped

18. Solitary predators generally stalk their prey by slinking and hiding, while many of these hunters have coats that blend with their surroundings.
    A) mix
    B) dissolve
    C) transfer
    D) reduce

19. In ancient Egypt, merchants hired criers to walk through the streets and announce the arrival of ships and cargo.
    A) spread
    B) report
    C) follow
    D) heed

20. Between the years of 1347 to 1352, a terrible plague epidemic, now known as the Black Death, killed about a fourth of Europe's population.
    A) vast
    B) careful
    C) desperate
    D) practical

Intensive Practice

01. Animals live on impulse, and are happy as long as external conditions are favorable.
    A) escapable
    B) preferential
    C) pleasing
    D) exceptional

02. Buddhist mystics may meditate for hours or even days without moving.
    A) intervene
    B) plan
    C) contemplate
    D) conciliate

03. The unfinished Executive Mansion stood in isolated splendor amid a dismal, swampy landscape.
    A) near
    B) grumpy
    C) feeble
    D) secluded

04. If an individual's conduct threatened the safety or harmony of a group, that person was banished.
    A) disapproved of
    B) exiled
    C) silenced
    D) restrained

05. Water molecules cling together so tightly that water can support objects that are much heavier than itself.
    A) adhere
    B) fuse
    C) separate
    D) strike

06. The PH scale is used to measure the degree of acidity or alkalinity.
    A) study
    B) discern
    C) handle
    D) assess

07. Witnesses generally give their testimony in response to questions asked by an attorney.
    A) advice
    B) perjury
    C) evidence
    D) requisition

08. Many workers are not reluctant to move to a different country, or even to a different part of their own country, to receive a higher wage.
    A) obdurate
    B) unwilling
    C) negligent
    D) palpable

09. Iron and steel corrode easily when exposed to the atmosphere.
    A) vanish
    B) mold
    C) wear away
    D) bend

10. In cases that have received a lot of publicity, the jurors may be sequestered from other people, including their families, throughout the trial.
    A) isolated
    B) leaved
    C) ostracized
    D) forced

11. Lipids are fatty or oily substances that are insoluble in water.
    A accountable
    B unpaid
    C does not dissolve in a liquid
    D reimburse

12. The force of an earthquake depends upon how much rock is broken and how far it shifts.
    A transforms
    B burnings
    C deteriorates
    D moves

13. Errors were introduced as when copies were made, so that the content of the works were often inaccurately summarized.
    A thoughtfully
    B appropriately
    C strictly
    D incorrectly

14. In many cases, chemotherapy may dramatically decrease the number of white blood cells, leaving the patient vulnerable to infection.
    A conceivable
    B susceptible
    C deceivable
    D protectable

15. Cold air is denser than warm air, so that cold air advances by moving under and pushing up the retreating warm air.
    A standstills
    B forward movements
    C withdrawals
    D rises

16. The Mexican government neglected its northern territories, and many Mexicans living in California resented the interference from the government officials of Mexico City.
    A dispersed
    B diminished
    C considered
    D disregarded

17. As one of the most prominent mammals of the pleistocene period, the elephant-like mammoth, roamed the frozen plains of the Northern Hemisphere.
    A hunted
    B detected
    C traveled
    D settled

18. The Social Security Act provided pensions for the elderly and insurance for the unemployed.
    A villas
    B annuities
    C pressures
    D safeguards

19. Two of the most outstanding characteristics of a human being are its large brain and its ability to walk upright.
    A pending
    B indecent
    C uncertain
    D extraordinary

20. Autoradiography is very useful when localizing specific classes of molecules as well as for tracing their movements through the cell.
    A encouraging
    B connecting
    C seeking
    D restricting

Related Words 16-20

의류	- attire, clothing, apparel, custom, garment
인내	- patience, endurance, tolerance, fortitude, perseverance
모욕	- indignity, humiliation, insult, scorn
구제, 구원	- relief, deliverance, alleviation, help, assistance, aid
대성공	- bonanza, boom, jackpot, windfall, boon, good fortune
측정	- measure, means, indication, gauge, rule, extent, dimension
미생물	- microorganism, germs, microbe, bacterium
철회하다	- withdraw, quit, retire, retreat, secede
모험하다	- venture, dare, risk, challenge, defy
우회하다	- circumvent, avoid, evade, bypass, elude, sidestep
빠지게 하다	- plunge, immerge, submerge, dip
호의적인	- benevolent, kind, altruistic, benign
순수한	- pure, clear, immaculate, unadulterated, spotless, clean
지루한	- tedious, irksome, wearisome, tiresome, monotonous, boring
비참한	- wretched, dejected, miserable, pitiable, distressed, pitiful
녹지 않는	- insoluble, inexplicable, baffling, impenetrable
수직의	- vertical, perpendicular, erect, upright, plumb
관련 없는	- irrelevant, unconnected, inappropriate, beside the point
상처 입기 쉬운	- vulnerable to, susceptible to, weak, feeble
탄성 있는	- resilient, rebounding, elastic

Knowledge based Vocabulary 16-20

EMILY ELIZABETH DICKINSON

Emily Elizabeth Dickinson (1830 – 1886) was an American poet, born in ❶ rural Amherst, Massachusetts. Emily Dickinson lived a mostly introverted and ❷ reclusive life in the household of her parents. Because she became known for her penchant for white clothing and her ❸ reluctance to greet guests or, later in life, even leave her room, she was thought as an ❹ eccentric by the locals. Most of her friendships were therefore carried out by correspondence.

Dickinson was a ❺ prolific private poet, fewer than a dozen of her nearly eighteen hundred poems were published during her lifetime. The work that was published during her lifetime was usually altered significantly by the publishers to fit the conventional poetic rules of the time. Dickinson's poems are unique for the era in which she wrote; they contain short lines, typically lack titles, and often use slant rhyme as well as ❻ unconventional capitalization and punctuation. Many of her poems deal with themes of death and ❼ immortality, two recurring topics in letters to her friends.

Although most of her acquaintances were probably aware of Dickinson's writing, it was not until after her death in 1886—when Lavinia, Dickinson's younger sister, discovered her cache of poems—that the ❽ breadth of Dickinson's work became apparent. Her first collection of poetry was published in 1890 by personal acquaintances Thomas Wentworth Higginson and Mabel Loomis Todd, both of whom heavily edited the content. A complete and mostly ❾ unaltered collection of her poetry became available for the first time in 1955 when The Poems of Emily Dickinson was published by scholar Thomas H. Johnson. Despite some ❿ unfavorable reviews and some skepticism during the late 19th and early 20th century as to Dickinson's literary prowess, she is now almost universally considered to be one of the most important American poets.

What is closest meaning to left word?

1. rural	Ⓐ urban	Ⓑ rustic	Ⓒ boisterous	Ⓓ roar
2. reclusive	Ⓐ sociable	Ⓑ elusive	Ⓒ monotonous	Ⓓ secluded
3. reluctance	Ⓐ unwillingness	Ⓑ voluntariness	Ⓒ obedience	Ⓓ resistance
4. eccentric	Ⓐ introverted	Ⓑ normal	Ⓒ outlandish	Ⓓ natural
5. prolific	Ⓐ expanding	Ⓑ peculiar	Ⓒ fruitful	Ⓓ unproductive
6. unconventional	Ⓐ atypical	Ⓑ regular	Ⓒ uncomfortable	Ⓓ uneasy
7. immortality	Ⓐ ethics	Ⓑ perpetuity	Ⓒ afterlife	Ⓓ honesty
8. breadth	Ⓐ span	Ⓑ generosity	Ⓒ amplitude	Ⓓ latitude
9. unaltered	Ⓐ unconfirmed	Ⓑ unrestricted	Ⓒ undercover	Ⓓ unchanged
10. unfavorable	Ⓐ warm	Ⓑ hostile	Ⓒ amicable	Ⓓ acclaimable

에밀리 엘리자베스 디킨슨

에밀리 엘리자베스 디킨슨(1830-1886)은 매사추세츠 엠허스트의 시골에서 태어난 미국의 시인이었다. 에밀리 디킨슨은 부모의 집에서 내성적이고^{mostly introverted} 은둔한 삶^{reclusive life}을 살았다. 그녀가 흰 옷을 매우 좋아했고^{her penchant for white clothing}, 손님을 맞이하는 것을 꺼려하거나^{her reluctance to greet guests}, 심지어 말년에는 방에서 나가는 것도 꺼린 것으로 알려졌기 때문에^{became known for} 그녀는 그 지역 사람들에게 별난 사람으로 여겨졌다^{thought as an eccentric by the locals}. 따라서 대부분의 그녀의 교우 관계는 서신왕래에 의해 이루어졌다^{carried out by correspondence}.

디킨슨은 일생 동안 거의 1800개의 시 중에서 12개 미만^{fewer than a dozen of her nearly eighteen hundred poems}을 출간했던, 다작의 비밀스런 시인^{a prolific private poet}이었다. 일생 동안 출판되었던 그 작품들도 대부분 그 당시의 보편적인 시의 규칙에 맞도록^{to fit the conventional poetic rules of the time} 출판업자가 상당히 바꾸었다^{altered significantly by the publishers}. 디킨슨의 시는 그녀가 썼던 그 시기에는 유일무이한 것이었는데,^{are unique for the era in which she wrote} 짧은 행을 포함하고, 으레 제목이 없고 종종 불완전한 운(韻)과 게다가 판에 박히지 않은 대문자와 구두점^{unconventional capitalization and punctuation}을 사용하였다. 많은 그녀의 시들은 그녀의 친구들에게 보낸 편지에서 반복되는 두 개의 주제인^{two recurring topics in letters} 죽음과 영원한 삶을 다루었다^{deal with themes of death and immortality}.

비록 그녀의 지인들 대부분은 아마 디킨슨의 작품을 알고 있었지만^{were probably aware of Dickinson's writing} 1886년에 그녀가 죽은 후 디킨슨의 여동생인 라비니아가 그녀 시의 저장고를 발견하고 나서야^{discovered her cache of poems} 비로소 디킨슨 작품의 폭넓음이 명백해졌다^{the breadth of Dickinson's work became apparent}. 그녀의 첫 번째 시집^{collection of poetry}은 개인적 안면 있는 두 사람인^{both of whom heavily edited the content} 토마스 웬트워스 히긴슨과 메이블 루미스 토드에 의해 1890년 출간되었는데, 두 사람 모두 내용을 심하게 편집했다^{both of whom heavily edited the content}. 완전하고 대부분이 고쳐지지 않은 그녀의 시집^{a complete and mostly unaltered collection of her poetry}인 The Poems of Emily Dickinson은 학자인 토마스 H. 존슨이 출간했을 때인 1955년에 처음으로 가능하게 되었다. 디킨슨의 문학적 훌륭함에 대해서^{as to Dickinson's literary prowess} 19세기 말과 20세기 초 동안에 일부 비판적인 평론과 어떤 회의론이 있었음에도^{despite some unfavorable reviews and some skepticism} 그녀는 가장 중요한 미국 시인 중 한 사람으로 지금은 거의 보편적으로 여겨지고 있다^{now almost universally considered to be}.

1. Ⓑ   2. Ⓓ   3. Ⓐ   4. Ⓒ   5. Ⓒ
6. Ⓐ   7. Ⓑ   8. Ⓒ   9. Ⓓ   10. Ⓑ

TOEFL iBT [Step-up] 2
정답 · 해설

TOEFL DAY 01

Daily Checkup 01

1. ⓓ	2. ⓑ	3. ⓓ	4. ⓑ	5. ⓒ
6. ⓐ	7. ⓓ	8. ⓑ	9. ⓒ	10. ⓒ
11. ⓐ	12. ⓑ	13. ⓓ	14. ⓑ	15. ⓒ
16. ⓓ	17. ⓐ	18. ⓐ	19. ⓐ	20. ⓓ

1. ~로부터 훈계를 받다
2. 교재의 핵심
3. 여행을 연장하기로 결정하다
4. 개인 사건을 변호하다
5. 명쾌한 설명

6. 쇠락의 징후를 보이다 / 말기적인 현상을 보이다
7. 집을 가게로 변경하다
8. 손가락 끝 부분끼리 가볍게 두드리다
9. 아주 진기하고 이국적인 새
10. 점차 나아지다

11. 매우 믿을 수 있는 정비공
12. 낙담하여
13. 난공불락의 요새
14. 학교 입학용 지원서
15. 소년을 전학시키다

16. 거대한 돌덩이
17. 무언가 벽에 긁어 대는 것이 있다.
18. 방안의 공기에 퍼지다
19. 비난을 받다 / 혼나다
20. 변하지 않는 관습

6. 대부분의 종교는 구원이 한 번만 오고 그것이 영원하다고 가르친다. (salvation 구원)
7. 천문관은 대중을 위하여 천문학자를 고용하여 강의하고 수업을 지도한다. (planetarium 천문관)
8. 아담스는 미국이 중립을 지키도록 결정하였고 해밀턴과 그의 추종자의 정책을 통탄했다.
9. 노새는 암말 및 수컷 나귀의 붙임이 된 새끼이다.
10. 바람에 날린 모래입자는 바위 표면을 문질러대고 닳아 없앤다.

11. 이슬람교에서는 사람들이 오직 신만을 숭배하고, 신의 계명을 가르치고, 미래를 예언하지 않도록 신이 예언자를 선택한다고 생각한다.
12. 1910년에 헐리우드는 세계 영화의 중심이 되었다.
13. 리히터 스케일에서는 지진 규모에 있어 각 숫자의 증가는 지진의 에너지 방출이 대략 32배 더 크다는 것을 의미한다. (Richter scale 미국의 지진학자 이름에서 따왔으며 지진의 진도를 1에서 10까지로 구분하였음)
14. 인터넷에 배포된 많은 정보가 신뢰할 만하더라도, 그것의 일부는 편견이거나 거짓이다.
15. 대부분의 비행기 날개는 금속으로 만들지만, 뼈대는 보통 알루미늄 합금으로 만든 얇은 덮개로 되어 있다.

16. 오늘날 중국 정부는 종교의 풍습을 허용하여 신봉자들의 수가 점차적으로 증가하고 있다.
17. 베르길리우스는 로마의 기원을 그리스인들에 의한 트로이의 격한 파괴가 뒤따랐던 사건들과 연결하고자 시도했다.
18. 한 나라의 역사를 이해하기 위해서 개개의 유명한 남성들의 생활과 일을 연구하는 것은 필요치 않다.
19. 오랑우탄은 길고 구부러지는 손가락과 발가락을 가지고 있어 가지를 잘 붙잡고 나무에서 생활하기에 편리하도록 돕는다.
20. 지구의 내부에서는 온도가 급속하게 상승하여 대양 내에서 약 2300°C 및 암반 핵에서 7000°C에 도달한다.

Practice Test 01

1. ⓒ	2. ⓑ	3. ⓐ	4. ⓑ	5. ⓓ
6. ⓓ	7. ⓓ	8. ⓑ	9. ⓐ	10. ⓐ
11. ⓐ	12. ⓒ	13. ⓐ	14. ⓑ	15. ⓐ
16. ⓐ	17. ⓒ	18. ⓓ	19. ⓒ	20. ⓓ

1. 사람은 육지의 거의 모든 곳에서 살 수 있다.
2. 너무 많은 소금은 음식의 진정한 풍미를 감추게 한다.
3. 구리와 다른 무기물은 전기분해로 불순물을 깨끗이 한다.
4. 화산은 마그마, 뜨거운 가스 및 바위의 파편이 지표면을 꿰뚫고 파열할 때 형성된다.
5. 체로키족 여자는 '여전사'의 지위를 얻을 수 있고 전쟁회의에 참가할 수 있다.

TOEFL DAY 02

Daily Checkup 02

1. ⓒ	2. ⓑ	3. ⓐ	4. ⓑ	5. ⓓ
6. ⓐ	7. ⓐ	8. ⓑ	9. ⓓ	10. ⓓ
11. ⓑ	12. ⓒ	13. ⓐ	14. ⓑ	15. ⓒ
16. ⓑ	17. ⓓ	18. ⓒ	19. ⓑ	20. ⓓ

1. 포근한 겨울
2. 지지하다
3. 벌떡 일어서다
4. 관례를 지키다
5. 가상의 적

6. 지방 자치 단체
7. 아주 신나는 파티
8. 폭동을 선동하다
9. 여행하기에는 너무 허약하다
10. 우유를 농축하다

11. 엄한 목소리
12. 누구의 일을 질질 끌다
13. 다정한 가정
14. 탐욕에 눈이 멀다
15. 슬픈 소식에 망연자실하다

16. 수면을 줄이다
17. 사업에서 두드러진 인물
18. 피할 수 없는 결과
19. 김빠진 맥주
20. 궁핍한 가족을 돕다

Practice Test 02

1. ⓒ	2. ⓐ	3. ⓐ	4. ⓑ	5. ⓐ
6. ⓑ	7. ⓐ	8. ⓐ	9. ⓑ	10. ⓓ
11. ⓒ	12. ⓓ	13. ⓒ	14. ⓓ	15. ⓒ
16. ⓑ	17. ⓐ	18. ⓐ	19. ⓒ	20. ⓓ

1. 말은 대략 기원전 3000년경에 탈 수 있도록 길들여졌었다.
2. 격렬한 활동을 할수록 더 많은 열량이 연소된다.
3. 약 1900년경에 라틴아메리카 예술가는 명백하게 라틴아메리카의 회화 스타일을 개발하기 시작했다.
4. 대부분의 세균은 진핵의 세포막에 붙는 세포벽에 의해 둘러쌓여 있다.
5. 주정부는 세금으로 공립학교를 지원하고 현지 학군을 통해서 관리한다.

6. 비록 세계가 전체적으로는 담수가 풍부함에도 몇몇 지역에서는 여전히 물이 부족하다.
7. 애덤스는 잭슨의 외교정책과 무효화에 대한 그의 강경한 반대를 지원했다.
8. 멀리뛰기를 시작하기 위하여 경쟁자들은 긴 도움닫기 길에서 전력 질주하고 테이크오프보드(발구름판)에서 도약한다.
9. 장관은 월요일의 투표에서 의외의(놀랄 만한) 패배 후에 지난밤에 사직했다.
10. 부적당하거나 부적절한 식단은 각종 질병의 위험을 증가시킨다.

11. 인디언 아이들은 예의 바르게 행동할 때 칭찬받고 무례한 행동을 할 때 창피 당한다.
12. 비행기는 날개 주위의 공기 흐름으로 떠받치는 공기를 통해서 비행할 수 있는 엔진구동의 기계이다.
13. 온난할 때 축축한 공기는 산바람이 불어오는 쪽 사면 위쪽으로 이동하고 수증기가 물방울로 응축되는 동안 냉각된다.
14. 개척지 생활에서 가장 크게 물의를 일으키는 부분만을 보여주면서, 질이 안 좋은 많은 작업들이 진실에서 멀리 빗나갔다.
15. 워터게이트는 개인의 욕심이 명백하게 중요한 역할을 하지 않았기 때문에 대부분의 이전 정치적인 물의와는 달랐다.

16. 건조한 지역에서 모래 토양은 보호적인 덮개기능의 초생물이 제거된 후에는 빠르게 침식한다.
17. 고대의 지질 기록은 약간 애매하게 남아있지만, 아직도 많은 지질학자들은 해수면이 지금보다 대략 5미터 정도 더 높았다고 믿고 있다.
18. 대부분의 국가 정부는 해외 여행자가 백신주사와 접종 증명서를 그들 국가로 들어오는 것을 허락하기 전에 보여줄 것을 요구한다.
19. 젊은이들은 강요적으로 특정 행동을 취하거나, 특정 가치를 받아들이거나, 그렇지 않다면 집단으로 받아들여지기 위하여 순응해야 하는 것에 거의 공감하지 않는다.
20. 금성이 태양 주위를 순회함에 따라 금성은 태양의 중심으로부터 그어진 가상의 선인 축을 따라 천천히 자전한다.

TOEFL DAY 03

Daily Checkup 03

1. ⓑ	2. ⓓ	3. ⓒ	4. ⓐ	5. ⓓ
6. ⓒ	7. ⓐ	8. ⓒ	9. ⓑ	10. ⓓ
11. ⓑ	12. ⓑ	13. ⓓ	14. ⓐ	15. ⓑ
16. ⓓ	17. ⓒ	18. ⓑ	19. ⓓ	20. ⓑ

1. 일하기 **편리하다**
2. 화학 **실험**
3. 법망을 **피하다**
4. 널찍한 집
5. **뛰어난** 재능

6. 대학교에서 파트타임과 **부수적** 강의(겸임강사) 자리
7. 모든 사무실에서 흡연을 **금지하다**
8. **조화되지 않는** 색
9. 하나님께 자비를 **빌다**
10. 계절은 **돌고 돈다**.

11. 갓 태어난 동물들을 **죽이다**
12. 우리 지식의 **집약 [전체]**
13. 누구의 직업(경력)을 **망치다**
14. 방법을 **채택하다**
15. 오렌지 **조각**

16. **극도의** 위험에서
17. ~의 **방법**으로 / ~을 매개로 / ~을 **통하여**
18. **비분의** 눈물
19. 걱정하지 않아도 될 **사소한** 손실
20. **전심전력으로** 공부하다

6. 지구는 남극과 북극을 잇는 가상선을 축으로 **자전하는** 데 하루에 한 번 걸린다.
7. 경도(단단함)는 다른 물질을 긁거나 다른 물질에 의해 긁히기를 **견뎌내는** 물질의 특성이다.
8. 빛은 결정의 평면에 의해 **분산되었다**.
9. 현미경에서 거울은 **표본**을 비추기 위하여 검경대에 있는 개구를 통해 들어온 빛을 반사시킨다. (the stage 무대, 검경대)
10. 이제까지는 서남극 대륙의 운명에 있어 **사소한** 역할을 한 지구온난화는 미래에 더 중대한 영향을 끼칠 것이다.

11. 1906년에 다른 불완전한 **구역**에 따른 이동은 결과적으로 샌프란시스코 대지진을 초래했다. (faulty 불완전한, segment 구획, 단편, 부분)
12. 고전음악 작곡가들은 그들의 작업에 민요가락을 **포함시켰다**.
13. 많은 **우화**에서 교훈은 이야기의 끝부분에 격언의 형식으로 전해진다.
14. 의사는 장애를 **진단하고** 치료하고자 다양한 전자기기와 기계들을 사용한다.
15. 우리 자신의 경제시스템에서 돈은 우리가 거의 무엇이든 사거나 팔 수 있는 편리한 교환 **수단**으로서 가치의 보편적인 수단을 제공한다.

16. 난독증을 가진 사람들은 수시로 글자나 단어를 **혼동하고** 틀린 순서로 단어나 문장을 읽거나 쓸지도 모른다.
17. 전세계 사람들은 수천 마리의 코끼리들이 상아보석과 조각물을 제공하기 위하여 매년 **학살되고** 있다는 사실을 인지하게 되었다.
18. 포도당과 같은 단당류는 6개의 탄소원자로 된 **뼈대**를 갖고 있어 수소와 산소원자가 붙게 되고 화학기호 $C_6H_{12}O_6$를 제공한다.
19. 청량음료는 금속 캔과 많은 유형의 유리와 플라스틱 용기와 같은 더 **편리한** 포장으로 유용하게 제작되어 왔다.
20. 그 연극들은 영국 왕위의 지배를 위한 요크가와 랭카스터가 사이의 일련의 유혈 충돌인 장미전쟁을 생생하게 **반영한다**.

Practice Test 03

1. ⓐ	2. ⓒ	3. ⓓ	4. ⓑ	5. ⓒ
6. ⓓ	7. ⓒ	8. ⓓ	9. ⓐ	10. ⓑ
11. ⓒ	12. ⓑ	13. ⓓ	14. ⓒ	15. ⓐ
16. ⓒ	17. ⓓ	18. ⓑ	19. ⓒ	20. ⓐ

1. 종량세율은 단위당 **총액**으로서 수입한 특정제품에 부과한다.
2. 로마 도로의 대부분은 연이은 수세기 동안 **파괴되었다**.
3. 혜성을 발견하고자 시도하던 누군가는 성운을 혜성으로 쉽게 **잘못 알 수 있다**.
4. 많은 통신사는 통신위성을 **통해** 언론기관에 보고를 전달한다.
5. 훌륭한 운전사는 다른 사람과 도로를 공유할 마음이 있음을 의미하는 훌륭한 **마음가짐이** 있다.

DAY 04

Daily Checkup 04

1. ⓑ	2. ⓒ	3. ⓓ	4. ⓐ	5. ⓑ
6. ⓓ	7. ⓑ	8. ⓒ	9. ⓐ	10. ⓓ
11. ⓐ	12. ⓒ	13. ⓑ	14. ⓑ	15. ⓓ
16. ⓒ	17. ⓐ	18. ⓐ	19. ⓓ	20. ⓑ

1. 문명의 초기 단계
2. 판자에 구멍을 뚫다
3. 검을 단조하다
4. 삶의 의미에 대해 곰곰이 생각하다
5. 상을 타려고 경합하다

6. 암묵적으로 통하다
7. 반제국주의자의 정서
8. 재목이 썩어가고 있다.
9. 무례한 대답
10. 허약한 마음

11. 축하의 쇄도
12. 인간의 힘을 초월하다
13. 경치의 아름다움에 매료되다
14. 방탕한 생활을 하다
15. 조상을 존경하다

16. 과실을 인정하다
17. 상당히 많은 피를 흘리다
18. 휴면 중인(활동을 중단한) 싹을 깨우다
19. 시장이 극도로 침체되어 있다.
20. 자신의 꾀에 자기가 말려들다 / 자업자득이다

6. 몇몇 인도 예술가들은 그들의 세상이 변해왔음을 인식했고 그들의 작업에 그러한 발달(그 변화)을 반영했다.
7. 라틴아메리카의 경제는 1960년대와 1970년대 사이에 빠르게 성장하였지만 1980년대에 급격하게 둔화되었다.
8. 고대의 따뜻함은 현재보다는 조금 더 온화한 조건을 야기했을지도 모른다.
9. 물은 지구 표면의 약 70%를 차지하며 땅은 대략 30%를 차지한다.
10. 집이란 거주인에게 피난처이자 안락한 곳과 보호를 제공하는 건물이다.

11. 줄거리는 비올라의 쌍둥이 형제인 세바스찬이 나타날 때까지 점점 엉키게 되었다.
12. 미항공우주국은 7에서 76나노미터의 파장을 연구하기 위하여 1992년에 Extra Ultraviolet Explorer를 공중으로 보냈다.
13. 많은 상상이 풍부한 작가들이 우주 여행을 위한 기발한 기술을 제시했다.
14. 접혀지는 수레는 어떤 크기든지 될 수 있고, 때때로 자체적으로 열어서 앞 전경을 넓게 한다.
15. 현대사회에서 사람들은 연대감을 느끼는 어떤 그룹에게 종종 가족에게 사용하는 말을 쓴다.

16. 기억 B 림프구는 만일 동일한 유형의 항원을 나중에 만나게 되면 감염에 면역체계가 더 빠르게 반응하는 것을 가능하게 한다.
17. 빙원의 가장 두꺼운 부분은 해수면 아래로 잠겨 있는 깊은 바닥에 위치해 있다.
18. 1960년대 이래로 많은 가족들이 경제적으로 침체된 전원지역에서 새로운 정착지로 이동해 왔다.
19. 공기는 지구로부터 멀어질수록 점차 엷어지고 지구 위로 대략 1,000킬로미터를 넘어서면 우주로 사라져간다.
20. 산소는 약 2억 년 전에 상당한 양이 처음으로 대기 중으로 들어가서 약 1억 5천만 년 전에 안정적 수준까지 단계적으로 증가하였다.

Practice Test 04

1. ⓒ	2. ⓓ	3. ⓓ	4. ⓒ	5. ⓐ
6. ⓓ	7. ⓒ	8. ⓐ	9. ⓑ	10. ⓒ
11. ⓐ	12. ⓑ	13. ⓑ	14. ⓓ	15. ⓒ
16. ⓓ	17. ⓒ	18. ⓑ	19. ⓑ	20. ⓑ

1. 술은 강력한 흥분제로 습관적인 음주는 많은 건강문제를 일으킬 수 있다.
2. 오늘날 피자식물은 지구상에 가장 수가 많은 식물이다.
3. 미토콘드리아처럼 이러한 세포기관들은 구조가 복잡하다.
4. 이동하는 비행기는 비행 중에 압력으로 인해 흔들림을 야기한다.
5. 오존은 태양으로부터 오는 대부분의 자외선을 흡수하여, 지구에 도달하지 못하도록 방지한다.

TOEFL DAY 05

Daily Checkup 05

1. ⓑ   2. ⓑ   3. ⓓ   4. ⓓ   5. ⓐ
6. ⓐ   7. ⓓ   8. ⓑ   9. ⓑ   10. ⓓ
11. ⓐ   12. ⓓ   13. ⓒ   14. ⓓ   15. ⓑ
16. ⓒ   17. ⓑ   18. ⓓ   19. ⓑ   20. ⓐ

1. 자연의 놀라운 광경
2. 야만적인 풍습
3. 친한 친구
4. 재해로 고통을 받다
5. 근소한 차이로

6. (부정적인 의미로) 거의 활용되지 않다
7. 눈먼 사람
8. 봉변 당하다
9. 그것은 어느 정도 다르다.
10. 과제를 복잡하게 만들다

11. 그의 시선을 피하다
12. 화학반응을 일으키다
13. 주요 갈등으로 악화되다
14. 자유로운 의견
15. 친절한 선물로 달래다

16. 사람의 정직성을 확신하다
17. 바른 자세를 유지하다
18. 연어의 산란기
19. 그녀의 시간과 노력을 배상하다
20. 인간 고유의 감정

Practice Test 05

1. ⓒ   2. ⓐ   3. ⓒ   4. ⓑ   5. ⓓ
6. ⓑ   7. ⓐ   8. ⓐ   9. ⓐ   10. ⓑ
11. ⓓ   12. ⓓ   13. ⓐ   14. ⓐ   15. ⓑ
16. ⓑ   17. ⓒ   18. ⓓ   19. ⓑ   20. ⓒ

1. 모두가 그녀가 아주 아름다워질 거라고 정말로 확신했다.
2. 많은 신화들이 불이나 홍수와 같이 어떤 중대한 재해에 의해서 세상이 끝난다고 예언한다.
3. 생방송의 스포츠행사에서 비디오테이프는 스포츠 방송인이 일어난 주요 장면을 즉시 분석하고 되돌리는 것을 가능하게 한다.
4. TV 뉴스서비스는 방송뉴스에 대한 세계의 소식을 시각적으로 제공한다.
5. 많은 이전 오페라와는 다르게, 라트라비아타는 복잡한 감정을 가진 현실적인 등장인물들이 나온다.
6. 과학자들은 큰 동물들, 특히 거대한 공룡들은 몸의 열이 천천히 감소했다고 지적했다.
7. 비록 많은 귀신이 사악하고 불쾌하지만, 일부는 도움이 될지도 모른다.
8. 많은 출판사들은 어떤 그룹의 사람들이 자신들의 잡지를 읽는지를 알아보기 위해 설문조사를 한다.
9. 태양은 특히 태양의 극 근처에서 막대자석 형태와 어느 정도 비슷한 자기장이 있다.
10. 시간과 공간을 절약하기 위해, 전투부대 식량은 건조되어 밀폐 용기에 포장된다.

11. 불충분한 두뇌의 발달이나 시력 또는 청각장애는 읽기를 어렵게 할 수 있다.
12. 대부분의 동물성 지방은 고도로 포화된 상당히 많은 양의 지방을 함유한다.
13. 알레르기 전문의사는 피부 아래의 별도 영역에 적은 양의 알레르기 유발 항원을 주입한다.
14. 그 관점은 현재 지구의 놀랍고도 복잡한 진화에 관한 몇 가지 놀랍고 새로운 통찰력을 제시한다.
15. 백과사전의 모든 지식의 분야를 최신으로 하려면, 출판사는 정기적으로 수정해야 한다.

16. 이 직립 자세는 공룡이 배를 바닥에 끌지 않고 네 발로 걸을 수 있게 하였다.
17. 헌팅턴 질병으로 고통을 받으면, 사람들은 더욱 멍해 있고, 정신적 혹은 육체적 스트레스 상황에서는 비자발적 행동을 보이기 시작한다.
18. 기후 변화와 해수면의 영향에 관한 남극 빙상의 반응을 예측하는 것은 언제나 간단하지 않다.
19. 1900년대 중반의 남아메리카 원주민들은 사회, 정치, 경제와 토지개혁을 요구하는 무장시위에 참여하였다.
20. 육식을 즐기는 사람들은 고기를 자르고 썰기 위해 날카로운 이빨 부위가 있고, 채식을 즐기는 사람들은 섬유질이 많은 야채들을 분쇄할 수 있는 넓고, 무딘 이빨이 있다.

DAY 01-05

Exercise 01-05

1. ⓓ	2. ⓒ	3. ⓒ	4. ⓑ	5. ⓐ
6. ⓓ	7. ⓑ	8. ⓒ	9. ⓑ	10. ⓐ
11. ⓒ	12. ⓒ	13. ⓐ	14. ⓑ	15. ⓑ
16. ⓕ	17. ⓓ	18. ⓐ	19. ⓒ	20. ⓐ

1. 부당한 방법으로 일을 하다
2. 완벽한 경지에 이르다
3. 불충분한 장비
4. 경기가 나쁘다.
5. 농사를 짓기에는 너무 건조한 지역

6. 국민 다수의 목소리
7. 일의 중요도
8. 이름을 열거하다
9. 불필요한 방해
10. 속이 썩은 사과

11. 평소의 예의바름
12. 혼합물을 정제하다
13. 마음 태도
14. 다른 회사와 통합하다
15. 질문에 무뚝뚝하게 대답하다

16. 매우 지루한 파티
17. 뚜렷한 변화
18. 기골이 있다
19. 땅에 있는 거대한 구멍
20. 가면을 쓰다

Practice Test 01-05

1. ⓓ	2. ⓒ	3. ⓑ	4. ⓐ	5. ⓑ
6. ⓑ	7. ⓐ	8. ⓓ	9. ⓐ	10. ⓒ
11. ⓒ	12. ⓒ	13. ⓒ	14. ⓓ	15. ⓐ
16. ⓐ	17. ⓒ	18. ⓓ	19. ⓐ	20. ⓑ

1. 1600년대 말에 영국은 세계의 총 석탄 생산의 대략 80%를 생산했다.
2. 오늘날, 유황은 다양한 제품과 산업공정의 과정에 사용된다.
3. 1860년대 초기에 미국 정부는 철도선을 전국 각지로 확장하기로 결정했다.
4. 아기들은 성장과 발육의 방식과 속도에 차이가 있다.
5. 다이아몬드는 아주 단단한 금속을 빠르고 정확하게 자르고 갈고 구멍을 뚫을 수 있다.

6. 축축한 열대지역에서 습기는 수년 내에 나무로 만든 오두막을 썩게 하는 원인이 된다.
7. 많은 개인회사는 국가와 국제기관과 경쟁할 출시 서비스 개발을 시작해왔다.
8. 1977년에 FDA는 미국에서 사카린의 사용을 금지하는 절차를 취했다.
9. 수소는 액체 형태로 저장될 수 있지만 에너지의 상당 양은 수소를 극도로 낮은 온도(– 253 ℃ or – 423 ℉)로 차갑게 하는 데 필요하다.
10. 20세기 과학혁명은 과학의 여러 많은 분야에까지 확대되었다.

11. 영국은 극도로 추운 래보라도보- 멀리 북쪽에 위치해 있긴 하지만, 온화한 기후를 가지고 있다.
12. 연구소에서 수학과 그 응용수학에 대한 강의를 하였다.
13. 화석기록은 동식물의 복잡성에 대한 점진적인 증가를 설명한다.
14. 유럽에서 가장 유명한 열차 중 ㅎ-나인 오리엔트 특급열차는 1883년부터 프랑스의 파리와 터키의 이스탄불 사이를 운행했다.
15. 포유류는 사람들에게만 중요한 거 아니라 지구상의 모든 생명체에게도 중요하다.

16. 대부분의 빛은 눈에 백색으로 보여도 사실은 청색, 녹색, 적색의 3가지 기본 색으로 혼합되어 있다.
17. 가장 단순한 생물은 단 하나의 세포로 이루어졌지만 개와 인간과 같이 복잡한 생명체는 수십억 개의 세포로 이루어졌다.
18. 대부분의 언론기관의 경영자들은 정치적으로 보수적이지만, 많은 기자들은 진보적인 성향이 있다.
19. 스펙트럼의 연구는 화학자가 물질을 분석하는 것을 가능하게 하고 어떤 원소를 포함하는지를 결정한다.
20. 과학자들은 행성의 모든 지점과 접촉하는 가상의 표면인 궤도면의 직각에서 행성의 상대적 기울기를 측정한다.

Intensive Practice Test 01-05

1. ⓑ	2. ⓒ	3. ⓒ	4. ⓐ	5. ⓓ
6. ⓓ	7. ⓐ	8. ⓑ	9. ⓐ	10. ⓑ
11. ⓐ	12. ⓑ	13. ⓑ	14. ⓒ	15. ⓓ
16. ⓓ	17. ⓐ	18. ⓑ	19. ⓒ	20. ⓑ

1. 부유한 이집트인은 벽돌과 나무로 만든 아름답고 공간이 넓은 집을 지었다.
2. 최근의 성공에도 불구하고 줄기 세포치료는 아직도 대단히 실험적이다. (highly는 부사로 대단히, 매우)
3. 면역반응을 유발하는 물질을 항원이라고 한다.
4. 고백시 시인들은 성관계와 정신병 같은 사적인 개인의 경험에 대한 글을 집필하였다.
5. 존 애덤스(1735-1826)는 독립선언문의 채택에 선도적인 역할을 하였고 그 역사적인 문서에 서명하였다.

6. 세금을 올리려는 정부의 노력들은 국민들로부터 격렬한 항의를 불러일으켰다.
7. 시체 냄새가 공기 중에 머물렀고, 쥐가 큰 문제가 되었다.
8. 농부들은 주거지, 연료와 건물의 펜스를 만들기 위한 목재를 찾는 데 어려움이 있었다.
9. 가득 찬 온실가스를 하늘로 끌어올린 필연적인 결과가 지구 온난화이다.
10. 대부분의 중성자 별은 태양보다 8배에서 20배 더 무거운데, 거대하지만 그 이외에는 평범한 별에서 생겨났다고 여겨진다.
11. 기독교인의 도덕적인 관점은 국민의 대다수가 기독교인인 미국의 법에 주요한 영향을 끼쳐왔다.
12. 작가는 항상 신뢰할 수 있는 자료를 사용해서 문서에 정확한 정보를 나타낼 수 있어야 한다.
13. 모든 무슬림들은 무하마드와 알리와 같은 영웅을 성자로 인정한다.
14. 자코모 푸치니가 작곡한 '보헤미아인'의 비극적 오페라에서는 4명의 가난하지만 근심 없는 젊은이들과 건강이 안 좋은 연약한 어린 소녀인 미미가 그들의 이웃으로서 1830년 파리에서 자유분방한 삶을 산다.
15. 역사상 가장 잔인한 인종 박해 중 하나는 1930년대와 1940년대 사이 독일 나치군이 6백만 유태인을 학살하였을 때 일어났다.
16. 오늘날 경전철은 도시의 거리와 함께 지어지거나 고가 선로나 지하철로 땅속을 달린다.
17. 역사학자들은 1850년대 미국의 정당 시스템의 혼란과 정치인들의 실수에 대해서 더욱 많이 언급하고 있다.
18. 타이피스트가 원고를 준비할 때는 공간을 두 배로 만들고 모든 페이지의 상단, 하단, 측면에 여백을 둬야 한다.
19. 우리는 가끔 날씨에 관한 징후와 지식을 통해 쉽게 질병을 진단할 수 있게 된다.
20. 미국항공우주국(NASA)의 설립은 군과 대학, 항공산업 및 정치인들의 경쟁적인 이익집단 사이에서 협력관계를 구축하는 데 도움이 됐다.

TOEFL DAY 06

Daily Checkup 06

1. ⓒ	2. ⓑ	3. ⓐ	4. ⓒ	5. ⓓ
6. ⓐ	7. ⓑ	8. ⓓ	9. ⓒ	10. ⓒ
11. ⓐ	12. ⓑ	13. ⓒ	14. ⓑ	15. ⓒ
16. ⓑ	17. ⓓ	18. ⓐ	19. ⓑ	20. ⓓ

1. 투표권이 있다
2. 개척하여 길을 표시하다 / 새로운 길을 열다
3. 광범위한 명령
4. 엄격한 법
5. 달팽이의 지나간 자국

6. 누구를 확신시키다
7. 꾸러미 만드는 일을 돕다
8. 소박하지만 영양가가 높은 음식
9. 당신은 재산을 증여 받았다.
10. 대학의 지위로 승격되었다

11. 자비로
12. 식물이나 동물이 번창한다면
13. 가벼운 식사
14. 거리가 30피트 정도로 판단됐다
15. 일산화탄소의 유독한 연기 [유독가스]

16. 편리한 의복
17. 큰 부담을 지다
18. 문제를 숙고하다
19. 두 원수를 화해시키다
20. 거의 들리지 않는

Practice Test 06

1. ⓒ	2. ⓑ	3. ⓐ	4. ⓓ	5. ⓓ
6. ⓐ	7. ⓓ	8. ⓒ	9. ⓒ	10. ⓓ
11. ⓒ	12. ⓑ	13. ⓑ	14. ⓓ	15. ⓐ
16. ⓒ	17. ⓓ	18. ⓑ	19. ⓒ	20. ⓑ

1. 1800년대 이후 과학의 발전은 농업을 점점 더 생산적으로 만들었다.
2. 축구경기 시즌에는, 매주 토요일에 수천 명의 축구 관중들이 경기장을 메운다.
3. 여우는 종종 교활하게 올빼미는 현명하게 묘사된다.
4. 미국 인디언들은 민요를 아름다움이 아닌, 힘의 기준으로 판단한다.
5. 전미 광고심의위원회는 광고산업의 자율규제를 조장한다.

6. 일부 백화점과 가구매장은 인테리어 디자이너를 고용하여 고객을 **지원하고** 제품 판매를 돕는다.
7. 고대 로마사회는 약 2천 년 전에 **번성하였다**.
8. 유럽중앙은행으로 알려진 중앙은행은 유럽연합의 경제통화연맹의 모든 **통화**정책을 수행한다.
9. 뉴욕의 해안선은 대서양을 따라 204킬로미터 **펼쳐진다**.
10. 연합군은 1945년 8월 일본이 항복에 동의하기 전까지 일본 제국을 **조금씩 갉아먹었다**.
11. 로라 잉걸스 와일더는 1800년대 후반, **개척자**의 삶에 관한 9개의 소설집을 저술하였다.
12. 의류는 실용적이어야 했기에 대부분의 사람들은 매일 단조로운 같은 **의복**을 입었다.
13. 대부분의 가면은 신화나 민속에서 모범적인 인물을 표현하고 관객들에게 **널리** 알려졌다.
14. 1840년대의 대지주는 **토지**를 작은 독립적인 농장으로 나누는 과정을 진행했다.
15. 타운센드 계획의 광범위한 인기는 미국 의회로 하여금 1935년 사회보장법을 통과시키도록 **설득하는 데** 도움이 되었다.
16. 잉카인들은 그들로부터 멀리 떨어진 제국을 연결하기 위해 안데스산맥을 관통하여 **광범위한** 도로시스템을 건설하였다.
17. 가봉은 아프리카에서 **이례적으로** 상대적으로 부유하며 정치적으로 안정된 국가이며 중앙아프리카에서 가장 인구밀도가 낮다.
18. DNA 염기서열의 결정과 자료처리의 발전은 최근 생명과학에서의 가장 큰 **혁신**을 주도했다.
19. 베르니니는 감정과 **감각적인** 자유를 극적인 표현과 사실적인 자연주의와 함께 결합하였다.
20. 저작권이 침해된 저작권 소유자는 더 이상의 **저작권 침해**를 막기 위해 소송을 제기할 수 있다.

TOEFL DAY 07

Daily Checkup 07

1. ⓒ	2. ⓒ	3. ⓑ	4. ⓑ	5. ⓒ
6. ⓐ	7. ⓒ	8. ⓑ	9. ⓓ	10. ⓐ
11. ⓑ	12. ⓑ	13. ⓒ	14. ⓒ	15. ⓐ
16. ⓐ	17. ⓒ	18. ⓓ	19. ⓑ	20. ⓐ

1. **근본적** 차이
2. **간결한** 진술
3. **풍부한** 작물
4. **공석인** 자리
5. **빛나는** 미소

6. **결론**에 다다르다
7. **투명한** 유리 문
8. 과학의 **영역**에서
9. **종교** 음악회
10. 납은 몸에 **축적될** 수 있다.

11. 국가를 **분할하다**
12. 계약을 **수정하다**
13. 공기의 **양**
14. 여러 **측면**을 가진 문제
15. 아주 **상당한** 추가 수입

16. **오만한** 냉소
17. 마음의 **풍요**
18. **적절한** 발언
19. 의회를 **소집하다**
20. 사람을 다루는 데 **서투르다**

Practice Test 07

1. ⓐ	2. ⓑ	3. ⓐ	4. ⓒ	5. ⓑ
6. ⓐ	7. ⓑ	8. ⓒ	9. ⓓ	10. ⓑ
11. ⓓ	12. ⓐ	13. ⓒ	14. ⓐ	15. ⓑ
16. ⓓ	17. ⓒ	18. ⓐ	19. ⓒ	20. ⓓ

1. 외부 행성의 **희미한** 빛은 카메라의 긴 노출이 필요하다.
2. 세균 심내막염은 항생제로 치료되지 않으면 **치명적**이다.
3. 나트륨원자는 염소원자가 수용할 수 있는 전자를 **제공한다**.
4. 카우보이들은 항상 그들의 가축들을 퓨마와 가축 도둑들로부터 **보호했다**.
5. 어떠한 물체에서든지 움직이는 원자나 분자는 **복사**에너지의 파동을 생성한다.

6. 일부 광물들은 색이 있는 반짝이는 유리와 같은 표면이 있다.
7. 작곡가들은 음악적 아이디어를 개발하기 위한 기본으로 동기(모티브)라고 부르는 여러 개의 짧은 악보를 사용한다.
8. 쐐기가 위쪽으로 뾰족한 구멍에 위치해 있다.
9. 한국은 1945년에 두 개의 국가로 분리되었다.
10. 1616년 초에 갈릴레오는 그의 견해의 정통성에 관한 청문회로 로마에 소환되었다.
11. 만일 부사장이 사망 또는 사임하거나 업무를 수행할 수 없으면 공석이 된다.
12. 지구에서 가장 익숙한 관측이 이루어지는 것은 달의 상의 변화로 보름달, 반달, 초승달을 포함한다.
13. 산업용 등급의 다이아몬드는 불완전하게 형성되거나, 기타 여러 결함이나 색에 결함이 있는 돌들을 포함한다.
14. 빛이 공기에서 투명한 보석과 같이 밀도가 높은 물질로 통과할 때 속도가 감소된다.
15. 미주리 강과 로키산맥 사이의 광대한 평야는 1860년대까지 사람이 살지 않았다.
16. 어떤 원시사회에서는 사냥하는 도중에 동물이 죽게 되면, 사냥꾼의 친척들은 죽은 고기를 나누어 가질 권리를 갖는다.
17. 많은 유전정보가 실제로 세포의 많은 효소와 구조 단백질을 위한 암호라는 데 이견이 없다.
18. 과학자들의 결론의 정확도는 그가 사용하는 원칙과 규칙의 정확성과 완전성에 의존한다.
19. 고대 과학자들은 별과 태양과 달과 행성들의 관측된 움직임을 설명하기 위한 정교한 천상도를 만들었다.
20. 로큰롤은 상당한 인기가 있음에도 불구하고, 많은 어른들은 여전히 로큰롤의 가사나 공연 스타일을 외설적이라고 여겼다.

TOEFL DAY 08

Daily Checkup 08

1. ⓒ	2. ⓑ	3. ⓓ	4. ⓐ	5. ⓓ
6. ⓑ	7. ⓓ	8. ⓒ	9. ⓓ	10. ⓐ
11. ⓒ	12. ⓓ	13. ⓑ	14. ⓑ	15. ⓓ
16. ⓑ	17. ⓑ	18. ⓒ	19. ⓑ	20. ⓐ

1. 순항 속도
2. 우아한 벨벳 가운
3. 결혼한 한 쌍
4. 장엄한 광경
5. 황홀해하다

6. 언어는 인간 특유의 것이다.
7. 학생을 퇴학시키다
8. 예측할 수 없는 날씨
9. 무모함을 회개하다
10. 잘생긴 학교 소년

11. 공중도덕을 오염시키다
12. 외과 전문의사
13. 열차에서 기관차를 분리하다
14. 하품을 참다
15. 우리의 실수

16. 명령을 따르도록 강요 당하는 느낌을 받다
17. 자기 자신을 축으로 회전하다
18. 치료를 받다
19. 독창적인 사상가
20. 깃발이 미풍에 흔들리다

Practice Test 08

1. ⓓ	2. ⓒ	3. ⓑ	4. ⓐ	5. ⓒ
6. ⓑ	7. ⓒ	8. ⓐ	9. ⓐ	10. ⓓ
11. ⓐ	12. ⓓ	13. ⓒ	14. ⓒ	15. ⓐ
16. ⓒ	17. ⓓ	18. ⓑ	19. ⓒ	20. ⓓ

1. 해석기하학의 발견은 일반적으로 데카르트와 페르마 덕분이다.
2. 1900년 전에는 자동차회사들은 개별 자동차를 조립하기 위해 숙련된 노동자들을 고용하였다.
3. 대통령이 대외원조와 국제활동을 다루는 입법을 제안하였다.
4. 스페인의 농업은 경제의 가장 취약한 부분으로 남아 있으며, 농업은 다른 대부분의 유럽국가보다도 뒤떨어져 있다.
5. 사진 역사에 관한 전문가를 채용하는 박물관들이 점점 늘고 있다.

6. 성장은 생물이 성숙되어 가는 과정을 겪으면서 크기가 점점 자라는 과정이다.
7. 정치적·사회적 격변은 기반이 확고한 많은 정부를 전복시켰다.
8. 혜성은 보통 상대적으로 빠른 속도로 지구를 지나간다.
9. 대부분의 학자들은 뉴딜정책이 대부분의 경제적 고통을 완화시켰고 경제 회복을 위한 대책을 가져왔다는 것에 동의하였다.
10. 땅다람쥐, 프레리도그 및 많은 작은 동물들은 굴이나 다른 숨을 장소로 돌진한다.
11. 의료 사진사들은 의사들이 병을 진단하고 치료하는 데 사용할 정보를 제공한다.
12. 종교적 개념은 삶과 우주의 근본에 대한 초기의 철학적 추론을 제공했다.
13. 땅속에 서식하는 사막 흰개미들은 나무로 만든 건물, 기둥, 울타리에 종종 피해를 준다.
14. 역광조명은 실루엣을 만들기 위해 의도적으로 사용될 수 있다.
15. 오늘날 생산된 위대한 작품은 과거의 명작을 대신할 수는 없다.
16. 시인으로서 셰익스피어의 천재성은 그의 생각을 간결하고 화려하게 표현할 수 있게 하였다.
17. 아무도 왜 우리가 웃었는지 또는 재미있다고 생각한 것에 우리가 이상한 소리를 낸 이유를 정확히 알 수 없었다.
18. 은하수는 하늘을 가로질러 밝고 어두운 부분이 넓게 퍼진 얼룩이 있는 띠이다.
19. 식민지 시대에 번성하였던 세속 음악은 출판되지 않고 구두로 전달되었다.
20. 종합 해충관리체계는 최적화된 해충 통제방법을 통하여 해충의 수를 경제적 한계점 이하로 감소시키는 개념이다.

TOEFL DAY 09

Daily Checkup 09

1. ⓓ	2. ⓐ	3. ⓓ	4. ⓑ	5. ⓒ
6. ⓒ	7. ⓒ	8. ⓑ	9. ⓑ	10. ⓓ
11. ⓓ	12. ⓐ	13. ⓑ	14. ⓒ	15. ⓐ
16. ⓒ	17. ⓑ	18. ⓐ	19. ⓒ	20. ⓓ

1. 건강을 증진시키다
2. 잘못 짚은 냄새 [단서]
3. 회사의 유능한 사원
4. 이 계획은 당신의 승인을 받아야 한다.
5. 악담을 퍼붓다

6. 한 개인의 행동을 모욕하다
7. 가장자리 / 빠듯한 비용으로
8. 표현을 과장하다
9. 소중한 친구
10. 일정한 줄거리에 따라 언쟁을 하다

11. 타는 고무의 매캐한 냄새
12. 그 증거로 유죄가 명확해지다
13. 건강에 손상을 주다
14. 무서운 감정
15. 그 계획에 사소한 반대의 목소리를 내다

16. 그대로 두다
17. 실패할 징조가 있다
18. 신임 투표
19. 피아노 소나타 작품 1, No. 2
20. 다 허물어져가는 가구

Practice Test 09

1. ⓓ	2. ⓓ	3. ⓑ	4. ⓒ	5. ⓐ
6. ⓐ	7. ⓑ	8. ⓒ	9. ⓓ	10. ⓓ
11. ⓑ	12. ⓐ	13. ⓒ	14. ⓓ	15. ⓓ
16. ⓑ	17. ⓐ	18. ⓑ	19. ⓒ	20. ⓒ

1. 혼자 사냥하는 포식자는 떼를 지어 사냥하는 포식자보다 먹잇감을 더 조용히 사냥할 수 있다.
2. 대부분의 사람들은 더 많은 일을 해서 가족의 삶을 개선하고 싶어한다.
3. 다이아몬드는 (결정의) 벽개성 때문에 날카롭고 정확한 타격으로 깨끗하게 부서질 수 있다.
4. 큰 분화구는 산에 의해 가장자리가 형성되고 가파른 계단식 벽들을 갖게 된다.

5. 다이오드는 통합회로에 내장될 수 있으며 기존 회로의 개별 부품으로 형성될 수 있다.

6. 온실에서 재배되는 산딸기는 야생 산딸기보다 쓴맛이 덜하다.
7. 나일강이 북쪽방향의 이집트를 통하여 흘러감에 따라 큰 사막 한가운데에 좁은 리본 모양의 비옥한 토지를 만든다.
8. 커피와 차는 아주 드문 경우를 제외하고는 개척자 가족이 마시기에는 너무 비쌌다.
9. 하이에나는 자신의 영역을 표시하기 위해 고체의 배설물과 특별한 분비샘으로부터 만들어진 냄새를 남긴다.
10. 작품의 공식 이름은 작품의 형태를 식별하고 종종 작품번호를 포함할 것이다.

11. 주요 연사는 그 시대의 가장 위대한 웅변가들 중 한 사람인 에드워드 에버렛이였다.
12. 링컨은 전쟁의 시련을 겪으면서 자신의 판단이 옳았다는 조용한 자신감을 얻게 되었다.
13. 일부 과학자들은 대기 중 이산화탄소 CO_2의 생성은 인간 활동으로 인해 온난화현상을 일으켜왔다고 논쟁한다.
14. 유엔군의 힘은 강대국을 강요할 만큼 큰 힘은 아니더라도 도움이 될 것이다.
15. 철학적 질문에 대한 성찰이 시간 낭비라고 주장하는 사람도 본질적으로 무엇이 중요하고 가치 있고 소중한지를 표현한다.

16. 후보자들과 그 지지자들은 홍보, 광고 및 개인적인 등장을 통해 투표자의 지지를 얻으려고 노력한다.
17. 늦은 여름비가 부족했을 때 농부들은 은신처, 연료 및 건물 울타리를 만들기 위한 나무를 찾는 데 어려움을 겪었다.
18. 많은 귀신 이야기는 독자들의 죽음에 대한 두려움과 고립된 맨션이나 중세의 성처럼 불편하고, 낯선 장소의 두려움을 이용한다.
19. 보존이란 수행자가 그의 힘을 보유하고 그의 역할을 절정에 이르도록 고조시키는 방법들을 포함한다.
20. 산은 강력한 (지질) 구조적 힘의 작용이 가장 선명하게 나타난 징후이며 이러한 힘이 광대한 시간의 흐름을 통해서 나타나는 것이다.

TOEFL DAY 10

Daily Checkup 10

1. Ⓒ	2. Ⓒ	3. Ⓐ	4. Ⓓ	5. Ⓐ
6. Ⓐ	7. Ⓒ	8. Ⓑ	9. Ⓒ	10. Ⓒ
11. Ⓑ	12. Ⓓ	13. Ⓓ	14. Ⓓ	15. Ⓐ
16. Ⓒ	17. Ⓓ	18. Ⓐ	19. Ⓒ	20. Ⓑ

1. 그녀는 배우는 데 소질이 있다.
2. 나는 사실을 설명할 수 없다.
3. 그는 오락가락했으며 생각에 잠겼다.
4. 당신은 톰을 믿을 수 있다.
5. 물고기가 풍부한 산호초

6. 빛바랜 사진
7. 책을 버리다
8. 다양한 책들
9. 건조기의 시작과 일치하다
10. 다루기 힘들다

11. 상처 입기 매우 쉬운
12. 그는 막대한 빚을 졌다.
13. 그녀의 바쁜 일정 중에
14. 하루에 50페이지까지 완전히 익히다
15. 절차를 옳게 수행하다

16. 은하는 1천억 개의 별로 구성된다.
17. 그리스어에서 파생된
18. 장비를 주문하는 것에 더하여 허가하다
19. 초콜렛은 카카오 나무에서 온다.
20. 경비는 특허의 비용으로 줄어들 수 있다.

Practice Test 10

1. Ⓐ	2. Ⓐ	3. Ⓓ	4. Ⓑ	5. Ⓐ
6. Ⓑ	7. Ⓒ	8. Ⓑ	9. Ⓓ	10. Ⓑ
11. Ⓓ	12. Ⓒ	13. Ⓒ	14. Ⓑ	15. Ⓑ
16. Ⓓ	17. Ⓐ	18. Ⓒ	19. Ⓐ	20. Ⓒ

1. 살아있는 언어는 끊임없이 변화를 겪는다.
2. 이당류는 2개의 단당류가 함께 결합되어 이루어져 있다.
3. 고등동물에서 각각의 중요한 생명의 기능은 함께 작동하는 일련의 기관에 의해 수행된다.
4. 교육은 사람들이 변화에 적응하도록 돕는다.
5. 고래상어는 거대한 크기에도 불구하고 플랑크톤과 작은 물고기만 먹는다.

6. 이 책은 우리 시대의 문학을 다루고 있다.
7. 민주주의에 대한 아프리카인의 개념은 현재 미국인이 가진 개념과 일치하지 않는다.
8. 조류의 한쪽 끝에는 두 개의 긴 편모조류가 뻗어있는데, 조류는 앞뒤로 퍼덕거림으로써 유기체가 물을 가로지르며 나아가도록 돕는다.
9. 공연과 예행연습을 위한 적당한 공간을 찾아내는 것은 제작자에게 달려있다.
10. 침팬지는 서쪽에서 동쪽 아프리카까지 광범위한 서식지에서 살고 있다.

11. 그들은 워싱톤이 첫 번째 대통령으로 선택될 것이라고 당연하게 받아들였다.
12. 빵, 곡물과 감자는 비타민과 무기물과 섬유질 이외에도(뿐만 아니라) 탄수화물을 공급한다.
13. 붕괴되는 초신성은 기존의 가스 구름이 합쳐진 가스를 방출한다.
14. 많은 과학자, 경제학자 및 다른 전문가들은 식량 생산이 인구밀도와 더 이상 보조를 맞출 수 없게 될 것을 두려워한다.
15. 플레이트 텍토닉스 (판구조론)는 아직도 지구의 표면을 가로지르는 산맥의 분포에 대하여 설명하는 기본적인 뼈대를 제공한다.

16. 컨트리음악은 미국 남부의 시골 백인의 민속음악과 다른 미국 전통음악에서 유래되었다.
17. 매일 몸의 적혈구가 대략 0.8% 정도 마모되고 파괴된다.
18. 「오델로」와 「로미오와 줄리엣」은 공적인 일이나 왕권을 다루지 않는다는 점에서 셰익스피어의 다른 비극들과는 다르다.
19. 개인별 독서 프로그램은 폭넓은 독서능력과 필요성을 고려한다.
20. 체코 교육자인 존 아모스 코메니우스는 아이들의 책은 교육적일 뿐만 아니라 즐거워야 한다고 믿었던 최초의 작가 중 한 명이었다.

DAY 06-10

Exercise 06-10

1. ⓒ	2. ⓓ	3. ⓐ	4. ⓒ	5. ⓓ
6. ⓓ	7. ⓐ	8. ⓓ	9. ⓑ	10. ⓓ
11. ⓒ	12. ⓒ	13. ⓑ	14. ⓓ	15. ⓒ
16. ⓑ	17. ⓓ	18. ⓑ	19. ⓓ	20. ⓒ

1. 천박한 언어
2. 직장을 그만두다
3. 새로운 프로그램을 육성하다
4. 그는 1등 선수와 보조를 맞추려고 노력했다.
5. 정교한 작업

6. 손톱을 물어뜯다
7. 당신은 이러한 부분을 고려해야 한다.
8. 그 책은 걸작으로 간주된다.
9. 무성 영화
10. 치명적인 질병

11. 그의 형제와 비교하다
12. 그녀의 목소리에서 고통을 듣다
13. 사회적·경제적 격변
14. 쐐기 모양의 파이
15. 수확이 많은 하루

16. 당혹하여 꾸물거리다
17. 새로운 방법을 제안하다
18. 감각적인 기쁨
19. 통화 가치
20. 이상을 실현하려고 노력하다

Practice Test 06-10

1. ⓒ	2. ⓒ	3. ⓑ	4. ⓓ	5. ⓑ
6. ⓑ	7. ⓒ	8. ⓐ	9. ⓐ	10. ⓑ
11. ⓒ	12. ⓓ	13. ⓑ	14. ⓒ	15. ⓒ
16. ⓒ	17. ⓑ	18. ⓒ	19. ⓐ	20. ⓓ

1. 이것은 본래의 그림 [원작]이 아니라 복사본이다.
2. 블루릿지 상단의 스카이라인 드라이브는 셰넌도아 계곡의 멋진 광경을 보여준다.
3. 843년에 스코틀랜드 왕, 케네스 맥캘파인은 픽스의 왕국과 그의 왕국을 통일했다.
4. 포경선의 많은 선원들은 금을 찾기 위해 포경선을 버렸다.
5. 현대 과학은 우리가 어떻게 시간의 흐름과 관련한 방법의 문제를 간신히 고려하기 시작했다.

6. 삭막월 기간에 우리는 달의 갸름한 초승달에서 보름달까지의 달의 주기 변화를 볼 수 있다.
7. 신경과학자들은 수십 년간 뇌손상이나 뇌질환을 치료할 방법을 찾아내기 위해 노력해 왔다.
8. 진드기와 응애는 살진드기제보다 살충제에 덜 민감하다.
9. 건강은 인생을 즐기고 자신들의 목표를 달성할 수 있는 기회를 준다.
10. 기계화는 광부들이 더 생산적이 되도록 도왔다.
11. 세포질은 근원섬유라는 구조로 채워져 있으며 미토콘드리아와 밀접하게 연결되었다.
12. 생명체는 주변 환경의 변화를 감지하고 적응한다.
13. 4천 년 동안 인도 조각가는 영적 내용과 기술적 재능으로 특정지어진 영향력이 있는 작품을 만들었다.
14. 원자량은 탄소원자 12개의 중력과 비교되는 원자의 중력이다.
15. 푸에블로 사람들은 사냥하고 농사를 지으며 옥수수, 콩, 호박 등의 작물을 재배하였다.
16. 국가 라디오프로그램은 무료 오락물을 제공하고 불경기의 부담을 가볍게 한다.
17. 최근 접객업 및 여행업계의 성공은 증가하는 소비자 요구가 원활한 공급과 연결된 것이 원인이 되었다.
18. 은하 기원과 관련된 중요한 단서는 은하의 현지 밀도와 종류 사이의 놀라운 상관관계로부터 나온다.
19. 혼자 사냥하는 포식자는 일반적으로 자신의 모습을 숨기며 살며시 먹잇감에 접근하는데, 이러한 대부분의 사냥꾼들은 주위 환경과 섞이는 보호막이 있다.
20. FTA(자유무역협정)를 맺은 국가들간에는 관세가 없지만 각 회원국들은 비회원국이 생산한 상품에 대하여 관세를 설정할 수 있다.

Intensive Practice Test 06-10

1. Ⓐ	2. Ⓑ	3. Ⓒ	4. Ⓒ	5. Ⓑ
6. Ⓐ	7. Ⓓ	8. Ⓑ	9. Ⓓ	10. Ⓑ
11. Ⓐ	12. Ⓑ	13. Ⓑ	14. Ⓓ	15. Ⓑ
16. Ⓑ	17. Ⓒ	18. Ⓐ	19. Ⓒ	20. Ⓓ

1. 대부분의 영양소들은 사용됨에 따라 화학적 변화를 겪는다.
2. 전투가 심해지면서, 영국과의 화해의 희망은 사라졌다.
3. 과학자들은 물질의 특성을 물리적 성질과 화학적 성질로 나눈다.
4. 트랙터와 기타 현대 농장기계의 사용이 농업인력의 필요성을 급격하게 감소시켰다. (farm labor 농업인력)
5. 세포는 기능에 따라 변화되며, 어떤 세포는 며칠을 살고 다른 세포는 몇 년을 산다.

6. 원시 사회에서 음식을 만들거나 소유한 사람들은 종종 가장 좋은 부분을 다른 사람들에게 일부러 전달했다.
7. 자동차는 도시 교통체증의 주요 원인이며, 배출되는 연기는 도시의 대기 오염을 심각하게 악화시킨다. (exhaust fumes 배기가스)
8. 지구가 태양 주위의 공간을 이동하면서 축을 중심으로 자전한다.
9. 지하수에 스며든 오염물질은 오염된 지표수나 하수 배관 및 정화조 탱크 및 화학 유출의 결과이다.
10. 혜성의 궤도는 지구의 궤도에 비해 종종 가파르게 기울어져 있다.

11. 일반적으로 예레미야와 이사야와 같은 초기 예언자들은 사람들이 죄를 회개하고 하나님 안에서 믿음을 새롭게 하라고 호소하였다.
12. 지구온난화는 산호초뿐만 아니라 그들에 종속된 군락을 근본적으로 변하게 할 수 있다.
13. 세포 분열에 대한 초미세구조 및 면역학적 자료의 빠른 축적에도 불구하고, 많은 이론들이 문헌적으로 풍부하다.
14. 대부분의 상어는 그들의 먹이를 통째로 먹거나, 큰 덩어리의 살로 찢어 먹지만 나머지들은 큰 물고기로부터 작은 살점을 뜯어먹는다.
15. 아프리카인은 그들이 기타 다른 지역으로부터의 정복 위험에 직면해있다고 느끼지 않는다.

16. 바위가 형성될 때 살았던 동물들과 식물들이 바위 층이 층층이 쌓였을 때 매장되고 보존되어졌다.
17. 오늘날 긴 다리를 가진 동물들처럼 긴 다리를 가진 선사시대의 동물들은 아마도 민첩했으며, 짧고 굵은 다리를 가진 동물들은 천천히 움직였을 것이다.
18. 허드슨이 그린 초상화에는 그가 그리는 대상의 인간성을 담으면서 여러 다양한 재료들로 작업하는 그의 천재성을 보여준다.
19. 할로윈과 겹치게 하기 위해서, 젊은 연기자이며 감독인 올슨 웰스는 그의 주간 라디오프로그램인 '방송 중인 화성 극장'을 위한 소설을 각색하였다.
20. 단백질은 만들어지면서 리보솜으로부터 분리되어 소포체의 시스터네를 통해 나중에 변형이 될 수 있는 곳인 활면소포체로 이동한다. (ribosome 세포 안의 RNA로부터 단백질을 만드는 곳, endoplasmic reticulum 소포체, smooth ER 활면소포체, cisternae 막이 겹겹이 쌓여 있는 구조로 된 곳)

TOEFL DAY 11

Daily Checkup 11

1. ⓒ	2. ⓒ	3. Ⓐ	4. Ⓑ	5. ⓒ
6. Ⓐ	7. Ⓓ	8. Ⓓ	9. ⓒ	10. ⓒ
11. ⓒ	12. Ⓐ	13. Ⓐ	14. Ⓑ	15. Ⓑ
16. ⓒ	17. Ⓐ	18. Ⓑ	19. Ⓑ	20. Ⓓ

1. 난파선에서 생존하다
2. 자신의 재산을 낭비하다
3. 독실하고 신앙심이 깊은 기독교인
4. 우리의 삶의 방식에는 낯설다
5. 요구를 준수하다

6. 절망의 행위
7. 자발적인 기부
8. 미숙한 의견
9. 프로젝트 규모를 축소하다
10. 여성 권리의 지지자

11. 게으른 요리사를 위한 편리한 음식
12. 하루하루 급격하게 변동하다
13. 여론을 무시하다
14. 젊은이를 지도하다
15. 이전 기호를 대체할 수 있는 새로운 도형

16. 화려한 준비를 하다
17. 행위의 결과를 받아들이다
18. 토양은 겨울 눈으로 뒤덮였다.
19. 의도적인 미소 / 억지 웃음
20. 생물적 과정이 독립적으로 기능을 계속하게 하다

Practice Test 11

1. Ⓑ	2. Ⓑ	3. Ⓓ	4. Ⓓ	5. ⓒ
6. Ⓓ	7. Ⓐ	8. Ⓑ	9. ⓒ	10. Ⓓ
11. Ⓐ	12. ⓒ	13. ⓒ	14. Ⓐ	15. Ⓑ
16. Ⓓ	17. ⓒ	18. Ⓑ	19. Ⓐ	20. Ⓐ

1. 캘리포니아사막의 야생생물에는 코요테, 도마뱀, 방울뱀을 포함한다.
2. 그 (실험) 기구는 교수님이 내린 지시에 따라 만들어졌다.
3. 전사들은 영광을 위해서 싸우고 용감한 행위의 상징으로 종종 몸에 문신을 했다.
4. 침전물이 지질 연대기가 오래될수록 지구의 보다 깊숙한 곳에 파묻힘에 따라 퇴적물들은 점점 더 다져졌다.
5. 일부 남옥과 황옥의 푸른 색들은 거의 동일하게 보인다.

6. 작문이란 거듭되는 연습이 필요한 기술이다.
7. 200년이 넘게, 중세 후기의 예술의 어떠한 주제도 성모 마리아의 대중성과는 경쟁이 될 수 없었다.
8. 지진이 일어나는 도중에는 높은 건물들이 통제할 수 없을 정도로 진동하여 서로 부딪칠 수 있다.
9. 연역적 추론은 특정 가정에 필요한 결과를 연구하는 데 사용된다. (deductive reasoning 연역적 추리 inductive reasoning 귀납적 추리)
10. 가벼운 심장발작은 사람들에게 덜 활동적인 삶을 살게 하지만 심한 심장발작은 사망에 이르게 할 수 있다.

11. 그리스신화에서는 인간과 동물을 닮은 신과 여신들을 포함한 많은 신화적인 존재가 나온다.
12. 다른 사람에게 상해를 입힐 유해한 행위는 민법 위반으로 간주된다.
13. 캘리포니아 북부와 중부의 해안 기후는 따뜻하지만, 이 지역은 일반적으로 남쪽 해안보다 시원하다.
14. 청소년들이 자신들에게 갖는 감정은 특히 초기 청소년 시기에 불안정할 수 있다.
15. 비극의 리어왕은 '마치 파리가 장난꾸러기 아이들과의 관계처럼 우리가 신들과의 관계 같다'고 절망 속에서 울부짖었다.

16. 아프리카 중심주의 지지자들은 그 접근방법이 아프리카계 미국인 아이들 사이에서 자존감을 세우고 학업 성취도를 높이는 역할을 할 것이라고 믿는다.
17. 대부분의 대형 야생 포유류가 현재 수적으로 적고, 어떤 경우에는 보호를 거의 제공해주지 않거나 생활공간이 협소한 공원에 갇혀있다.
18. 원자들의 대부분의 요소는 다른 원자들과 결합할 수 있지만, 그중 대부분은 독립적으로 존재할 수 없다.
19. 빙하기 말부터 지난 만 년 동안 지속되어 온 높은 지구 온도로 인한 온난화는 빙하를 천천히 달구어 왔다.
20. 보고되는 뉴스에 더해, 「트리뷴」지는 책의 비평과 시를 출간하였고, 노예를 반대하고 여성권익을 지지하는 사설을 게재했다. (book review 서평)

TOEFL DAY 12

Daily Checkup 12

1. ⓒ	2. ⓐ	3. ⓒ	4. ⓒ	5. ⓓ
6. ⓓ	7. ⓒ	8. ⓑ	9. ⓐ	10. ⓓ
11. ⓐ	12. ⓒ	13. ⓐ	14. ⓒ	15. ⓐ
16. ⓒ	17. ⓑ	18. ⓓ	19. ⓑ	20. ⓑ

1. 용서를 구하다
2. 내키지 않은 동의
3. 기이한 사람
4. 우울한 가을 날들
5. 슬퍼하는 아이를 달래려고 노력하다

6. 세상의 조롱거리
7. 위장을 하다
8. 격론이 벌어지다
9. 사람의 미덕을 극찬하다
10. 샴페인 병을 흔들다

11. 엄격한 관점
12. 법을 효력이 없게 하다
13. 시간을 원망하다
14. 철강을 제조하는 방법을 배우다
15. 거짓 보고서를 배포하다

16. 공정한 결정
17. 규칙을 설명하다
18. 거대한 정치적 위험을 수반하다
19. 키가 작은 나무
20. 훌륭한 광경

Practice Test 12

1. ⓑ	2. ⓐ	3. ⓐ	4. ⓓ	5. ⓐ
6. ⓓ	7. ⓐ	8. ⓒ	9. ⓓ	10. ⓒ
11. ⓐ	12. ⓑ	13. ⓒ	14. ⓓ	15. ⓒ
16. ⓒ	17. ⓒ	18. ⓑ	19. ⓑ	20. ⓓ

1. 돌격대는 남북전쟁의 결과에 거의 영향을 주지 못했다.
2. 한 별이 백색왜성이 되면, 별의 존재의 최종 단계에 들어선다.
3. 인지질은 살아 있는 유기체에서 발견되는 모든 (생체) 막의 중요한 구성요소이다.
4. 세포는 매우 작기 때문에 다 자란 유기체에서 나타나는 그 수는 천문학적이다.
5. 영국과 프랑스는 제1차 세계대전이 끝난 직후 다른 전쟁의 위험을 무릅쓰기를 꺼렸다.

6. 다수의 전기발전소는 보조 발전기를 구동하려고 가스 터빈이나 디젤 엔진을 가지고 있다.
7. 빙하가 요세미티 계곡의 깎아지른 듯한 화강암 절벽을 만들었다.
8. 위생은 질병을 일으키는 많은 병원균이 더러운 곳에서 번식하기 때문에 중요하다.
9. 카펫과 바닥깔개는 따뜻하고, 편안한 분위기를 만드는 데 도움이 된다.
10. 3도 화상은 모든 피부층에 스며들고 그 아래 표피층에 영향을 준다.

11. 연구용 또는 학술적인 사전은 고대 영어 및 후기 라틴어의 경우처럼 언어의 초기 어휘를 포함할 수 있다. (a scholarly dictionary 학술사전, a scholarly journal 학술잡지)
12. 진피는 피부에 혈액을 공급하는 동맥과 정맥을 포함하고 있다.
13. 지리학자들은 종종 유럽과 아시아를 하나의 대륙으로 간주하여 유라시아라고 부른다.
14. 공중위생 관리자는 전염병이 있는 사람을 격리시킬 수 있다.
15. 대륙이동설은 위스콘신 주의 산호초 화석과 북쪽 북극권 지역의 열대 식물화석의 존재를 설명하는 데 도움을 준다. (the theory of continental drift 대륙이동설, coral reef 산호초)

16. 철학이 세상의 모든 현상과 지식을 다루고 있기 때문에 철학적 탐구는 어떠한 주제라도 만들 수 있다.
17. 한 선구자 가족이 정착하고자 한 장소에 도착했을 때, 지체하지 않고 영구주택을 지을 만한 시간을 할애할 수 없었다. (right away 곧, 지체하지 않고 permanent house 영구주택)
18. 육지에서는 공기가 리터당 210밀리리터의 가스로 동식물들이 살 수 있도록 매우 일정한 양으로 제공된다. 바다에서는 산소가 바다표면과 가까운 곳에만 제공된다.
19. 빛, 전자 또는 영상 등 어떤 형태건 간에 현미경은 무수히 많은 '세포 이하의' 구조(소기관)로 구성된 단위로서 세포를 보여준다.
20. 지구온난화와 인간이 만든 온실가스의 영향에 대한 최근의 우려는 기후 변화를 야기하는 기본적이면서 자연적인 과정을 이해하도록 하는 필요성을 증가시켰을 뿐이다.

TOEFL DAY 13

Daily Checkup 13

1. ⓒ	2. Ⓐ	3. Ⓓ	4. Ⓐ	5. ⓒ
6. Ⓑ	7. ⓒ	8. Ⓐ	9. Ⓓ	10. ⓒ
11. Ⓑ	12. Ⓐ	13. ⓒ	14. Ⓐ	15. Ⓑ
16. Ⓑ	17. Ⓑ	18. Ⓓ	19. Ⓐ	20. ⓒ

1. 건너뛰며 읽다 / 띄엄띄엄 읽다
2. 건방지게 굴다가 벌을 받다
3. 최선의 노력을 하다
4. 침대에 급히 가다
5. 비둘기는 평화를 상징한다.

6. 논쟁을 방지하다
7. 베인 상처
8. 법으로 규정하다
9. 목걸이는 그녀에게 아주 잘 어울린다.
10. 자신의 호기심을 채우다

11. 건강을 해치는 습관
12. 뉴스 미디어의 편견
13. 우리의 실수를 검토하다
14. 선견지명이 없는 학생들은 공부를 하지 않는다.
15. 튼튼한 상자에 책을 포장했다

16. 스마트폰의 단점
17. 두 회사 사이의 연관
18. 불화로 이어지다
19. 히스테리 기질
20. 자신의 위치를 잡다

Practice Test 13

1. Ⓓ	2. Ⓑ	3. Ⓑ	4. Ⓐ	5. Ⓐ
6. Ⓓ	7. ⓒ	8. Ⓐ	9. ⓒ	10. Ⓑ
11. Ⓐ	12. Ⓑ	13. ⓒ	14. Ⓐ	15. Ⓓ
16. Ⓐ	17. Ⓐ	18. ⓒ	19. ⓒ	20. Ⓑ

1. 물리과학은 우주의 본질을 조사한다.
2. 아마추어 천문학자들은 자신들의 아마추어협회와 지방 및 지역 클럽(소속)을 유지한다.
3. 왕은 국가의 중요한 외교 및 행사에서 국가를 대표한다.
4. 인간의 눈은 0.1mm의 작은 물체도 분별할 능력이 있다.
5. 일부 학교는 미리 정해진 프로그램을 이수한 후 인증서를 수여한다.

6. 쌍둥이 별자리에 태어난 사람은 아마도 수다스럽고 재치가 있을 것이다.
7. 배들이 다른 나라의 항구에 들어서면, 그 물품에 병이 있는지 검사를 받는다.
8. 그 출판사는 영어연구소로부터 발음에 관한 문서의 첫 번째 초교를 받았다. (the first draft 초교)
9. 제한효소는 실제로 쉽게 끊어지는 자리를 공격하여 DNA 분자를 더 작은 DNA 조각으로 잘라낸다. (restriction endonuclease DNA를 절단하는 효소)
10. 직접 공격이 실패하자, 그는 도시를 포위하였다.

11. 아프리카 미래에 대해 만들어진 일반화의 많은 부분은 불충분한 지식에 기초하여 결국 가치가 없다.
12. 우주선은 높은 온도를 견뎌낼 수 있는 방열판과 엄청난 가속력을 견딜 수 있는 튼튼한 구조가 필요하다.
13. 카르멘은 거리낌 없는 자유의 삶에 열정적이었던 아름다운 집시 여인이었다.
14. 비록 그 소설이 많은 역사적 사실을 담고 있지만, 작가는 환상과 비범한 인물들, 기괴한 사건, 긴장감과 특이한 유머도 넣었다.
15. 쿠바 난민들을 그들의 고향에 귀환시키고자 하는 노력에도 불구하고, 미국은 매년 수천 명을 받아들이고 있다.

16. 따뜻한 공기가 상승하면서 온도가 떨어지고 상대 습도가 증가하여 구름과 아마도 강우가 형성될 것이다.
17. 책은 쓰여졌거나 인쇄된 종이들로 구성되거나 또는 한쪽 부분을 다른 재료로 고정시켜 어느 부분에서라도 펼칠 수 있게 하였다.
18. 색채의 배합이 백열등과 형광등의 불빛 아래에서 다르게 보이기 때문에 사람은 이러한 불빛 아래에서 주위 깊게 선택을 해야 한다.
19. 과학자들은 빙상 바닥에서 온도가 일단 상승하게 되면 얼음은 부드럽게 될 것으로 보이며 더 빠르게 흐르게 하고 결과적으로 재앙적인 붕괴로 이끈다고 말한다.
20. 열역학 제1법칙은 에너지는 증가하거나 감소할 수 없어 일정하지만 한 형태에서 다른 형태로 변환한다고 설명한다.

TOEFL DAY 14

Daily Checkup 14

1. ⓒ	2. ⓓ	3. ⓐ	4. ⓑ	5. ⓒ
6. ⓐ	7. ⓒ	8. ⓑ	9. ⓒ	10. ⓓ
11. ⓒ	12. ⓒ	13. ⓐ	14. ⓒ	15. ⓑ
16. ⓐ	17. ⓐ	18. ⓓ	19. ⓑ	20. ⓒ

1. 음주의 법적 제한 수치
2. 외과 수술을 하다
3. 엄밀한 구별
4. 속이 빈 나무
5. 자라는 나무를 방치했다

6. 국가를 해방시키다
7. 질투로 고통스러워하다
8. 열이 가라앉았다.
9. 좋은 신문은 진실을 알려야 한다.
10. 옛 친구를 환호로 맞이하다

11. 법에 대한 허위 정보
12. 생존권을 위협하다
13. 변덕으로 가득한
14. 목적을 이루지 못하다
15. 모호한 대답을 하다

16. 어떤 사람이 그가 스파이라고 경찰에 신고하였다.
17. 일에 대해 보상을 하다
18. 아프리카 출신
19. 컴퓨터공학의 전문 지식
20. 차를 몰아 차고에 넣다

Practice Test 14

1. ⓓ	2. ⓓ	3. ⓐ	4. ⓑ	5. ⓓ
6. ⓒ	7. ⓑ	8. ⓐ	9. ⓒ	10. ⓒ
11. ⓐ	12. ⓒ	13. ⓐ	14. ⓒ	15. ⓒ
16. ⓓ	17. ⓒ	18. ⓑ	19. ⓐ	20. ⓓ

1. 광물은 지구에서 찾을 수 있는 가장 흔한 고체 물질이다.
2. 영양실조는 질병에 대한 몸의 저항성을 낮춘다.
3. 대부분의 원유는 휘발유, 난방유, 기타 연료로 정제된다.
4. 우리가 먹는 음식은 책을 읽는 것부터 달리기를 하는 데 필요한 모든 활동의 에너지를 제공한다.
5. 기원전 200년 이후, 그리스 연극은 쇠퇴하였고 예술의 선두 자리를 로마에 넘겨주었다.

6. 중력은 지구상의 모든 물체에 무게를 주고 아래로 자유낙하하는 물체의 하향 이동을 가속화시킨다.
7. 링컨은 9월에 노예를 해방시킬 예비 명령을 내렸다.
8. 많은 사람들은 행성과 별들 사이의 관계를 분석하여 미래의 사건을 예언하려고 한다.
9. 큰 규모의 조각은 그 크기 때문에 종종 기념비적이라고 한다.
10. 미국에는 7백만 명 이상의 아시아계 후손이 살고 있다.

11. 포물선 모양의 접시시스템은 접시라 불리는 그릇 구조의 윤곽에 따라 배열된 반사경이 있다.
12. 독일군은 1941년 11월에 레닌그라드를 포위했었고, 모스크바를 에워싸기 시작했었다.
13. 시간의 화살은 시간의 흐름이나 비대칭이 아닌, 세계가 시간의 비대칭이 있음을 나타낸다.
14. 남극대륙은 원래 아프리카, 오스트레일리아, 인도와 남아메리카를 포함하는 거대한 땅덩어리에 속해 있었다.
15. 몸에 혈액을 전달하는 심장의 능력을 방해하는 어떠한 질병도 이런 병의 원인이 될 수 있다. (condition 건강상태, 병)

16. TV 방송국은 신호가 최대한 도달할 수 있도록 가장 높은 건물이나 타워에 안테나를 세운다.
17. 해부학에 대한 지식은 연구를 위해 동물의 사체를 해부했던 갈렌에 의해 크게 진보되었다.
18. 유럽에서 증가하는 설탕 수요는 노예와 새로운 설탕 농장을 위한 치열한 경쟁을 만들었다.
19. 일부 역사학자들은 뉴욕의 애칭인 '엠파이어 스테이트'가 조지 워싱턴의 발언으로부터 나왔다고 믿고 있다.
20. 법원은 미국 헌법의 권리장전에 국가가 '개인정보보호의 영역'을 침해하지 못한다는 원칙에 따라 판결을 내렸다. (Constitutional Bill of Rights 권리장전)

TOEFL DAY 15

Daily Checkup 15

1. Ⓐ	2. Ⓒ	3. Ⓓ	4. Ⓑ	5. Ⓐ
6. Ⓓ	7. Ⓒ	8. Ⓓ	9. Ⓑ	10. Ⓐ
11. Ⓒ	12. Ⓒ	13. Ⓐ	14. Ⓑ	15. Ⓓ
16. Ⓑ	17. Ⓒ	18. Ⓒ	19. Ⓐ	20. Ⓐ

1. 정확한 묘사
2. 창을 부수다
3. 정제되지 않은 맛
4. 도박에서 협잡하다
5. 장학금 우승자를 지정하다

6. 해로운 곤충을 박멸하다
7. 선거 결과에 대해 슬퍼하다
8. 꾸준한 체중 감량
9. 주식을 배당하다
10. 공정한 결정

11. 헛된 시도를 하다
12. 터무니없는 계획
13. 정권을 쓰러뜨리다
14. 의무를 이행하다
15. 그 제안이 내 마음을 끌었다.

16. 병을 극복하다
17. ~을 근거로 하여
18. 국내 산업의 판로
19. 냉담한 학생들
20. 선생님들이 학생들에게 숙제를 내준다.

Practice Test 15

1. Ⓐ	2. Ⓐ	3. Ⓑ	4. Ⓒ	5. Ⓒ
6. Ⓓ	7. Ⓒ	8. Ⓑ	9. Ⓐ	10. Ⓒ
11. Ⓒ	12. Ⓑ	13. Ⓒ	14. Ⓐ	15. Ⓒ
16. Ⓓ	17. Ⓒ	18. Ⓑ	19. Ⓐ	20. Ⓐ

1. 그 지역에 살고 있는 모든 동식물 개체군들은 공동체를 형성한다.
2. 습한 공기가 산맥의 경사면을 쓸고 올라가면서 공기가 차가워지고 구름이 형성된다.
3. 동종의 공동체라 하더라도 의견 차이가 발생한다.
4. 부를 얻기 위한 욕망은 제국을 건설하기 위한 거의 모든 노력의 동기였다.
5. 국가의 가장 큰 문제점 중 하나는 비오는 지역에서 물이 필요한 건조한 지역으로 물을 나르는 방법에 관한 것이다.
6. 오존분자(O_3)는 자외선이 산소분자(O_2)와 충돌할 때 만들어진다.
7. 중세 유럽의 영웅 드라마는 오늘날 듣기에는 터무니없는 것 같아도 그 시기에는 대중적인 인기가 있었다.
8. 뉴딜정책이 만들어지고 난 후에, 은행 및 공공복지에 대한 정부의 역할은 꾸준히 증가했다.
9. 리튬은 가장 가벼운 고체 원소이며 순수한 형태로 있을 때 떠오를 수 있다.
10. 전자플래시 장치는 배터리나 콘센트에서 전달된 전류로 작동된다.

11. 햄릿 아버지의 유령이 왕자 앞에 나타나 그가 클라우디우스에 의해서 살해되었다고 말한다.
12. 평원 인디언들은 주술인이 사람을 치료할 수 있고 어느 정도 영적 세상을 통제한다고 믿는다.
13. 현대 문명의 근로자들은 선사시대 사람들처럼 그들의 일상생활에 크게 관심이 없다.
14. 선사시대 사람들은 밤하늘의 특정 그룹의 별들이 특정 위치에 도달했을 때 매년 계절이 바뀐다는 것을 알게 되었을 것이다.
15. 만일 사람들이 자유의지가 부족했다면, 그들의 결정과 행동에 대하여 책임을 지게 하는 것은 불합리하게 보일 것이다.

16. 워싱턴은 군사훈련과 전술에 대한 책을 읽고 그의 새로운 임무를 준비하였을 것이다.
17. 컴퓨터화된 통제는 낮은 비용과 정밀한 기능 때문에 아마도 미래 자동차 내부에 더 많은 작업을 할 것이다.
18. 농부는 나무를 심고 농지와 미경지 사이에 자연 식생의 터를 남겨서 토양의 손실을 줄일 수 있다.
19. 단백질 섭취 후, 대부분 사람들의 위에 있는 염산이 단백질 분자로 하여금 뭉치도록 한다. (hydrochloric acid 염산)
20. 수소 및 질소 등 각각의 원소는 종종 라틴어로부터 유래된 지정된 기호가 있다.

DAY 11-15

Exercise 11-15

1. Ⓐ	2. Ⓒ	3. Ⓑ	4. Ⓑ	5. Ⓑ
6. Ⓒ	7. Ⓐ	8. Ⓓ	9. Ⓓ	10. Ⓐ
11. Ⓒ	12. Ⓒ	13. Ⓐ	14. Ⓒ	15. Ⓑ
16. Ⓓ	17. Ⓓ	18. Ⓒ	19. Ⓓ	20. Ⓐ

1. 인권 침해
2. 가축을 가두고 보호하기 위해 울타리를 만들다
3. 그 마을에서 낙서 예술이 만연한
4. 아늑한 방
5. 학술적인 논문

6. 6개월간 격리되어지다
7. 보조 모터를 돌리다
8. 지층을 뚫을 수 없다
9. 안전벨트를 고정하세요.
10. 그 오솔길은 여기부터 오르막이다.

11. 감추지 않는 기쁨
12. 진행을 방해하다
13. 사유지에 침입하다
14. 똑바로 서다
15. 우리의 속도를 높이다.

16. 그들을 유럽으로 이주시키다
17. 숲에 거주하다
18. 정확한 의미
19. 부당한 요구
20. 동시대의 작가들

Practice Test 11-15

1. Ⓒ	2. Ⓑ	3. Ⓒ	4. Ⓑ	5. Ⓐ
6. Ⓓ	7. Ⓓ	8. Ⓓ	9. Ⓑ	10. Ⓑ
11. Ⓐ	12. Ⓒ	13. Ⓑ	14. Ⓑ	15. Ⓒ
16. Ⓑ	17. Ⓐ	18. Ⓐ	19. Ⓐ	20. Ⓑ

1. 독자는 관심이 없는 이야기들을 읽지 않고 건너뛸 수 있다.
2. 강력한 지진이 먼 거리의 단단한 대지를 심하게 흔들 수 있다.
3. 자원자들의 대답은 틀렸다.
4. 담즙의 과잉은 아마도 사람을 우울하게 만들 것이다.
5. 소크라테스는 모호한 의견을 분명한 생각으로 대체하고 싶었다.

6. 영국은 프렌치 인디언전쟁(1754-1763)에서 프랑스를 격파했다.
7. 일부 심리학자들은 심리학의 주요 목적은 특히 감정과 감각 및 의식이 있는 경험을 묘사하고 분석하고 설명하는 것이라고 믿었다.
8. 암벽 등반가는 암벽에 단단히 매달려 있다.
9. 캘리포니아의 기후는 다양하다.
10. 식물은 단순한 분자를 흡수하고 그것을 화학적으로 복잡한 식물자원으로 변경하며 자란다.

11. 세계의 많은 지역에서 질병과 열악한 생활환경은 심각한 문제이다.
12. 엔지니어는 강철처럼 견고하거나 목화처럼 부드러운 플라스틱을 개발했다.
13. 세포의 발견은 17세기 현미경의 개발과 연관이 있다.
14. 많은 종들이 포식자로부터 자신을 보호하는 데 도움이 되도록 모색을 주위 환경과 뒤섞는다.
15. 알코올성 간경변증으로 사망한 사람들의 대형동맥은 관절경화증이 놀랍도록 없다.

16. 그 대륙은 아프리카, 오스트레일리아, 인도와 남아메리카를 포함한 곤드와랜드라 불렸던 큰 대륙의 일부분이었다.
17. 미국의 많은 학교에서 제2외국어로 불어를 가르치며 2개 언어를 구사하는 어린이들을 위한 특별교육을 제공한다.
18. 핵유전자의 기능은 리보솜 RNA분자를 생산하여 최종적으로 리보솜의 한 부분으로 만드는 것이다.
19. 원형질의 대략 96%는 탄소, 수소, 산소, 질소로 구성되며, 3%는 인, 칼륨, 황으로 구성된다.
20. 제2차 세계대전(1939-1945) 중에 조지는 그의 책임을 양심적으로 완수하였으며, 영국 공습 때 사람들은 그의 행동에 감탄하였다.

Intensive Practice Test 11-15

1. Ⓐ	2. Ⓑ	3. Ⓓ	4. Ⓒ	5. Ⓓ
6. Ⓐ	7. Ⓓ	8. Ⓑ	9. Ⓓ	10. Ⓑ
11. Ⓐ	12. Ⓒ	13. Ⓒ	14. Ⓓ	15. Ⓒ
16. Ⓒ	17. Ⓐ	18. Ⓑ	19. Ⓑ	20. Ⓓ

1. 각국의 많은 젊은이들은 전통적인 결혼 방식을 무시한다.
2. 성경의 여러가지 현대 영어 번역물이 이전 버전의 오래된 언어를 교체하려고 시도되어 왔다.
3. 지난 1~2백 년 동안에 산악 빙하가 감소하고 있어서 계곡과 강으로 흐르는 물이 바다와 합쳐져 왔다.
4. 만일 입자와 반입자가 충돌하면, 감마선과 기타 에너지를 방출하여 서로 소멸될 것이다.
5. 쿠빌라이 칸은 그의 전임자보다 다소 온화한 성품이었으며, 실제로 유럽인들과의 교류를 권장하였다.

6. 일부 환자는 단순하고 일상적인 업무를 할 수 있는 능력을 잃게 되어 계획하기와 같은 지적 능력에 장애를 보였다.
7. 이순신 장군의 명량해전과 노량해전에서의 성공적인 전술은 일본 해군을 당황하게 하였다.
8. 어떤 사람들은 쓰나미 해일이라 부르지만, 과학자들은 파도가 조수간만에 의해서 발생하는 것이 아니기 때문에 이 용어는 오해의 소지가 있다고 생각한다.
9. 많은 비가(悲歌)들은 유명인이나 친한 친구의 죽음을 슬퍼한다.
10. 미국의 경우, 미국 원주민들에게 토지할당에 관한 연방정책은 1900년 초기까지 유효하였다.

11. 대부분의 인디언전쟁은 필사적이고 형편없이 장비를 갖춘 인디언들이 그들의 땅과 삶의 방식을 지키기 위한 무모한 도전에 불과했다.
12. 베르딩 방어를 조직한 앙리 페타 장군은 프랑스의 영웅으로 칭송되었다.
13. 일부 비타민은 비활성 형태로 음식과 약으로 생성된다.
14. 인류학자들의 목적은 어떻게 문화가 변화하고 차이가 생겨나는지 이해하는 것이다.
15. 우리 모두는 부당한 수색과 체포에 대해 보호 받을 권리가 있다.

16. 1800년대 후반에 많은 통계적 개념과 방법이 개발되었음에도 불구하고, 1920년대까지는 개선되지 않은 채로 있었다.
17. 1777년 10월, 프리먼 농장에서의 2차 전투에서 아놀드 장군은 버고인 장군에 대항하여 대담한 용기를 보였으며 다시 심각한 부상을 당하였다.
18. 남자들이 전쟁터에 나간 후 사무실과 공장의 일자리를 갖게 된 여자들은 새롭게 찾은 독립성을 포기하는 것을 달가워하지 않았다.
19. 복수심에 불타는 샤일록을 제외하고는 연극은 행복하게 막을 내렸지만, 이것은 명랑한 코미디는 아니다.
20. 과학자들은 궤도의 모든 지점과 접촉하는 가상의 표면, 즉 행성의 직각에서 행성의 상대적 기울기를 측정한다.

DAY 16

Daily Checkup 16

1. ⓓ	2. ⓒ	3. ⓓ	4. ⓐ	5. ⓓ
6. ⓐ	7. ⓐ	8. ⓑ	9. ⓐ	10. ⓑ
11. ⓐ	12. ⓑ	13. ⓒ	14. ⓑ	15. ⓒ
16. ⓒ	17. ⓑ	18. ⓐ	19. ⓓ	20. ⓐ

1. 단정한 복장
2. 비교가 안 될 정도로
3. 구름처럼 쓸쓸히 떠다니다
4. 만병 치료제
5. 반란군

6. 살려달라고 외치다
7. 제의를 철회하다
8. 파국으로 몰고 가다
9. 물결 모양의 움직임
10. 연금으로 생활하다

11. 수집 동전의 가치를 평가하다
12. 그 점을 보여주다
13. 기계를 작동시키다
14. 신을 공경하는(경건한) 마음
15. 마음 내키지 않는 조수

16. 인생의 의미에 대해 명상하다
17. 4개의 소설을 포함한 한 권의 책
18. 사과의 크기를 명시하다
19. 장대하고 아름다운 한강
20. 안이한 생각

Practice Test 16

1. ⓓ	2. ⓒ	3. ⓓ	4. ⓑ	5. ⓑ
6. ⓐ	7. ⓐ	8. ⓒ	9. ⓒ	10. ⓒ
11. ⓑ	12. ⓒ	13. ⓐ	14. ⓐ	15. ⓑ
16. ⓑ	17. ⓒ	18. ⓓ	19. ⓓ	20. ⓐ

1. 수학 문장은 일상적인 언어로 설명될 수 있다.
2. 과학자들은 열량계라는 기구를 이용해서 열의 양을 측정한다.
3. 낭만주의자들은 전통사회 및 정치적 제도에 저항하는 성향이 있었다.
4. 캘리포니아의 공립대학은 많은 훌륭한 의료시설과 연구소를 운영한다.
5. 참고문헌에서 학년 수준의 평가는 단지 일반적인 지침으로 의도된 것이다.

6. 기근, 전염병 및 기타 재난은 인구의 급격한 감소의 원인이다.
7. 과거에는 세계 경제지도자의 대부분은 지배적인 정치력과 군사력을 소유하였다.
8. 초음속수송기(SST)는 약 1,350mph(2,180kph) 높이에서 굉음으로 대기권을 비행할 수 있다. (roar 큰 소리를 내며 움직이다)
9. 물고기뿐만 아니라 양서류도 피부에 끈적끈적한 물질을 분비하는 분비선이 있다.
10. 잭슨의 동맹이 상원에 대한 통제에 이르렀고 결의안을 철회하였다.

11. 천문학자들은 태양계 너머의 많은 별들에서 생명이 존재할 수 있는 행성이 존재한다고 생각한다.
12. 양자물리학에서는 모든 입자와 필드는 페로미온과 보손이라는 극단적으로 다른 두 종류로 나뉜다.
13. 저작권 침해자들은 법에 의해 지정된 실제 손해 및 이익에 대해 손해배상의 책임이 있다.
14. 가을에 제임스 윌킨슨 장군과 웨이드 햄튼 장군은 몬트리올 공략을 위한 군사작전에 착수했다.
15. 포유동물은 먹이를 찾고 물을 마시고 숨을 곳을 찾기 위한 일상적인 활동으로 주변 지역을 어슬렁거렸다.

16. 3천만 년에서 4천만 년 전, 히말라야산맥과 남아시아에 인접한 티베트고원은 솟기 시작했다.
17. 인종차별, 높은 범죄율, 과도한 토지 가격 등은 투자자들에게 이러한 프로젝트 위탁을 경계하게 만들기 때문에 도시 부흥은 종종 정부의 도움이 필요하다.
18. 새로운 빵, 생크림과 딸기와 같은 일부 상품은 생산된 후 바로 소비해야 하며, 그래서 지역 시장으로 판매가 제한된다.
19. 로마제국과 중국제국은 2세기 동안 함께 공존하였지만 정치적으로나 경제적으로 직접적인 교류가 거의 없었다.
20. 고생대시대의 후반에 양서류의 많은 종들이 육지와 물로 나뉘어 호수와 강 기슭에서 서식하였다.

TOEFL DAY 17

Daily Checkup 17

1. Ⓐ	2. Ⓓ	3. Ⓐ	4. Ⓓ	5. Ⓒ
6. Ⓒ	7. Ⓒ	8. Ⓒ	9. Ⓐ	10. Ⓑ
11. Ⓑ	12. Ⓒ	13. Ⓐ	14. Ⓓ	15. Ⓑ
16. Ⓐ	17. Ⓐ	18. Ⓐ	19. Ⓐ	20. Ⓑ

1. 두 관점 사이의 큰 차이
2. 새로운 직장에 대하여 걱정하다
3. 어려운 시기를 보내다
4. 애매한 답
5. 어떤 외진 곳에서

6. 비탄에 빠지다
7. 즉흥적인 연주회를 개최하다
8. 색상의 조화
9. 학생들이 운동장으로 몰려들었다.
10. 폭풍이 가라앉다.

11. 얼음 송곳으로 가방에 구멍을 뚫다
12. 그의 변덕스러운 행동으로 혼란스럽다
13. 스케줄을 조정하다
14. 어떤 새들은 겨울에 따뜻한 나라로 이동한다.
15. 모든 이웃들에게 호의적인 감정

16. 적은 수입
17. 재즈의 선율을 융합시키다
18. 제철의 푸른잎 채소
19. 남에게 맡겨 기르다
20. 불침번 병사

Practice Test 17

1. Ⓐ	2. Ⓒ	3. Ⓐ	4. Ⓑ	5. Ⓓ
6. Ⓒ	7. Ⓑ	8. Ⓐ	9. Ⓒ	10. Ⓐ
11. Ⓓ	12. Ⓒ	13. Ⓓ	14. Ⓒ	15. Ⓒ
16. Ⓒ	17. Ⓐ	18. Ⓐ	19. Ⓑ	20. Ⓓ

1. 생존하기 위해서 생물은 환경의 장기적인 변화에 적응해야 한다.
2. 사람들이 육지생물에 치우친 시각으로 보면, 해양생물들은 이상하게 보일 수 있다.
3. 알렉산더 대왕이 죽은 기원전 323년 이후에 그의 제국은 작은 왕국들로 쪼개졌다.
4. 아동문학은 과학의 경이로움과 예술의 아름다움을 독자들에게 소개한다.

5. 1700년대 스페인의 브루봉 왕가의 통치자는 많은 정부 개혁을 수행했다.

6. 선거일이 다가오면서 캠페인의 속도는 몹시 빨라졌다.
7. 마그마(액화바위)는 분리판 사이의 간격을 채우는 연약권으로부터 올라왔다.
8. 원숭이와 코끼리와 같은 일부 동물은 열대지역에 서식한다.
9. 1402년, 간헐적인 전쟁이 스코틀랜드와 영국 사이에서 발생했다.
10. 아프리카는 미국에서 고수익 노예무역의 초창기 노예 공급지였다.

11. 직립원인의 일원은 결국 아프리카에서 아시아와 유럽으로 이주하였다.
12. 현명한 결정을 하기 위해서, 학생들은 자신들과 세계에 대한 완전하고 정확한 정보를 얻어야 한다.
13. 남북전쟁 후 엄청난 변화가 경제를 개조시켰다.
14. 세포는 활동이 멈춘 후에도, 전해질이 내용물을 먹어 치워 결국 구멍을 낼 것이다.
15. 처음에 록음악은 대체로 4/4비트를 따르며 멜로디에서 단지 2개 또는 3개의 화음을 사용했다.

16. 아프리카에서 코끼리 숫자 감소의 주요 원인은 불법 사냥이다.
17. 구조대원이 10킬로미터의 지역을 샅샅이 뒤졌다.
18. 컨트리음악은 종종 기억으로 또는 기존의 노래를 즉흥적으로 연주한다.
19. Hehe 농업에서, 맥주는 연간 토지를 개간하는 데 도움을 준 사람에게 지급하는 수단으로 사용된다.
20. 1932년 이후 윈스턴 처칠은 그의 연설과 글에서 나치 독일의 위험에 대한 국민과 세계의 관심을 끌려고 노력하였다.

TOEFL DAY 18

Daily Checkup 18

1. ⓒ	2. Ⓐ	3. Ⓓ	4. ⓒ	5. Ⓐ
6. Ⓓ	7. ⓒ	8. Ⓑ	9. Ⓓ	10. ⓒ
11. Ⓐ	12. ⓒ	13. ⓒ	14. ⓒ	15. Ⓐ
16. Ⓓ	17. Ⓐ	18. Ⓑ	19. Ⓑ	20. Ⓑ

1. 중립을 고수하다
2. 활발한 토론
3. 계약서에 서명하다
4. ~의 환심을 잃다
5. 설탕은 음식에서 흔하게 사용된다.

6. 가톨릭 교리
7. 가공하지 않은 석유 [원유]
8. 지식을 얻다
9. 대량으로 구매하는 것이 경제적이다.
10. 어디에나 존재하는 하나님

11. 흔적이 없어지다
12. 전망이 좋은 장소를 차지한 집(전망이 좋은 집)
13. 벽에 포스터를 붙이다
14. 출생의 권리(명문의 특권)
15. 비합법 노동조합

16. 위험을 감수할 준비가 되다
17. 불성실하여 그를 고발하다
18. 언쟁하다
19. 뛰어난 글을 쓰다
20. 열렬한 지지자

Practice Test 18

1. Ⓐ	2. ⓒ	3. Ⓑ	4. Ⓓ	5. Ⓓ
6. Ⓑ	7. ⓒ	8. Ⓑ	9. ⓒ	10. Ⓓ
11. ⓒ	12. Ⓐ	13. Ⓑ	14. Ⓓ	15. Ⓓ
16. Ⓑ	17. Ⓓ	18. Ⓐ	19. ⓒ	20. Ⓑ

1. 해마다, 장소마다 강수량이 적은 시기는 강수량이 높은 시기와 번갈아 나타난다.
2. 1763년의 발표는 짧은 시간 동안 서부 이동을 중단시켰다.
3. 일부 과학자들은 화성의 중심부에는 순수한 철 황화물, 황과 철의 화합물로 구성되어 있다고 믿는다.
4. 1940년대 후반에 기술자들은 제2차 세계대전 중에 만들어진 조잡한 제트엔진의 성능을 개선하기 위해 노력했다.

5. 시장의 한 부분에서 얻을 수 있는 가격은 시장의 다른 부분에서 지불하는 가격에 영향을 준다.

6. 많은 사회비평가들은 슬럼가의 삶을 연구하고 그곳의 비참한 생활조건을 보고했다.
7. 양극의 이온이 서로 접촉되었을 때, 이를 이온결합이라고 한다.
8. 남북전쟁 당시에 공화당은 민주당을 연합에 부정한 당이라고 비난하였다.
9. 일부 해양생물로부터 추출한 화학물질은 암과 기타 질병을 치료하는 의약품으로 사용된다.
10. 제퍼슨은 1796년 대통령 후보 출마 기회를 잃었지만, 존 애덤스 대통령 시절에 부통령이 되었다.
11. 목축업자들은 넓은 평온에서 방목을 하기 때문에 울타리 없이 단지 몇 개의 건물이 필요하다고 생각했다.
12. 돈키호테의 주인공은 오래된 옛 이야기의 기사에 대한 소설을 읽으면서 소설이 사실이며 정확하다고 믿으며, 그의 단조로운 삶에 활력을 넣고 싶어한 스페인의 지주이다.
13. 견본을 조립하는 것은 종종 디자인 문제를 드러내는데, 이를 고침으로써 차의 최종 조립이 좀 더 효과적으로 되도록 할 수 있다.
14. 각각의 종교에는 가르침을 전달하고 도덕적 교리를 설명할 수 있는 이야기가 있다.
15. 많은 학자들은 비평가들이 작가가 실제로 쓴 글에 더 다가갈 수 있도록 셰익스피어의 초기 원문을 연구하는 것에 집중해왔다.
16. 알파벳 시스템의 큰 장점은 상대적으로 적은 개수가 요구되는 기호를 통해서 보편적 문맹률을 낮게 한다.
17. 사람이나 야생집단에도 질병을 야기하는 유기체의 증식을 선호하는 환경특성으로 변경되어 전염성 질환이 나타나거나 널리 퍼질 수 있다.
18. 사람들이 개인식별번호(PIN)로 접근할 수 있는 자동화기기(ATM)는 수치 검증시스템의 사례이다.
19. 많은 과학자들이 지구, 태양, 풍력, 해양으로부터 얻는 에너지가 미래에 경제적인 전기에너지를 생산하기 위해 좀 더 광범위하게 사용될 수 있으리라고 믿는다.
20. 오늘날, 컴퓨터 기술은 지루한 수작업 인자작업, 채색 및 촬영작업을 대체하고 있다.

TOEFL DAY 19

Daily Checkup 19

1. ⓒ	2. ⓒ	3. ⓑ	4. ⓓ	5. ⓐ
6. ⓓ	7. ⓐ	8. ⓑ	9. ⓐ	10. ⓒ
11. ⓐ	12. ⓑ	13. ⓒ	14. ⓓ	15. ⓑ
16. ⓓ	17. ⓒ	18. ⓒ	19. ⓐ	20. ⓑ

1. 지방 공동체
2. 인공 얼음
3. 반역죄로 추방하다
4. 격리된 구역
5. 스스로를 격리시키다

6. 선전 포고를 하다
7. 전략을 밝히다
8. 태양 향점
9. 모욕을 당하다
10. 계곡의 깊은 곳

11. 누구에게 어떤 책임을 지우다
12. 전쟁의 그림자가 다가오고 있다.
13. 그들의 소득은 비참할 정도로 적다.
14. 연기 냄새를 탐지하다
15. 광상(鑛床)을 개발하다

16. 인내심을 가지고 고통을 참다
17. 부정확한 정보
18. 혹독한 고난
19. 무관심의 장막을 치다 / 모른 체하다
20. 모든 종류의 폭력을 혐오하다

Practice Test 19

1. ⓐ	2. ⓓ	3. ⓓ	4. ⓑ	5. ⓐ
6. ⓓ	7. ⓐ	8. ⓒ	9. ⓑ	10. ⓓ
11. ⓐ	12. ⓐ	13. ⓑ	14. ⓐ	15. ⓒ
16. ⓒ	17. ⓑ	18. ⓐ	19. ⓓ	20. ⓑ

1. 적당히 균형 잡힌 식단은 건강을 지키는 데 도움을 준다.
2. 혈관은 진피와 표피에 영양분을 제공한다.
3. 직립원인은 아마도 불의 사용을 완전히 익힌 최초의 인간일 것이다.
4. 많은 청각 장애인들은 음파를 증폭시키는 전자 청각보조장치에 의존한다.
5. 확률은 결과의 가능성을 수학적으로 연구하는 학문이다.

6. 영장류 가운데 인간만이 다른 색의 맨살을 갖는다.
7. 많은 국가들은 화석연료의 의존성을 줄이기 위해 다른 에너지 원천을 개발하려고 노력 중에 있다.
8. 세계화 계획에서 찰리 윤은 곤충시장의 국제산업화에 대한 그의 생각을 설명하였다.
9. 비행기는 승객과 화물의 가장 빠르고 효율적인 운송수단을 제공한다.
10. 먼로는 결국 애덤스의 충고를 받아들이기로 결정하고 먼로주의를 선언했다.
11. 신화를 연구함으로써 우리는 사람들이 왜 그렇게 행동하는지를 이해하기 위해 노력할 수 있다.
12. 만일 두 정당이 휴회 기간에 동의할 수 없다면, 대통령은 회기를 연기할 수 밖에 없다.
13. 축산목장, 과수원, 포도밭과 시장용 채소밭이 아름다운 계곡에 여기저기 흩어져 있다.
14. 또 다른 정부의 재정위기가 미국에서 나타나고 있다.
15. 많은 미국인들은 닉슨 대통령이 연방법을 위반하였다고 생각했고 공판에 세우고 싶어했다.
16. 타워 또는 높은 나무와 같은 수직적인 선은 품위와 웅장함을 전달해 줄 수 있다.
17. 1970년대에 석유수출국기구(OPEC)가 석유가격을 급격히 올리자 그 회원국들이 석유 생산을 제한하면서 국가소득을 증가시킬 수 있었다.
18. 인디언 전설은 인류 탄생 이전의 세상, 인류의 기원 및 부족의 기원, 부족 영웅의 설화에 대한 이야기를 포함하고 있다.
19. 정족수란 조직이 사업을 집행하기 위해 참석해야 하는 최소한의 인원을 말한다.
20. 한 국가가 자국민을 노예로 삼는 상황이면 국가는 다른 나라와의 관계에 있어서 완전히 통제 불능 상태가 될 수 있다.

TOEFL DAY 20

Daily Checkup 20

1. Ⓐ	2. Ⓓ	3. Ⓑ	4. Ⓒ	5. Ⓓ
6. Ⓐ	7. Ⓒ	8. Ⓑ	9. Ⓒ	10. Ⓐ
11. Ⓑ	12. Ⓐ	13. Ⓑ	14. Ⓒ	15. Ⓐ
16. Ⓑ	17. Ⓒ	18. Ⓓ	19. Ⓒ	20. Ⓐ

1. 식물에게 햇빛을 받게 하다
2. 감정을 억누르다
3. 인조견, 최초의 합성직물의 종류
4. 흥미로운 과학 현상
5. 나뭇가지에 매달리다

6. 경멸의 눈초리
7. 실험을 하기 위해 시간과 노력을 들이다
8. 어린 나무의 탄력 있는 나뭇가지
9. 경우에 꼭 맞는
10. 착지점

11. 임시 총회
12. 도시 생활
13. 내 인생에서 기억에 남는 시기
14. 숲의 소박한 통나무집
15. 삶의 다양한 측면

16. 실질적인 문제를 회피하다
17. 습기에 의해 부식되다
18. 책의 기원
19. 교잡된 옥수수 씨
20. 이런 와인들은 쓰며 다소 신맛이 난다.

Practice Test 20

1. Ⓑ	2. Ⓒ	3. Ⓓ	4. Ⓒ	5. Ⓐ
6. Ⓑ	7. Ⓒ	8. Ⓑ	9. Ⓐ	10. Ⓑ
11. Ⓑ	12. Ⓒ	13. Ⓓ	14. Ⓓ	15. Ⓐ
16. Ⓒ	17. Ⓑ	18. Ⓓ	19. Ⓐ	20. Ⓒ

1. 전설은 보통 문화와 역사의 어떤 측면과 연관된다.
2. 축축한 지의류(地衣類)가 햇빛을 흡수할 때, 조류부분은 광합성을 통해 당을 생산한다. (lichen 균류와 조류의 복합체)
3. 어떤 종들은 보호를 받더라도, 회복될 수 없을 것이다.
4. 합금은 새로운 합성 고분자보다 쉽게 만들어진다.
5. 이탈리아에서는 제1차 세계대전 이후의 경제적 고통이 파업과 폭동을 일으켰다.

6. 시대는 기간으로 나뉘어지고, 기간은 중요한 사건으로 나뉘어진다.
7. 질병을 일으키는 병원균은 휴식을 취한 사람보다는 피곤한 사람을 더 쉽게 공격한다.
8. 빅토리아 여왕은 이미 권력과 위엄과 명성을 잃은 채 왕권을 계승했다.
9. 무슬림은 이슬람 연도 9번째인 라마단 기간의 새벽과 일몰 사이에는 음식을 먹거나 마실 수 없다.
10. 소설가는 사건을 정리할 수 있고 장소를 설명할 수 있고 거의 무한한 방법으로 등장인물들을 묘사할 수 있다.

11. 워싱턴은 미국 대통령 재임기간 중 탁월한 용기와 명예와 지혜를 발휘했다.
12. 경제적·사회적 삶의 해석은 종종 실제 사건과는 무관한 생각에 기반을 둔다.
13. 매년 봄, 푸르고 하얀 제비꽃은 강의 계곡과 높은 고지대의 하부지역에 따라 꽃을 피운다.
14. 전통적인 사진 촬영기법에서 빛이 카메라의 이미지 센서에 노출되어 이미지를 데이터로 기록한다.
15. 거슈윈은 그의 작품에서 미국 남동부의 흑인이 부른 노래의 정취를 잡아냈다.

16. 청소년기는 인간 발달의 생물학적 현상으로서 항상 존재한다.
17. 화학요법은 환자를 감염에 취약하게 하고 백혈구의 숫자를 급격히 감소시킨다.
18. 1980년대에 많은 산업국가에서 비디오카세트의 인기는 하늘 높이 치솟았다.
19. 1970년대와 1980년대의 도시 정착과 체스피크 만을 따라 세워진 공장의 위치는 오염을 야기했고 식물과 야생동물들에게 약간의 피해를 입혔다.
20. 바닥 깔개를 사용하는 경우 카펫·양탄자와 탄성 바닥재로 알려진 경외장재 중에서 선택해야 한다.

DAY 16-20

Daily Checkup 16-20

1. ⓓ	2. ⓑ	3. ⓐ	4. ⓑ	5. ⓒ
6. ⓐ	7. ⓐ	8. ⓓ	9. ⓑ	10. ⓒ
11. ⓐ	12. ⓓ	13. ⓑ	14. ⓐ	15. ⓒ
16. ⓓ	17. ⓓ	18. ⓒ	19. ⓐ	20. ⓐ

1. 실험에 착수하다
2. 편파적이지 않은 의견
3. 군중을 흥분시키다
4. 지루한 연설
5. 낮과 밤이 교대로 왔다.

6. 식물과 관목과 나무의 꽃
7. 보스톤과 인접한 근교
8. 직설적인 화법을 조심하다
9. 수익성이 높은 사업을 창립하다
10. 간헐성 맥박 / 부정맥

11. 수직 운동
12. 롤스로이스와 같은 명차
13. 인구가 대도시에 집중하는 경향이 있다.
14. 우유는 아이에게 영양분을 준다.
15. 성공을 보장하다

16. 공습을 받기 쉬운 요새
17. 아마 / 십중팔구
18. 회의를 연기하다
19. 모든 관련 없는 사항을 제거하다
20. 치솟는 생활비

Practice Test 16-20

1. ⓑ	2. ⓐ	3. ⓒ	4. ⓑ	5. ⓓ
6. ⓑ	7. ⓓ	8. ⓐ	9. ⓑ	10. ⓐ
11. ⓑ	12. ⓓ	13. ⓐ	14. ⓓ	15. ⓒ
16. ⓐ	17. ⓒ	18. ⓐ	19. ⓑ	20. ⓒ

1. 고기소들이 계곡 목초지에서 풀을 뜯고 있다.
2. 황은 맛이나 냄새가 전혀 없다.
3. 많은 실업자들이 자신들의 문제들을 낮은 임금으로도 일을 하려는 중국인 노동자들을 탓하며 비난했다.
4. 선진화된 공군은 기습적인 미사일이나 적의 폭격을 감지하기 위하여 레이더 기지나 위성을 사용한다.
5. 법원은 규제라는 단어를 장려하고 촉진하고 보호하고 금지하거나 제한한다는 의미로 해석하였다.

6. 육지에 사는 사람들의 관점에서는 해양생물들이 이상하게 보일 수 있다.
7. 성인은 음식에서 매일 음료나 물의 형태로 23/10쿼트(2.4리터)의 물을 마셔야 한다.(1쿼트는 0.94리터)
8. 만일 재앙이 극심하고 널리 펴졌다면, 초식공룡은 굶어 죽었을 것이다.
9. 모든 다 자란 성체의 뼈대는 200개 이상의 뼈로 구성되는데 그 뼈의 일부는 단일한 구조로 형성되어 융합된다.
10. 화상은 차가운 물로 세척하거나 시원한 젖은 타월로 통증이 가라앉게 하거나 전문적인 도움을 받기 전까지는 화상을 입은 곳을 신속히 차갑게 해야 한다.
11. 고래의 젖은 육지 포유류의 젖에 비해 더 농축되고 지방, 단백질, 무기질이 매우 풍부하다.
12. 휴식을 취하는 연습을 하면서 긴장과 초조함을 피할 수 있다.
13. 다른 포유류와 마찬가지로, 어미고래는 새끼를 양육하고 최소 1년간은 새끼를 가까이서 보호한다.
14. 중성자 별은 인류에게 알려진 가장 고밀도의 물체인데, 지름이 단지 20킬로미터밖에 되지 않는 천체 안에 태양의 질량보다 약간 더 무겁게 채워져 있다.
15. 대부분의 국립공원은 뛰어난 아름다움과 자연 특유의 과학적 중요성으로 보호를 받는다.
16. 파충류에서 포유동물로의 변화는 너무 점진적인 과정이어서 파충류에서 포유류로 변화하는 시점을 결정하는 것은 거의 불가능하다.
17. 국경지역의 대부분의 사람들은 거의 벌거숭이로 지내거나 또는 추운 지역이더라도 옷을 거의 입지 않았다.
18. 혼자 사냥하는 포식자는 주위 환경에 조화를 이루는 털로 위장을 하며 대부분 먹잇감에 슬그머니 다가가 숨어서 접근한다.
19. 고대 이집트에서 무역상들은 길거리를 걸어 다니면서 배와 화물의 도착을 알리는 목소리가 큰 사람들을 고용하였다.
20. 1347년부터 1352년 사이에 지금은 흑사병이라 부르는 아주 끔찍한 전염병이 유럽 인구의 1/4 정도의 목숨을 빼앗았다.

5. 물 분자는 함께 견고히 붙어있어서 물이 자신보다 더 무거운 물체를 지탱할 수 있게 해준다.
6. 산도는 알칼리성이나 산성의 정도를 측정하는 데 사용된다.
7. 증인은 일반적으로 변호사의 심문에 대한 반응으로 증거를 제공한다.
8. 많은 노동자들이 더 많은 임금을 받기 위해 다른 나라로, 심지어 자신의 나라의 다른 지역으로 이동하는 것을 주저하지 않는다.
9. 철강은 대기에 노출이 되면 쉽게 부식된다.
10. 대중의 관심을 많이 받는 경우라면 배심원들은 재판이 진행되는 동안 가족은 물론이고 다른 사람들로부터 격리될 수 있다.
11. 지방질은 물에 녹지 않는 지용성 물질이다.
12. 지진의 힘은 얼마나 바위가 부서지고 얼마나 멀리 이동하는지에 따라 다르다.
13. 복사본이 만들어졌을 때 오류가 발생하였고, 작품의 내용이 종종 부정확하게 요약되었다.
14. 많은 경우, 화학요법은 백혈구의 감소를 급격하게 감소시켜 환자를 감염의 위험에 약하게 한다.
15. 찬 공기가 따뜻한 공기보다 밀도가 높기 때문에, 찬 공기는 물러나는 따뜻한 공기의 아래로 내려간 뒤에 이를 위로 올림으로써 나아간다.
16. 멕시코 정부가 북쪽 지역에 사는 사람들을 방치했고 캘리포니아에 사는 멕시코 사람들은 멕시코시티 정부 관료로부터의 간섭을 싫어했다.
17. 홍적세시대의 가장 대표적인 포유류로 코끼리처럼 생긴 맘모스는 북반구의 얼어붙은 평온을 돌아다녔다.
18. 사회보장법은 실업자에게는 보험을 노인에게는 연금을 제공했다.
19. 인간의 가장 뛰어난 두 가지 특징은 큰 뇌와 직립을 할 수 있는 능력이다.
20. 방사능 사진은 특정 분자를 국부화하며 세포에서 분자의 움직임을 추적하는 데 아주 유용하게 사용된다.

Intensive Practice Test 16-20

1. ⓒ	2. ⓒ	3. ⓓ	4. ⓑ	5. ⓐ
6. ⓓ	7. ⓒ	8. ⓑ	9. ⓐ	10. ⓐ
11. ⓒ	12. ⓒ	13. ⓓ	14. ⓑ	15. ⓑ
16. ⓓ	17. ⓒ	18. ⓑ	19. ⓓ	20. ⓒ

1. 동물들은 충동적으로 살며, 외부 환경이 좋은 한 행복하다.
2. 불교도 신비주의자는 움직이지 않고 몇 시간, 심지어 며칠 동안 명상할 수 있다.
3. 완공되지 않은 관저가 음울하고 습한 풍경 속에 외로이 웅장하게 서 있었다.
4. 만일 개인의 행동이 그룹의 안전과 화합을 위협한다면 그 사람은 추방되었다.

ALL ABOUT IELTS 실전문제집 시리즈

IELTS 급상승 Actual Test 1
[Reading &Writing] (Academic Module)

James H. Lee 저 | 210*280mm | 316쪽 | 16,800원

IELTS 급상승 Actual Test 2
[Listening & Speaking]

James H. Lee 저 | 210*280mm | 284쪽 | 16,800원

IELTS 급상승 Vocabulary

James H. Lee, Chang-man Yun 저 | 188*258mm | 440쪽 | 16,800원(mp3 무료 제공)

IELTS 급상승
기초다지기
시리즈

IELTS 급상승 Grammar 기초다지기
김재한 저 | 188*258mm | 172쪽 | 15,000원

**IELTS 급상승 Writing 기초다지기
[Academic Module]**
김재한 저 | 188*258mm | 320쪽 | 16,800원

**IELTS 급상승 Reading 기초다지기
[Academic Module]**
이수용 저 | 188*258mm | 248쪽 | 15,000원

IELTS 급상승 Listening 기초다지기
이수용 저 | 188*258mm | 224쪽 |
15,000원(mp3 파일 무료 제공)

IELTS 급상승 Speaking 기초다지기
이수용 저 | 188*258mm | 284쪽 |
15,000원 (mp3 파일 무료 제공)